Enabling Technology
for Inclusion

Enabling Technology for Inclusion

Edited by

Mike Blamires

P·C·P
Paul Chapman
Publishing Ltd

Paul Chapman Publishing Ltd
A SAGE Publications Company
6 Bonhill Street
London EC2A 4PU

SAGE Publications Inc.
2455 Teller Road
Thousand Oaks, California 91320

SAGE Publications India Pvt Ltd
32, M-Block Market
Greater Kailash-I
New Delhi 110 048

British Library Cataloguing in Publication Data

A catalogue record for this book is available from the British Library

ISBN 1 85396 436-0
ISBN 1 85396 394-1 (pbk)

Library of Congress catalog card number available

Typeset by Dorwyn Ltd, Rowlands Castle, Hampshire
Printed and bound by The Cromwell Press, Wiltshire

Contents

Contributors   vii

Preface   ix

Acknowledgements   x

The focus   xi

Introduction   xiii

Abbreviations   xiv

1   What Is Enabling Technology?   1
    Mike Blamires

Part I   Enabling Learning   17

2   Enabling Learning: The Vital Role of Theory   19
    Peter Dorman

3   Developing Literacy   27
    Mike Blamires

Part II   Enabling Socialization   35

4   Advocacy and Self-Advocacy   37
    Sally Paveley

5   Raising Self-Esteem   52
    Colin Hardy

6   Developing Social Communication   61
    Richard Walter

Part III   Enabling Physical Engagement   73

7   Scaling Physical Barriers   75
    Lesley Rahamim

8   Developing Curriculum Access Based on Sensory Approaches:
    Partial Sight and Blindness   83
    John Lodge

9   Developing Visual Approaches: Hearing Impairment and Deafness   96
    Ann McDevitt

Part IV   Summary   111

10   Summary Themes   113
     Mike Blamires

Appendix I: Sources   118

Appendix II: List of Suppliers   119

References   123

Bibliography   186

Name Index   192

Subject Index   193

Contributors

Mike Blamires is Principal Lecturer in Special Educational Needs within the Special Needs Research and Development Group of the Centre for Educational Research at Canterbury Christ Church University College. He is programme Director of the PG Diploma/MA course programme. He is also co-convenor of the Special Educational Needs Information Technology on-line discussion list and has published a diverse range of educational software, books and articles.

Peter Dorman is Senior Lecturer in Education within the Faculty of Education at Canterbury Christ Church University College. He was formerly an Advisor for Primary Education and Advisory Teacher for Special Needs and Information and Communications Technology (ICT) in Kent and Northumbria.

Colin Hardy is an education officer (inclusive education planning and support) for the London Borough of Newham. Formerly (to September 1998) he was the ICT co-ordinator at the Learning Support Service, London Borough of Newham.

John Lodge is currently Information Technology (IT) Co-ordinator at Dorton House School – an institution run by the Royal London Society for the Blind. Previously Royal National Institute for the Blind (RNIB) technology training officer, Senior Lecturer in IT at Roehampton College of Higher Education and primary school teacher. He has published widely on the topic of Visual Impairment and ICT.

Ann McDevitt is a consultant, advisory teacher and lecturer with an expertise in the support of learners with visual impairments and blindness and has published on ICT-based approaches in this area. She has also undertaken research for the National Council for Educational Technology (NCET) into the effective use of compact discs (CDs) in schools.

Sally Paveley is an Information and Communications Technology (ICT) (special needs) consultant at the Advisory Unit: Computers in Education where she has developed switch, overlay keyboard and on screen grid software with Chris King. Sally has recently completed a project, supported by the Joseph Rowntree Foundation, examining the use of symbols with adults who have learning difficulties.

Lesley Rahamim is an advisory teacher at CENMAC, the Centre for Micro-Assisted Communication in London, UK. She has spent many years in mainstream primary schools as a classroom teacher, Individual Support Teacher and Special Educational Needs (SEN) Co-ordinator. She has written 'Access to Words and Images' for BECTA and contributed to several other publications. She is currently co-convenor of the

SENIT mailing list which uses the Internet to share knowledge about the use of ICT to support learners with SEN.

Richard Walter is the Information Technology for Communication (ITC) co-ordinator and classroom teacher at Meldreth Manor school which is a Scope school near Cambridge for approximately 100 pupils aged between 7 and 19. The pupils in school have cerebral palsy, severe, profound and complex learning difficulties, and many also have additional medical needs including epilepsy and feeding difficulties. Meldreth recently won the Microsoft Road Ahead prize for the school's innovative design of an accessible web site. The school is at the forefront of enabling alternative access to ICT equipment and multimedia for people who have physical and cognitive difficulties.

Preface

The potential for technology to provide an accessible, motivating and collaborative learning environment has never been greater. We must be encouraged by the significantly increased awareness of the value of information and communications technology in education generally and in particular to enable all students to be included in the learning process in the classroom and beyond. However, the gap that exists between an awareness of its potential and the confidence to implement it means that much still needs to be done.

Educational technology is becoming easier to use and, although developments still present problems for some users, IT increasingly opens new doors for many others, enabling and empowering them. Inclusion can be supported and made a reality using technology and this book offers some practical ways to aid this process. There are nuggets of information, hints, tips and useful advice as well as inspiration which will help and enthuse teachers of a wide range of learners.

The contributors to this book all have significant experience of working with teachers and students. Each has a wealth of practical knowledge in assessment and identification of appropriate technological provision for learners. Having worked directly with many students both in mainstream and special education, they understand the real issues that confront teachers and the importance of providing manageable solutions that work in individual settings. It is important that they are now sharing this by providing both practical case studies and also research and pedagogic context in which teaching and learning strategies are applied. It is as important to understand why and when to use or not use technology, as it is to be able to go through the mechanics of using the software. Only when teachers possess all this knowledge will technologies be fully integrated into achieving learning objectives.

Dennis Stevenson in his report 'Information and Communications Technology in UK Schools' said, 'The role of ICT is to serve education in particular by helping students to learn more effectively and by helping teachers to do their professional job'. Nowhere is this more true than in the area of inclusion. Mike Blamires asks the question, 'Why then is this book so long?' The answer is simple – it needs to be to meet the needs of those working with technology to develop inclusive schools within an inclusive education system.

Terry Waller
Education Officer, SEN and Inclusion BECTA

Acknowledgements

Inclusion is about listening to unfamiliar voices . . .

(Barton, 1998, p. 85)

In this book I have endeavoured to create a space for the voices I have learnt from and grown greatly to respect. In spite of my editorial efforts they represent a diversity of styles and viewpoints but they have one thing in common. They came to use technology not for the sake of technology itself but for what it could help learners to do. Their knowledge has been derived from many years of critical experience and research. They redefine Schön's (1987) criteria for reflective practice but do not engage in solipsism. We could do worse than mirror them.

I would also like to thank my colleagues who took on the extensive burdens of course delivery and development while I was on the study leave that produced this book. I would also like to thank members of the autism and SENIT discussion lists on the Internet who have directly or indirectly contributed to this book. Sincere thanks go to the Senior Management of Canterbury Christ Church University College who gave me a term's leave to finish this book. Perhaps it needed a year? On that subject I take responsibility for any errors in fact that occur in the book.

I am totally indebted to Joanna and my children Robin, Kate and Oliver. The latter can now have the computer back to finish Caesar 3 . . . I think I might join them.

Mike Blamires
December 1998
M.Blamires@canterbury.ac.uk

The Focus

Successful and realistic implementation of computer technology for students with special needs depends on: teachers' commitment, computer awareness and knowledge of effective pedagogical principles; administrative support; and effecting matching of curriculum goals, teaching philosophy, validated instructional procedure, appropriate computer applications, and students' individual strengths and needs.

(Lindsey, 1993; Sitko and Sitko, 1995, pp. 1, 2)

So if the problem is that simple why is this book so long?

Introduction

We hope that in a few years' time there will be no call for a book devoted exclusively to the use of micros as a resource (for learners with special educational needs), but all books will refer to the use of new technology.

(Hope, 1986, p. 14)

If we accept Hope's view the book in your hands should not exist. As technology becomes more commonplace, more invisible in society, it should become more a part of everyday teaching and learning. Therefore, it should not need a separate consideration from other forms of learning and teaching. However, the possibilities of technology are changing and the requirements of good practice in responding to a diversity of needs are becoming more demanding and problematical. In fact, Hope recognized that this was likely to be the case and that it would be a topic worthy of further consideration. In the same introduction she contradicts her earlier assertion.

We live in exciting times . . . We are learning how best to use and integrate the micro in special needs education. If we are fortunate enough to be preparing a similar book in a few years time the content will no doubt be radically different. We are on a steep learning curve and long may it last.

(Hope, 1986, p. 19)

She was and she did two years later.

It is worth noting that twelve years later my colleague Phil Poole quite unintentionally begins his introduction to a booklet on micro-technology for trainee teachers and their tutor-mentors with the phrase, 'We live in interesting times' (Poole, 1998). I am gullible enough to believe that 'May you live in interesting times' is an old Chinese curse! 'Interesting times' are times of challenge and difficulty when many things change and people have to adapt and come to terms with what they have gained or lost.

The challenge we have set ourselves in this book is to identify emerging and enduring issues within the field of enabling technology, map out areas of concern and locate criteria which may determine success. From past mistakes, we aim to produce a book that will aid future success – a handbook on enabling technology which is not obsolete on publication.

To do this we do not say that 'such and such' device or software is 'the best thing since sliced bread'. We might suggest that 'sliced bread' may not have been such a good idea anyway. We consider generic types of software and devices and the features which make them useful for enabling different forms of learning. We also consider how the technology can facilitate inclusion – a demanding and controversial construct which can have differing meanings to those involved in its implementation or prevention.

We have kept the number of illustrations to a minimum as they are abundant in catalogues, magazines and web pages. When a word or phrase is printed bold you will find an entry for it in the References.

Abbreviations

BECTA	British Educational Communications Training Agency
CAST	Center for Applied Special Technology
CCTV	closed circuit television
CD	compact disc
CD-ROM	compact disc – read only memory
CENMAC	Centre for Micro-Assisted Communication
CRT	cathode ray tube
DART	directed activities relating to text
DES	Department of Education and Science
DfEE	Department for Education and Employment
DVD	digital video disc
GUI	graphical user interface
HTML	hypertext mark-up language
ICT	information and communications technology
IDEA	Individuals with Disabilities Act (1990) Public Law 101–476 (United States)
IEP	individual education plan
IHS	intelligent help system
IT	information technology
ITC	information technology for communications
LCD	liquid-crystal display
LEA	local education authority
LSA	learning support assistant
LVA	Low Vision Aid, e.g. a magnifier
NCET	National Council for Educational Technology
OCR	optical character recognition
PC	personal computer
RNIB	Royal National Institute for the Blind
RP	retinitis pigmentosa
RSI	repetitive strain injury
SEN	special educational needs
SLD	severe learning difficulties
SR	speech recognition
TTA	Teacher Training Agency
UN	United Nations
VAS	voice activated software
VDU	visual display unit
VR	virtual reality

1

What is Enabling Technology?

Mike Blamires

Enabling technology is concerned with the creative and sensitive application of appropriate technology in order to improve the quality of life of individuals and their range of life opportunities. The technology is appropriate whether or not it is at the leading edge of technological innovation or a piece of 'mass market' low technology. Appropriateness is judged as a result of periodic monitoring of progress by a partnership consisting of the individual, parents/carers and professionals. Enabling technology, therefore, is about participation in joint decision-making rather than 'off the shelf' quick fixes. People grow and change. Enabling technology by its nature can and should adapt to these changes.

To be enabled does not solely mean to have access. Enablement is about being helped to achieve something that could not be achieved at all without that aid or without great personal effort. An individual may be enabled to learn something, say something, do something, create something, go somewhere or join in some activity. Enabling technology is not just about access, it is about engagement and inclusion.

For example, a young girl can run across the shell beach to explore a rock pool that takes her fancy because she is wearing plastic sandals so that her feet are not hurt. Another girl enters a discussion about the opera 'Otello' on the **Internet**. She can do this as she is able to communicate with the relatively small number of people who want to discuss this topic because she is connected to the Internet. She can compose a message to send because she uses a computer program that writes using a single switch triggered by an eye blink. Both children utilise examples of enabling technology. Success for one will depend upon what is in the rock pool, for the other it depends upon how well she can put her ideas across and how well they aid the developing dialogue and discussion. Technology has enabled both their achievements. This book contains a number of examples of people using technology for you to consider and judge whether or not they are truly being enabled.

In addition to this physical support, enabling technology can facilitate understanding and engagement with knowledge and people. Speech, pictures, symbols, words and animation can be combined in interactive ways to structure concepts to suit the level of understanding of learners and their interests. Words which for some learners waited as dead print, black on white on a page in a busy classroom waiting to be explained by the teacher or helper can now be brought to life and spoken, illustrated or animated. These representations can be published or distributed to different audiences. This is provided the appropriate technology is employed appropriately. Peter Dorman discusses this in Chapter 2.

Models of learning

To consider the role of enabling technology within learning we need to know what is actually involved in learning. DeCorte (1990) has proposed a useful model of learning which is displayed in Figure 1.1.

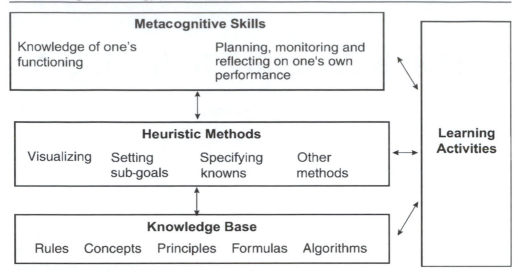

Figure 1.1   A model of learning

- The knowledge base is the subject to be learnt. Whether this is science, mathematics or English, it will invariably have its own concepts, rules and principles. It may also have algorithms and formulas for deriving information from other given data.
- The heuristic methods are general ways of problem-solving that can be applied to the knowledge base. They are the usual problem-solving skills of attempting to visualize the problem mentally, pictorially or diagramatically, breaking the problem down into sub-sections with sub-goals, specifying what is known and what is not known plus any of a range of other methods.
- Metacognition is the thinking we do about our thinking and how as a consequence we approach a learning task. Knowing what we are good at and what has worked before as well as monitoring our own performance enables us to change our approach if we are not being successful.

To be effective, enabling technology can impact on all aspects of this model.

Is technology available now 'intelligent enough' to develop all these aspects of learning? Or should the question be 'Will the growth in intelligence applications (software) result in more intelligent children?'

The focus of interest in more intelligent software over the last two decades has been on the development of expert systems, i.e. software that can learn to carry out decision-making normally undertaken by a human expert in their field. An expert system needs to have a knowledge base which it can apply to problems. It has to have goals, rules and an understanding of how things operate so that the knowledge it has is used efficiently. Good expert systems will evaluate how well they have solved a problem from the results they have achieved, and as a result, may change their knowledge base or how they do things according to established criteria (could we call these values?). Expert systems 'think' about what they have done and learn from experience.

Within education our aims are similar: we want to build experts but these systems have to operate within learners rather than machines.

Can an expert system teach a learner? This will depend upon what you consider 'teach' to mean. If you consider teaching to be the input of facts and simple skills which are then tested for 'mastery', I suppose the answer would be 'yes'.

The basics are important but they are only the basics

Because current educational expert systems rarely go beyond the building of a basic knowledge base, existing teaching software tends to impoverish learning. In other words, they are not that intelligent. Ironically, this fits with current metaphors for learning which are about curriculum delivery, school improvement through target-setting and observable outcomes. It is easy to print out graphs of test results but it is less easy to provide evidence of knowledge and experience gain.

Maybe our goal for expert systems should be to enable learners to become experts themselves? In which case children need to develop a knowledge base on a particular subject, become aware of this knowledge and how they have structured it. They need to be able to evaluate this knowledge, therefore they need criteria. They need to learn different ways to use this knowledge and apply it to real-life problems (metacognition).

Perhaps it is unrealistic to argue that all people should become experts. You might be really negative and argue that some people with learning difficulties are unlikely to become experts at anything so it is unfair and unrealistic to expect them to try. However, Warnock (1978) suggests that the aims of education should be the same for all children and the perception that a child may not achieve them at all, or achieve some of them only after a very long period and great effort by child, carer and teacher, should not stop us from aiming for them. How many children have learning difficulties because they have learnt facts and skills without understanding?

See also **integrated learning systems**.

A social/psychological/biological model of learning

The approach taken by this book moves away from a deficit view of special educational needs where there is 'something missing' within the individual, towards a model that takes into account individual biological and psychological strengths and deficits alongside community strengths and deficits. These include the availability and application of technology as well as many other issues beyond the scope of this book. Meeting special educational needs is about negotiating a way of dealing with 'what is missing between us'.

The model in Figure 1.2 may help show the different factors that contribute to the generation of diversity, parts of which will sometimes be described as special educational needs.

As Norwich (1990) notes, to attribute a strength or deficit to an individual does not mean that that characteristic has to be unchangeable. Similarly, characteristics of institutions and their practices do not have to stay the same for ever. An 'inclusive' institution may even become exclusive over time. Change for good or ill, will expand or diminish a person's horizons of personal growth and development. Enabling technology can be a catalyst or inhibitor in this context.

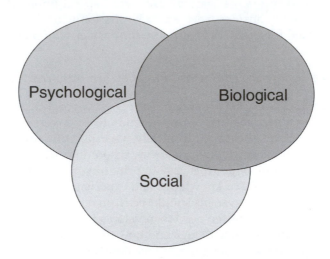

Figure 1.2   The social/psychological/biological model of special educational needs
Source: Cooper, P. (1998) after Norwich, B. (1990) after Engel, G. (1977).

A model of information and communications technology in education

The Teacher Training Agency, England and Wales, model (Table 1.1) categorizes the main areas where ICT can have a positive impact on learning. Enabling technology may utilize any or all of them.

Access technology

Day has suggested that

> Access technology . . . In its broadest sense, this means that IT can enable pupils to overcome the barriers to learning by providing alternative or additional methods of

Table 1.1   The Teacher Training Agency model of information and communications technology in education

Communication	Provisionality
Technology can aid the process of communication. Work can be published to a wide audience electronically.	The DELETE key and the Undo button mean that learners can be more experimental. Documents can be saved at different stages of development so that new possibilities can be explored with little risk of loss and with ease.
Presentation	**Accuracy**
Ideas can be presented in a wide range of formats including sound, video, music, pictures and graphics.	Editing is easier than with traditional technology. Proofing tools such as **spell checkers** and **autocorrect** can improve accuracy in work by taking over secretarial aspects of composition.
Information	**Speed**
Large amounts of information can be accessed from discrete encyclopaedias on CD-ROM to vast networks of interconnecting information such as the World Wide Web.	Laborious aspects of work can be eliminated such as letter formation and the duplication or movement of text, images and sound.

communicating within the learning process. It also means that IT can enable them to take advantage of their entitlement to a broad and balanced curriculum.

(Day, 1995. p. 4)

Day suggests three forms of access:

- Physical access: 'technology at its most dramatic, liberating the pupil from the physical barriers to learning' (ibid., p. 4) so that a learner is provided with alternative access to communication and learning', e.g. the use of a **communication aid** operated by **switches**.
- Cognitive access: 'IT enables us to present the curriculum in different ways, thereby encouraging the pupil who has difficulty grasping the concepts, skills and knowledge required of him' (ibid., p. 4), e.g. the use of floor **robots** to develop spatial skills. This can be considered as supporting the **universal design** for learning principle of multiple forms of presentation and engagement.
- Supportive access: 'the power of technology to support pupils in particular areas of difficulty' (ibid., p. 4), e.g. the use of **word-processing** in place of handwriting. This can be also be considered as temporary scaffolding which is discussed below.

Following the English and Welsh Code of Practice on Special Educational Needs (DfEE, 1994), Day goes on to to suggest that a continuum of needs should be considered alongside a continuum of provision. At one end are learners for whom IT provides 'access to the world of living and learning in a way that no other resource can' where 'IT is a lifeline' (ibid., p. 5) and at the other is where IT 'makes a difficult task easier by acting as a facilitator'. At different points along the continuum different levels of technology are required. This ranges from occasional access shared with other learners, through targeted access where the learner has individual use of technology for specific tasks towards designated individual provision allocated to a learner as part of a statement or individual education plan.

Day suggests that, for learners with special educational needs, technology can provide them with access to the curriculum if appropriately utilized within their individual education plans. However, this rather undersells the potential that technology can have in re-shaping the curriculum to create alternative ways of successful learning. Access technology may be necessary but alone not sufficient for inclusion. In fairness, this was not its intention, its emphasis being on the selection and monitoring of technology to meet individual special needs – a process of educational triage. The challenges of inclusion are not merely access but active engagement in learning tasks that are worth while alongside one's peers.

(See also **assistive technology** which has a slightly different scope and focus.)

The limits of 'access technology'
On the subject of lifelines: an analogy could be to the Titanic tragedy where the Captain had the technology to access New York but not to engage or avoid icebergs.

Extending horizons: a developmental model of inclusion

Figure 1.3 results from discussions with my colleagues Peter Dorman and Myra Tingle and builds upon the work of Day and her colleagues within the context of the model of learning illustrated in Figure 1.2 and the continuum of provision recognized in Warnock (1978), Department for Education and Employment Individuals with

Disabilities Act, 1990 and the DfEE *Code of Practice* (1994). The lines represent the different degrees of inclusion that an individual may have as a result of the three parameters. For example:

- A learner may be cognitively engaged in every lesson she attends through her use of a laptop computer but she may have no social involvement with the class or the life of the school.
- A learner may attend a variety of social activities and lessons in the school but not be included in the teaching and learning activities.
- A learner might attend a local school but his social and cognitive needs are not recognized or catered for.
- A learner may not attend his local college but is engaged in learning and social activities via mail, speech and video with tutors and peers who form a 'virtual' community. (But who are we to say this virtual community is not real?)

Thankfully, the following chapters present some more positive examples of people who are included.

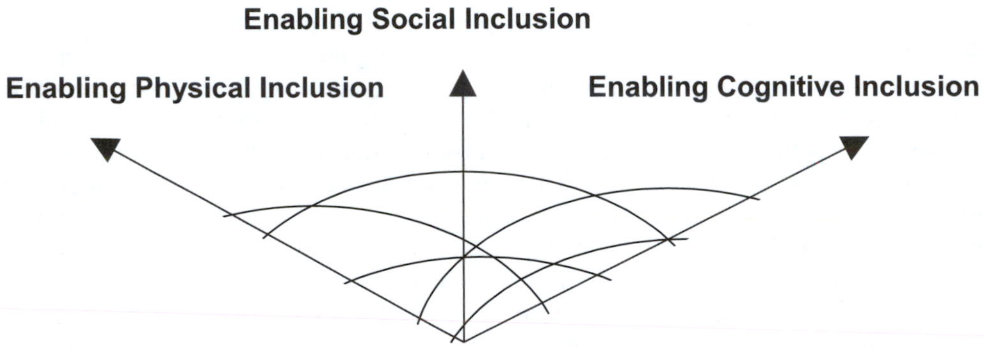

Enabling Social Inclusion

Enabling Physical Inclusion   ▲   **Enabling Cognitive Inclusion**

Figure 1.3   A developmental model of inclusion

Each dimension of inclusion within Figure 1.3 may be a result of the following very tentative equation:

Inclusion = Access + Engagement

But what is inclusion? Is it a binary switch or an analogue control (Figure 1.4)?

Figure 1.4   Binary switch and analogue control

Some of the practice within this book takes place in segregated settings. These may be mainstream or special schools but either may be to some degree segregated from one another. This is an acknowledgement of the reality that inclusion is a learning process under the influence of political will and the agendas of different interest groups.

From our model, inclusion is concerned with access and engagement at a physical, social and cognitive level with one's peers in tasks that are at an appropriate level and worth while. Inclusion is about increasing engagement with a menu of learning opportunities (Moore, 1992) that are a response to the needs and rights of a diversity of learners. Including means being part of a dynamic relationship rather than a fixed state.

> Inclusive education is thus about responding to diversity, it is about listening to unfamiliar voices, being open and empowering all members . . . This is a demanding task particularly where there are limited forms of communication on the part of some children. But also that listening requires us not to talk. Given that teachers spend a great deal of the time talking, it is not going to be an easy task.
>
> (Barton, 1998, p. 85)

This skill may be a key aspect of professional development for inclusion.

Some authors, e.g. Thomas, Walker and Webb, have argued that special needs expertise has been complicity employed to segregate learners with special needs and to de-skill mainstream teachers: 'experts and professionals have in the past promoted the idea that only those with special qualifications are equipped to assess, teach and make decisions about children significantly different from others' (Thomas, Walker and Webb, 1997, p. 13). The key phrase in this quote should be 'in the past'. The Teacher Training Agency (TTA) of England and Wales provides evidence in its proposed standards for specialist special needs teachers that this approach is changing. A key outcome of their requirements includes: 'SEN Specialists . . . Who are involved in the formulation of strategies to increase inclusiveness in mainstream schooling' (TTA, 1998, p.14).

Thomas, Walker and Webb go on to argue that mainstream teachers need to feel confident that they can teach learners with special needs and further suggest that one of the principles for successful inclusive schools is: 'de-professionalisation: an inclusive school is one where there is an assumption amongst staff (shared by students) that all staff share in the contribution they make to children's learning' (Thomas, Walker and Webb, 1997, p. 17). However, their use of 'de-professionalisation' as a name for this process is also de-skilling and misleading, giving credence to the practice where the least skilled person in a school ends up attempting to meet the needs or 'minding' the learner with the most complex needs (teaching assistants or learning support assistants). What I suggest they are actually referring to is the blurring of educational demarcations within an institution – a limited empowerment of all staff without qualified teacher status. The application of Enabling Technology for Inclusion requires more professional skills amongst all staff, not less, and ongoing professional development.

Within his consideration of 'Effective Schools for All', Ainscow (1995) emphasizes the importance of two factors that are central to inclusive practices; 'the opportunity to consider new possibilities' and 'the availability of support for experimentation'. But such experimentation needs the checks and balances that arise from the views and expertise of all the stakeholders being taken into account if 'Institutional Effectiveness for All' is not to become the 'Tyranny of the Majority'. In the context of competitive schools, the rhetoric and practice of 'School Improvement' and 'Zero Tolerance' on nonconformity have often resulted in exclusion with the cognitive/academic aims emphasized at the expense of aesthetic or vocational aims (e.g. Armstrong, 1998).

However, schools can improve and become more effective at the same time as they become more inclusive. This involves students having a stake in the learning and its outcomes, being engaged in tasks that are perceived as being worth while by the people involved, and having high expectations which do not lead to self-perception of being a failure. This process may be supported by the slow and slight trend away from needs which might or might not be addressed, towards recognizing the rights of future citizens as reflected in the following documents:

- the English and Welsh National Curriculum which included 'The entitlement to access to a curriculum which includes the National Curriculum and which is broad, balanced and relevant' (DES, 1988)
- the Salamanca Statement (1994)
- educational provision for learners with SEN should be provided in the 'Least Restricted Environment' (IDEA US, 1990)
- Articles 23 and 29 of the United Nations (UN) Convention on the rights of the child (1989).

Within this context inclusion is a process characterized by evolution rather than revolution, building upon existing knowledge and experience. The subliminal message from some advocates of inclusion might be 'forget the past and create the future'. We need to be wary of losing established critical frameworks or we might be approaching 'Year Zero' not the next millennium.

In Chapter 2 of this book Peter Dorman argues that educational technology is a central resource to support inclusion as it can create new opportunities for learning and engagement. Pencil and paper and chalk and talk alongside a vast amount of dead print on the page have long been the central tools of education. Dorman cites Resnick as stating that tools will dictate practice, 'If you only have a hammer everything will look like a nail.' Technology is now the versatile tool for **handling information** and communication. **Information and communications technology** is therefore a central tool for inclusion.

But like any tool ICT needs to be understood and evaluated. The model in Figure 1.5 illustrates how enabling technology can create new opportunities for inclusion.

Just as Dorman will argue in this book that the enabling use of ICT requires a creative mindset, Hart has proposed a method of 'innovative thinking' which she suggests may be employed to avoid the attribution of deficits to a child so that the teacher can act positively to include a learner within classroom activities. She suggests

> five questioning moves help us to *move beyond* what we already think and know about the situation by probing what has not so far been examined within our existing thinking about the situation . . .
>
> - Making connections: This move involves exploring how the specific characteristics of the child's response might be linked to features of the immediate and wider context. We ask ourselves: 'What might be helping to produce this response?'
> - Contradicting: This move involves teasing out the underlying norms and assumptions that lead us to perceive the child's response as problematic. It asks 'How else might

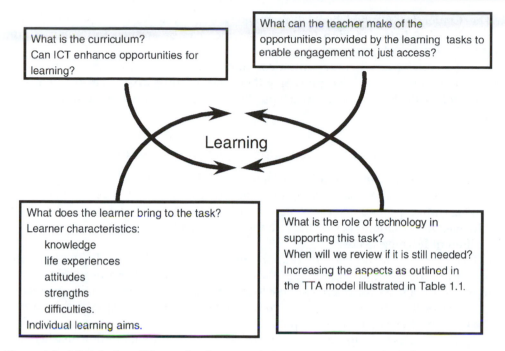

Figure 1.5 Model of enabling technology creating new opportunities for inclusion

this response be understood?' It seeks to uncover the norms and assumptions under-lying a judgement, so that these can be reviewed and evaluated
- Taking a child's eye view: This move involves trying to enter the child's frame of reference and see the meaning and logic of the child's response from the child's perspective. It asks 'What meaning and purpose does this activity have for the child?'
- Noting the impact of feelings: This move involves examining the part that our own feelings are playing in the meaning we bestow on the situation and in leading us to arrive at a particular interpretation. It asks 'How do I feel about this?' and 'What do these feelings tell me about what is going on here?'
- Suspending judgement: This move involves recognising that we may lack information or resources to have confidence in our judgements and therefore holding back from making judgements about the child's needs while we take the step to add to our resources.

(Hart, 1996, p. 103)

This approach is rather like that which a parental advocate might adopt in a meeting to discuss a learner's individual education plan. If it is not to take on the solipsism of Schön's Model of the Reflective Practitioner (1987), accountable only to his own con-science, then other voices need to be heard and responded to. The five questions provide us with a framework for listening to the voices we need to take into account. They are good questions to ask but one person is unlikely to be able to answer them.

From innovative thinking to universal design for learning

The response to issues arising from these questions and concerns can be framed in the context of universal design.

The Center for Applied Special Technology (CAST, 1998) have proposed three principles of **universal design** for learning which can be applied to the curriculum and which set a working agenda for inclusion. They take advantage of the fact that the **Internet** enables many people with a common interest to work together and share perspectives and resources despite being thousands of miles apart. It also builds upon the World Wide Web's design principle that content should not be bound up in structure.

Principle one: provide multiple representations of content

Key information is represented in alternative modalities – textually, visually or auditory. Unlike the printed page, computers can present information in multiple media formats. Unlike printed pages, content and structure are not locked together and unchangeable. Resources across the Internet can be combined in many different ways for different learning needs.

CAST note that some content cannot truly cross from one modality to another without loss of meaning, for example a painting, poem or piece of music, so it is important to consider the purpose of the learning task and the learner characteristics if compromises have to be made. A picture may be worth a thousand words but the right word may evoke a thousand pictures.

Because learners have more ways of representing their understanding, teachers will also have more information about that learning. 'Computer hardware and software often provide tools for both teachers and students to facilitate and strengthen cognitive and meta-cognitive strategies' (Sitko and Sitko, 1996, p. 4).

As a result of Weir's work using **Logo** with children with a variety of learning difficulties, she suggested that it was possible to examine the child's learning strategies and understanding. She argued that this resulted from the way they worked and that what they produced could be seen on the screen. Weir (1987) like many Logo researchers (e.g. Lawler, 1985) was able to work on an infrequent basis with individual children for substantial periods of time. Technology might not have been the significant factor which facilitated her investigation of learning needs. However, the application of **models** and **microworlds** have enriched the ways in which learners have been able to communicate their understanding. Instead of using verbal language or written text, there are now a variety of means in which a learner can build representations of her understanding of the world which can readily be changed and re-presented.

Principle two : provide multiple options for expression and control

The dominant mode of expression on web pages has been through the production of text but there has been a move towards the use of **multimedia authoring** which encompasses artwork, photography, drama, music, voice recording and animation because these can be stored digitally and manipulated. This convergence of digital media facilitates different ways for learners to explore and build understandings. They can then demonstrate what they have learnt through publication in a variety of forms.

In addition differences among students' ability to use different kinds of tools mean that a wide range of ways of using the computer have to be considered. These are discussed in the References and in Lesley Rahamin's and Richard Walter's respective chapters.

Many current curriculum-based activities are locked into one method of expression and control. This is probably a result of the limitations of systems of assessment as well as an artefact of technology, e.g. 'Write a story' rather than 'create narrative'.

The 'problem' of generalization and 'transfer'

When learners with special needs first used computers the emphasis was on the 'need' to encourage transfer and generalization (Hope, 1986, p. 16). It was as if any achievement of a child with special needs using a computer was in doubt until they could achieve the same feat with more prevalent technology such as pen and paper. For example, 'There is the need to show . . . That the skills learned together on the word-processor are in fact transferable to the realm of everyday writing' (Patrick Keane in Hope, 1986, p. 85). For Keane in 1986 word-processing was not part of 'everyday writing'. Technology was then at the margins of education but we argue that it has since earned its place as a powerful tool for inclusive learning and participation in society.

Within the principle of multiple forms of expression the problem of generalization and transfer is a problem of metacognition. What has the learner actually learnt about applying the rules and concepts she has used? Does she have a framework for applying this knowledge to other problems presented in different ways? Transfer and generalization are not about proving you can carry out a task in a preferred medium.

> With appropriate technology I can get across the Atlantic in twelve hours. It isn't cheating, honest ! But please do not ask me to generalize the achievement using a rowing boat.

Principle three: provide multiple options for engagement and motivation

This acknowledges the diversity of backgrounds, hopes and purposes of learners, and that learning has an important emotional component. Learners need to feel safe and confident in their ability to respond to the challenges presented to them.

> For any given student, teachers need to be able to provide content that is interesting; an appropriate level of challenge; appropriate supports and scaffolds that can be withdrawn as skill improves; timely, personally relevant feedback so that the student can observe progress and make adjustments; options for learning context (e.g. exploratory versus structured, individual versus collaborative; real-life versus fictional); and a clear purpose for learning.
> (CAST, 1998, Http://darkwing.uoregon.edu/~uplan/UDEPweb/MainUDEP.html)

Without the flexibility resulting from innovative use of technology this task might not be possible.

Learning activities supporting engagement

These are activities which can facilitate engagement in learning. They are not specific pieces of software or technology but are ways in which learning is organized or emphasized. These activities may be tentatively categorized as shown in Figures 1.6 to 1.9.

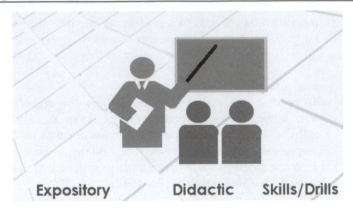

Figure 1.6   Expository activity

Figure 1.7   Creative activity

Figure 1.8   Exploratory activity

Figure 1.6 shows the use of technology to directly teach in a structured and directed way, e.g. **ILS**, some **early learning** software, **typing tutors**. Figure 1.7 is the use of technology to create new artefacts, e.g. **word-processing, painting and drawing** and **multimedia authoring** (see also Chapters 1, 2, 5, 6 and 9). Figure 1.8 is the use of

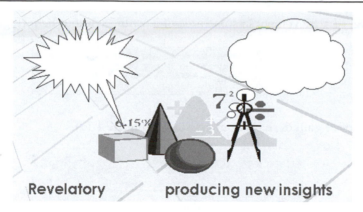

Figure 1.9   Revalatory activity

technology to explore new concepts or knowledge bases, e.g. **microworlds, cloze procedure, talking books** (see also Chapters 3, 6 and 9). Figure 1.9 is the use of technology to reveal patterns and exceptions. Making abstract information more visible or tangible, e.g. **information handling, spreadsheets, modelling** and **microworlds** (see also Chapters 2 and 5).

Enabling software and devices
These software and devices would include **communication aids, speech synthesis** and **magnification**, which enable access to the activities which support engagement through physical, social or cognitive scaffolding (Figure 1.10) (see also Chapters 2, 3, 4, 5, 6, 7, 8 and 9)

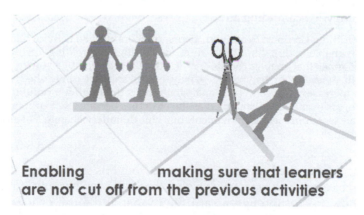

Figure 1.10   Enabling software and devices

Enabling engagement: scaffolding across proximal zones
It may be useful to consider the concept of the proximal zone (Vygotsky, 1978) 'in which a distinction is made between what has been learned independently until the present and what could be achieved in the future in a specific context and field with environmental assistance and facilitation' (Norwich, 1990, p. 107). This would involve the measurement of the following three aspects:

(1)   The level of achievement in some area of learning without help (Figure 1.11).

(2)   The extent of gain derived from assistance (Figure 1.12).

(3)   The degree of help required to achieve the gain (Figure 1.13).

Figure 1.11   A model of learning

Scaffolding is the environmental help or assistance that helps someone to achieve what they have not been able to until now (Bruner, 1986). Sitko and Sitko elaborate the role of technology in scaffolding as

> providing additional support to allow students to accomplish an activity that they would otherwise be unable to do without that support. Through scaffolding, instruction is provided in a manner that enables the student to carry out a cognitive strategy or learning activity, with guidance or temporary structure and support diminished gradually as competence increases. The concept is analogous to scaffolding on a building site where the scaffolding is eventually dismantled as the structure becomes self supporting . . . The supports may be temporary or permanent, but will definitely change as student's skills and needs change.
>
> (Sitko and Sitko, 1996, p. 3)

But what if the learner needs prolonged support from this scaffolding? Or perhaps the scaffolding takes care of an aspect of learning that will soon become inauthentic, such as knowing how to sort through a card file by hand, the use of logarithms or the correct way to multiply with Roman numerals. Does this permanent scaffolding become a prosthesis for learning? Does this mean we are becoming dependent upon technology?

What is independence?
When educators talk of the aims of becoming an independent learner they should take into account the technological tools they are assuming to be available. Today, we can assume the availability of pen and paper but tomorrow what other technology will be readily available?

Inauthentic labour

Underwood and Underwood (1990) have suggested that IT can free learners from the 'inauthentic labour' within a learning activity. For example, a learner can search through a database with thousands of records in seconds using a computer, whereas this might take hours by hand. She is therefore freed to concentrate on the essence of the task rather than the method.

Smith (1982) has made a similar distinction within the process of writing, that between composition and transcription. The latter is concerned with the secretarial aspects of writing, the letter formation, punctuation, capitalization, spelling and layout, whilst the former is concerned with the shaping of meaning through the use of words, syntax and genre. Smith suggested that too much concentration on the transcription can be at the expense of composition. For many people, the increasing capability of computers to look after the transcription involved in writing has been one of the most enabling aspects of technology. A basic word processor can form the letters in the way you want, allow you to put spaces between words, indent and justify your text, and change your words.

Target drift and the inauthentic labour within learning

Using the Underwoods' language, transcription is 'inauthentic labour' which can be carried out by the micro-technology whereas composition is the authentic labour. However, if one is writing for an audience, one can anticipate that transcription, which is concerned with the way writing appears to the reader, may become important. Therefore at different stages of a learning activity some aspects may be more important than others. An excessive focus upon one element of the task may divert the learner from achieving other learning outcomes. We call this 'target drift' and it can occur when the teacher is not confident with the technology, or when the goals of the activity are not clearly defined. For example:

- printing a coloured graph out as a bar chart, pie chart and three-dimensional chart because it is possible rather than considering what it is showing
- spending an inordinate amount of time choosing fonts for a piece of writing outlining a project.

Target drift occurs when a superficial aspect of the learning task becomes the focus of the learner's efforts.

Guidance for training teachers in England and Wales in the use of ICT states that teachers need to be trained in 'Avoiding giving the impression that the quality of presentation is of overriding importance and supersedes the importance of content' (Circular 4/98). So content must not be sacrificed for presentation. But how do we judge content?

What is authentic learning on a computer?

If the computer can take over many inauthentic labours of learning, how can we tell when it has taken over the authentic labour of learning as well? To what extent are the learning outcomes resulting from computer use, the achievements of the learner or those of the technology (i.e. the various people who designed the system)?

Yet again, this difficulty has been recognized in guidance for the use of ICT in initial teacher training in England and Wales: 'Trainees should be taught to identify . . . criteria to ensure that judgements about pupil attainments are not masked because ICT is used' (Circular 4/98).

Miles (1998) suggests that there is an ethical dimension to be considered when supplying voice dictation systems for writing to learners identified as being 'dyslexic'. He reports that learners without difficulties and without access to the same technology are starting to complain of their lack of access to similar technology and to suggest that the dyslexic learners have an unfair advantage.

Perhaps this is not a problem but a rich learning opportunity for these children to discuss degrees of disadvantage as well as what is fair and unfair in teaching and learning. (There is of course another ethical area to consider – that of equality of access to resources across disability which may appear divisive to some. There do appear to be 'blue chip disabilities' which may be considered more worthy of inclusion in some quarters.)

The following chapters outline a range of approaches which illustrate different aspects of the application of enabling technology to aid inclusion within a wide range of contexts. For convenience they are categorized under 'Enabling Learning', 'Enabling Socialization' and 'Enabling Physical Engagement' but within each chapter different forms of access and engagement may also be covered. Many of the terms, approaches and resources that they refer to are explored at greater length in the References.

Part I
Enabling Learning

In Chapter 2 Peter Dorman confronts one of the main causes of learning difficulties: the reluctance of some educators to re-evaluate their understanding of teaching and exploit the versatility that even simple technology may offer in enabling learning. He argues that meaning is built and not delivered and that 'Resistance to the use of enabling technologies may therefore be an unconscious response to an implied overall philosophy rather than resistance to the practical demands of time, organization or resource management'. In consequence, the reliance on 'curriculum bought in boxes' could be a 'bolt on' that will ultimately 'drop off', the bits that drop off being traditionally labelled as having learning difficulties.

In Chapter 3 I consider the models of literacy and the tools than can support its realization within a framework of whole class and small group activities. More subject-specific uses of technology are also considered in the References.

2

Enabling Learning: The Vital Role of Theory

Peter Dorman

In considering the role of ICT within learning contexts we must recognize that both ICT and the context in which it is used are not value-free. Wherever teaching takes place assumptions are made about the very nature of the learning process. Such assumptions may, however, not be made explicit by the teacher, indeed the teacher may not even be aware of the model which informs their teaching (Jones and Mercer, in Scrimshaw, 1995). However, the teacher's epistemological beliefs, even if implicit, have powerful implications for the organizational structures, techniques employed, tasks presented and selection of software. Such beliefs regarding objectives, strategies, problem-solving, metacognition etc. have similarly significant consequences in the parallel context of software design (Perry *et al.*, 1995).

Whilst there have been many attempts to categorize the software types and styles which are appropriate for use with learners (e.g. Hope, 1987; Self, 1985), the central issue is that of control. The question is posed, does the user control the software or is the user controlled by the software or, more precisely, by the unseen hand of the software designer? Differing learning paradigms have clear implications for the design and use of software within educational settings.

The behaviourist view of the learning process emphasizes behaviour and the strategies by which it may be modified: 'Learning according to this paradigm is a change in the behavioural dispositions of the organism *and can be* shaped by selective reinforcement' (Jonassen, 1995, p. 5). In this model the teacher takes the lead role as a didactic leader as: 'The teaching-learning event is seen as a process within which the teacher attempts to mediate objective knowledge and the learner is to possess this mediated knowledge at the end of the knowledge transport in exactly the same form as the teacher' (Mandl and Reinmann-Rothmeier, 1995, p. 7).

This view of learning emphasizes behaviour which can be both observed and measured but, as mental processes are not by their nature directly open to observation, they are not considered to be legitimate areas of study. Indeed, behaviourists 'believe that the construct of mind does more harm than good; that it makes more sense to talk about overt behaviours than about ideas, concepts or rules' (Gardner, 1985, p. 35).

At the centre of this paradigm is the assumption of the existence of an objective reality in which knowledge structures can be described, analysed, simplified and then modelled. The role of the software designer is to create a product which would then map on to learners this objective reality.

The implications for software design of such a model can be shown diagrammatically (Figure 2.1). At stage 1 concern is with identification of relevant learning content and the pre-specification of hierarchical links. Through a process of task analysis, the software designer would endeavour to decompose the task into a series of linked sub-tasks (stage 2), which are presented to the learner at stage 3. The observable outcomes at stage 4 are judged against predetermined criteria; unsuccessful outcomes result in the re-presentation of tasks at A or presentation of new tasks at B. The key task of the teacher within this model will be the reduction of all variables within the learning environment. To remain in line with Skinner's (1938) concept of operant conditioning the product would include positive reinforcement of correct responses. In contrast, incorrect responses would be ignored in the belief that they would gradually disappear or, in Skinner's terms, be extinguished.

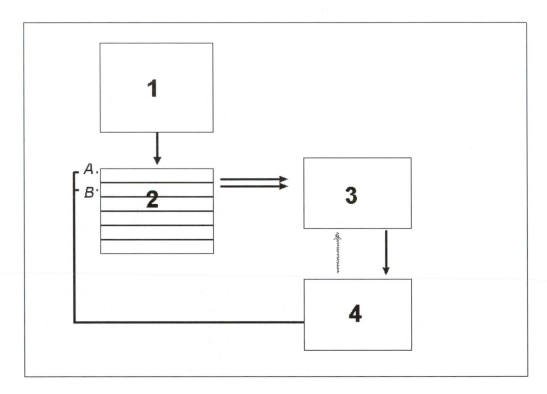

Figure 2.1   Four-stage model of software design

At the core of this approach is the assumption that meaning is independent of understanding and that mental processes can be disregarded on the presumption that knowledge is perceived in the same way by all learners. The role of language within this model is as an abstract symbolic system in which words act as referents carrying explicit knowledge through precise meanings. A key task within the model is the clarification of such meanings.

The Cognitive and Technology Group at Vanderbilt give a useful definition of the nature of the instructional software design (ID) process: 'ID is a discipline that is concerned with understanding and improving the process of instruction . . . The purpose of design activities is to prescribe optimal methods of instruction that could induce desired changes in student knowledge' (Xiaodong *et al.*, 1995, p. 55).

The purpose of the ID process is the creation of an 'architect's blueprint' comprising the following key steps:

(1)   Identify key learning objectives – that is, what do we want children to be able to do as a result of this programme of instruction?
(2)   Assess students' prior knowledge and skills.
(3)   Specify the content to be taught.
(4)   Identify key learning strategies and instructional methods to be used.
(5)   Develop instructional materials – tests, learner's manual, instructor's manual.
(6)   Test, evaluate and revise on the basis of the degree to which students have met the performance objectives.

This is clearly a systematic process based on the principle that, if we know enough about a learner and can control the learning environment sufficiently, we can bring about predictable changes in learning outcomes. Such an approach underpins the use of networks of dedicated computer terminals running so-called 'individualized learning packages' designed to teach basic mathematical and language skills. A vision of the entire school-aged population linked through the Internet to centrally commissioned learning packages swims uncomfortably before the eyes.

A limitation of this approach is that, in the process of attempting to improve instructional efficiency through the atomistic decomposition of the tasks, the inherent complexity of the learning process is ignored. There are few contexts in which the learner in real-life situations is simply required to re-present information in the exact form in which it was learned. If we consider the context of language, for example, each language interchange is a unique experience requiring creative responses based upon an understanding of implicit rules. Such system-mediated learning (Mandl and Reinmann-Rothmeier, 1995) it is argued (Resnick, 1987) has little or nothing to do with experiences in daily life. Knowledge may have been conveyed but unless it becomes part of the vocabulary of the learner which can be enacted in meaningful contexts it remains inoperative knowledge. Traditional instructional design models (Gagné and Briggs, 1979; Reigluth, 1983) fail to contend with this question and, by lacking a theory of learning, encourage passivity on the part of the learner.

In contrast to the behaviourist standpoint the constructivist philosophy emphasizes the active nature of the learning process. It is a positivist approach based upon Kantian beliefs which affirms that reality is 'constructed by the knower based upon mental activity' (Jonassen, 1995) in Piagetian terms, through the processes of accommodation and assimilation. Rather than asserting that knowledge exists independently of the individual and that, through a process of controlled instruction, the blank slate of the mind is conditioned, the constructivist predicates the active construction of knowledge.

The focus of attention therefore moves from instructional activities to constructional processes. Effective learning is seen not simply as a process transporting knowledge to the learner but rather as being developed through a series of negotiated objectives within *real* problem-solving contexts. Concern turns from the mediation of subject content towards the process and situations through which personalized constructs are acquired then related to existing conceptual frameworks. Within this model of *situated learning* (Mandl and Reinmann-Rothmeier, 1995) the learner is engaged in an active process in which knowledge, as a function of prior experiences, is mapped on to prevailing mental structures. The role of the educator within this paradigm is to provide the tools with which, the techniques through which and contexts in which this process can effectively take place.

It would be a misconception that a constructivist standpoint argues for the 'intellectual anarchy' (Jonassen, 1994) of individual realities or that it invalidates all instructional activities: '*It* does not mean that, from the constructionist point of view, memorisation and rote learning are considered useless. There are, indeed, matters that can and perhaps must be learned in a purely mechanical way' (von Glaserfeld, 1995, p. 11). Indeed, von Glaserfeld thinks that such activities are simply matters of 'generating the right discipline in students . . . *this* is essentially a task with which teachers have far more experience than any theoretician' (ibid., p. 5).

An instructional approach may, for example, be the most effective strategy in the development of automaticity of simple response skills, such as knowledge of mathematical tables. It is at a deeper level of learning that such approaches are less appropriate.

A limitation of the model lies in the individualization of the process. Whilst as with the behaviourist approach the action of mind is at its centre, it may fail to acknowledge meaning-making, imagination and motivational aspects of an essentially interactive process. It continues to predicate a model which 'does things to' rather than 'does things with' the learner. Additionally, it does not acknowledge the social and cultural aspects of the learning process, for most learning is a 'social enterprise' (Bonk, 1995) and it is within this social context that the powerful learning medium of language is developed. As Vygotsky (1978) reminds us, language has a vital role in enabling children to solve practical tasks, not simply with their eyes and hands, but also with speech.

Such social constructivist principles have had a significant impact in current educational thinking (Brooks, 1990). The model of knowledge construction which is mediated through the use of cultural artefacts (Wells and Chang-Wells, 1992), of which computers are a powerful example, is clearly at variance with a model which stresses competitive, individual learning of isolated didactically delivered facts and the teaching of unrelated sub-skills. Rather, it embraces the Vygotskian socio-cultural theories of intelligence (Wertsch, 1991) which emphasize 'conditionalized knowledge' in which knowledge and skills acquired through problem-solving activities can be more effectively reflected upon, transferred to and utilized within other problem-solving contexts. These principles are crucial elements in the field of Cognitive Flexibility Theory which stresses the importance of the ability to constantly '*restructure* one's knowledge, in many ways, in adaptive response to radically changing situational demands' and 'knowledge that will have to be used in many ways should be taught in many ways' (Xiaodong *et al.*, 1995, p. 57). Such a model of learning reaffirms the importance of coaching, contingent teaching, scaffolding and fading proposed by Bruner (1986).

Duffy and Jonassen (1996) have suggested that constructivist principles have had less impact on instructional software designers than would have been expected and that this is because a series of precise rules governing the design have not been produced. They contend that:

> Instruction, we believe, should not focus on transmitting plans to the learner but rather on developing the skills of the learner to construct (and reconstruct) plans in response to situational demands and opportunities . . . plans must be constructed, tested and revised as a function of the particular encounters in the environment.
>
> (Duffy and Jonassen, 1996, pp. 1–16)

Whilst it could be argued that precise guidelines cannot be provided in the same way that behaviourist blueprints can (Papert, 1991), a number of attempts have been made. A model proposed by Dijkstra (Dijkstra, 1995) incorporates such social constructivist principles of cognitive constructs, exploration, discovery, imagination, research, and development of learning strategies, into a traditional instructional design framework which pre-specifies content subject-matter and conceptual links within a specified subject-domain. The proposal attempts to balance what may be termed system-mediated learning and situated learning in a model of software design in which goals at three levels of performance are identified. In this model the acquisition of knowledge and skills within a specific context is achieved prior to the use of such skills in non-specific, everyday, contexts.

At the first level Dijkstra identifies problems of categorization. Skills developed at this level would include those of identification, recall and recognition through which individual examples are assigned to specific categories. This is followed at the second level by problems of interpretation in which relationships between concepts must be identified. The final level is marked by design problems of construction in which artefacts re-present the newly acquired understanding.

An example of this process in operation might be centred on the development of understanding of varying forms of trees. At level one the concepts of conifer and deciduous trees are developed through the presentation of a range of examples, key differences being identified. At the second level users are presented with a procedure to enable them to reach a pre-specified conclusion. For example, an attribute table may be used to assign specific examples to categories. Finally, a new artefact is created which is designed to enable other users to follow similar procedures; in this way new knowledge and skills are both reinforced and demonstrated, for the completion of products which allow the learner, or more likely an external assessor, to compare the user's understanding within a particular subject-domain with that of an expert is viewed as the end point of a cyclical process. In a similar manner, the development from intelligent help systems (IHS) (Breuker, Winkels and Sandberg, 1987) into '*Intelligent Courseware* is distinguished from (presumably unintelligent) Courseware, in that it creates a dynamic model of the student's understanding and compares it with an ideal model, an expert solution to the problem' (Eklund, 1997). In this way the support traditionally provided by the teacher is built into the system.

More general principles of design which can be used to support the development of packages within a constructivist framework have been outlined by Mandl and Reinmann-Rothmeier (1995). The principles and justifications they propose are that:

- learning takes place in a social context to ensure enculturization through discussion and shared action
- learning is based upon authentic problems in order to enhance motivation
- learning is carried out in many contexts to avoid skills becoming rigidly fixed
- learning takes place from multiple perspectives in order to facilitate greater flexibility in the application of the knowledge which is acquired.

In this way they focus attention on the way in which: 'technology-using educators are interested in instruction that focuses on developing the skills of the learner to construct and reconstruct context-based knowledge, problem-solving strategies, or plans of action to guide successful performance' (Knox-Quinn, 1995, p. 244)

Within this framework the role of the community – both the teacher and other learners – is to provide the setting challenges and to offer the support that will encourage learning to take place (Eklund, 1997). Such a conceptualization of learning which requires the construction of public artefacts through a process of social discourse can better be termed social constructionism.

The most commanding proponent of software designed to be used within this paradigm is Seymour Papert whose development of the programming language of **Logo** and whose seminal work *Mindstorms* (Papert, 1980) has been arguably the most influential book on the role of IT within an educational context. He defines constructionism in the following terms:

> ConstructioNism – the N word as opposed to the V word – shares constructivism's connotation of learning as 'building knowledge structures' irrespective of the circumstances of the learning. It then adds that this happens especially felicitously in a context where the learner is consciously engaged in constructing a public entity, whether it's a sand castle on the beach or a theory of the universe.
>
> (Papert, 1998)

The language he has designed allows the creation of a computer microworld which enables pupils to interact directly with the computer and through such interactions develop a range of mathematical skills and concepts, including estimation, knowledge of shape and space. In the process of developing such domain-specific skills, a context in which proficiency in problem-solving, planning and metacognitive skills is effectively encouraged.

The introduction of increasingly powerful computer systems together with the development of simple to use programming languages such as Logo, or the availability of multimedia and **web authoring** tools, has important implications for the teaching-learning situation. We are no longer simply considering how packages enable instruction or support teaching, for drill and practice packages alone cannot tap the developing potential of computers. Rather such tools move children from being mere consumers of predetermined packages to actual producers of software. The introduction of simple multimedia authoring packages, for example, moves children from the passivity of readers and responders to the activity of writers and authors. The centre of the activity and particularly control of the activity has been fundamentally changed; where Dijkstra would argue that a well-structured problem is a problem that can only be right or wrong, Papert would argue that learning takes place when we contend with the issues of the rightness of right and wrongness of wrong within any problem-solving context. Rather than having a series of predetermined answers which can simply be utilized in and mapped upon uniquely evolving situations, we are constantly involved in a process of 'bricolage' (Papert, 1992) of flexibly applying knowledge, skills and understanding through a process of reflective action.

Within this model teachers aim to identify present preconceptions and understanding, to increase the learner's repertoire of learning, processing and presentation styles, and to develop the learner's capacity to select between them (Resnick, 1987). The role of ICT within such a model is to provide learners with alternative tools to facilitate iterative learning through the support and encouragement of experimentation, inquiry and risk-free decision-making. A graphics package which allows children to fill a space with a solid colour then replace it moments later with a complex pattern is one such example of this enabling process.

At the simplest level developing technologies provide alternative methods of approaching known problems and alternative methods of carrying out traditional tasks; the enhanced interactivity of the package providing an increased level of stimulation and motivation. The best ICT tools, however, provide unique approaches which cannot be achieved in any other way. They allow completely different ways of thinking and allow tasks to be recouched in radically different forms. The importance of the inclusion of such tools is vital, for as Resnick reminds us: 'If a person has only a hammer, the whole world looks like a nail.'

The multiple possibilities provided by the developing technologies place the focus in an educational setting on supporting the ability to learn. The possibility of tensions within those schools which place great emphasis on the transmission of knowledge but neglect the development of heuristic methods, metacognitive skills or learning strategies is clear. The use of constructivist techniques implies increased time for their effective utilization and this has to be weighed against the proposed advantage of the development of other skills. 'Teachers who give so much autonomy to their students are declaring their belief in a radically different theory of knowledge, one that entails far more work for them as well as their students' (Papert, 1992, p. 63).

Pragmatic concerns are a legitimate part of class-level organization. Resistance to the effective use of technologies may, however, be grounded in unspoken issues of educational philosophy. Information and Communication Technology has a crucial role in facilitating the interactive learning process, but it is the use of the technology not its mere selection which is important. A word processor can be a liberating tool for creative self-expression. On the other hand, if its sole use is to carry out the repetitive tasks of copy-typing it becomes an educationally dehydrateded means of child control.

It is important to recognize that ICTs do not exist in a neutral way but are value-laden symbols. This study of the deeper meanings of things is called semiotics – let us take Logo as an example of the effect of such deeper meanings. In his discussion of the semiotics of Logo, Arnold (1995) highlights Lemke's statement that, 'In social semiotics, nothing has meaning: not a word, not a text, nor an action. Its meaning must be made by social practices that establish its relations to other words, texts, and actions. Different sub-communities make different meanings for words, texts, actions' (Lemke, 1988, p. 1).

Discussions of Logo use in schools are often based not on a discussion of program specifications, characteristics and learning outcomes, that is, specific features of Logo, but rather an interpreted meaning of the underpinning Logo philosophy, that is, an exploratory, non-didactic, experiential and, above all, progressive approach not to teaching but to learning. Users become part of a Logo community, a community from which non-users are excluded. Logo therefore functions, according to Pierce, 1973, (in Arnold, 1995), as a signal. At one level, it is a computer language, a system of ordering and controlling through the use of specific words or 'primitives', but at a deeper level it is a symbol of an educational approach.

I find that his arguments resonate powerfully with my own experiences. Some of my fiercest debates with teachers in England who are reluctant to incorporate ICT into their class curriculum have focused on the lack of the final *me* in the English spelling of the phrase *computer program*. Clearly, it is totally irrelevant for practical purposes if we use the spelling *programme* or *program*; for some staff, however, it clearly has particular significance. In Arnold's terms the debate is with the field of reference rather than the referent, with what the word signifies rather than with the word itself

(Crystal, 1995). In this example the final *me* acts as a trigger mechanism within the teacher's personal lexicon, activating for them a whole range of related and largely negative ideas including, perhaps, liberalism, non-standard spellings, Americanisms.

Whilst some (Papert, 1998; Resnick, 1997) would argue that the traditional school context is no longer appropriate for the development of the skills which will be required for the next generation, it is within such contexts that developments are planned to take place. Clearly the use of enabling technologies will require not simply an organizational restructuring to accommodate their effective use but a specific educational approach based on particular principles of learning for their successful implementation. Resistance to the use of enabling technologies may therefore be an unconscious response to an implied overall philosophy rather than resistance to the practical demands of time, organization or resource management. If we believe that such technologies can indeed revolutionize the learning potential for users, it is with such barely spoken views that we must therefore contend.

3

Developing Literacy

Mike Blamires

We could take a definition of literacy from any curriculum in the world and argue at length about what it included or excluded, what it prioritized or glossed over. However, being literate essentially means being able to respond successfully to the information demands of the society you are part of.

If you have to deal with a heavily print-oriented society the curriculum for literacy for the English and Wales National Curriculum is a good example of established priorities. It states that pupils should be taught to

- read accurately and fluently
- understand and respond to literature of increasing complexity drawn from the English literary heritage and from other cultures and traditions
- analyse and evaluate a wide range of texts.

The guidance goes on to describe key skills.

Pupils should be taught to read with fluency, accuracy and understanding. They should be taught the alphabet, phonic skills, the basic conventions of books and print, and effective techniques of reading, understanding and responding.

Pupils should be introduced to and taught to make use of, the various sources of information in order to establish meaning. They should be taught to apply various approaches to word identification and recognition, and use their understanding of grammatical structure and the meaning of the text as whole to make sense of the print.

(DfEE, 1988, 2.1, p. 8)

The areas are listed as follows:

- Phonic knowledge: the relationship between print symbols and sound patterns including their inconsistencies and modifying interaction, e.g. final e and soft c.
- Graphic knowledge: focusing on what can be learned about word meanings and parts of words from consistent letter patterns (these used to be called morphemes, i.e. units of meaning).
- Prefixes and suffixes, verb endings, plurals and root words.
- Word recognition: the development of a sight vocabulary aiding the automation of reading.
- Grammatical knowledge: focuses on the order and structure of written language (syntax).
- Using reading ahead and rereading to make sense of a sentence.
- Contextual understanding: focuses on meaning derived from the text as a whole, making use of their background knowledge and understanding of the book.

However, being literate means more than simply the ability to decode print, getting hold of the surface message. It means being able to bring experience and knowledge to bear on any text which is presented; being able to 'read the small print'; read between the lines. It does not take much imagination to appreciate the deeply damaging effects of not having access to literacy; lack of confident literacy affects not only learning opportunities but the fundamental human rights of any individual or group.

(Bearne, 1996, p. 53)

In contrast a booklet by the British Dyslexia Association covers the same topic:

What is Literacy?

Literacy aims
We want to read for enjoyment and information.
We want to write (using spelling and other skills) to express what we know or think, for ourselves or for communication with other people.

The task
The English Language has 26 letters and 44 sounds.
Many letters and letter-groups can be read in several ways.
Many sounds can be spelled in different ways.
Except for those few people with a photographic memory, we all have to work to learn reading and spelling. Some find it easier than others.

. . .

Reading and spelling skills
When we read, we look at a letter, letter group or word and think, 'What sound can those letters have?'
When we want to write a word, we perceive the sounds and then think 'Which letter(s) can we use to represent those sounds?'

(Hutchins, 1998, p. 4)

Here, the long-term aim of literacy is similar to Bearne's but the method of getting there is by decoding print to sound. If that is the case, reading is no more than learning the tricks that a programmer uses to turn text into synthetic speech (see **speech output**) but that is nonsense as the speech synthesizer does not understand what it has read. The curriculum requirements above acknowledge that other skills are involved, that the reader brings understandings to the text which are extended, contradicted or clarified by his or her engagement with the text.

So what is the authentic and inauthentic labour involved in being literate within the current age of technology? We no longer need to have good handwriting skills to write letters to important people. We can make telephone calls or use fax or electronic mail (email) after we have word-processed our letter. Having a 'good hand' is 'inauthentic' labour. If this is the case, then perhaps decoding and spelling skills are next. If so, we need to question educational practices that result in learners spending a significant part of their school life failing for little reason other than tradition.

For example, a National Literacy Hour has been introduced in England and Wales in schools for children between the ages of 5 and 11. This is intended to happen every day and consists of the following:

15 minutes   Class discussion of a text on a set topic.
15 minutes   Class work on words and sentences including phonics and spelling words.
20 minutes   In five groups set by reading ability working on shared or directed tasks, taking it in turns to be supervised by a teacher or another adult.
10 minutes   Class session discussing the work that has been done.

(DFEE, 1998, p. 5)

Similarly, in North America, Musselwhite and King-DeBaun (1997) suggest an approach to the development of literacy where writing, speaking and listening develop concurrently and interrelatedly, not in a sequence. This refutes previous notions that a learner should develop speaking and listening first with reading and eventually writing to follow and is in line with current practices in **augmentative communication** and the principles of **universal design**. It has been argued that the broad curriculum is irrelevant to a learner with low levels of literacy and that they should learn to read and write before they can join in. In this model the learner joins in by learning to read and write. (In the universal design model the learner just joins in.)

The basics of the four-block model are: guided reading, writing, self-selected reading and working with words. This has similarities to the approach of the English and Welsh National Literacy Strategy. However, in a whole class and group setting each area receives an equal portion of instructional time. The order in which the blocks are completed during a given day is thought to be unimportant.

Four-block model: block 1
In guided reading, students must understand that reading requires thinking and meaning-making; learning to use strategies and comprehend printed text, and to use a variety of types of books and other print materials.

ICT resources may include **word processors**, **cloze procedures** and **talking books**.

Making texts more accessible: supporting engagement with the meaning

A special needs teacher suggested on an Internet discussion list that all the texts that have to be encountered by children with reading difficulties should be simplified to make them more accessible. Is simplification the solution to this problem of inclusion?

What the reader brings to the text is as important as what the text can offer the reader. Bob Moy (1984) noted that many poor readers had difficulties with crudely simplified texts. He suggested that they were drowning in the shallow ends of language. Their own knowledge, values and ways of explaining the world were not being used to enable them to encounter new knowledge that was meaningful to them. Rather than overly simplifying text, we need to encourage teaching that enables poor readers to engage with the text, understand the ideas held within the text and evaluate the implications of these ideas.

A number of activities have been used to support groups of readers in dealing with texts. The 'Effective Use of Reading' project (Lunzer and Gardner, 1979) suggested the term 'directed activities relating to texts' (DARTs) as a description of these activities. These support the principle of universal design for learning as they are different ways that a learner can engage with a text.

DARTs

Classic DARTs
The first DARTs were paper-based activities.

SQ3r
This is a procedure for dealing with new texts. It consists of

- surveying the text: scanning through the text
- questions: identifying questions to be addressed by the text
- reading the text to see if the questions are answered
- recite: going over the points established
- review: another reading to check that nothing has been missed.

Prediction
Sections of the text are read and then the students discuss what will happen next.

Sequencing
Sections of texts are photocopied and then placed in a random order. Students discuss and provide evidence for the ordering of the text.

Cloze procedure
Usually every sixth or seventh word is blanked out or deleted. Real names and place-names should be avoided and the next word should be chosen for deletion. A more strategic selection of words or even phrases for deletion can facilitate more discussion leading to a better understanding of the text. However, cloze procedure can be over-applied and be used to literally 'fill in' time. Alternatively, if the task is about building the meaning of a whole text rather than just guessing the right word, then it can become a worthwhile task. Word processors now allow children to take more risks with their suggestions, as what they write in the gap can be changed easily. Banks of suggested words can be produced on a computer using an onscreen keyboard or overlay keyboard.

Hypertext: the World Wide Web
Surfing the web is a metaphor that conjures up superficiality and excitement at the same time. Maybe this metaphor needs to be upgraded to stress the possibilities of a greater engagement with readable materials on the web.

Instead of just surfing, the principles of **universal design** suggest that there should be alternative methods to support engagement with material on the web. Some of the targets of the National Literacy Project are entirely compatible with this view.

Ken Barker notes the problem of using web pages that do not support different forms of engagement when children are asked to do a research task such as 'find out about volcanos'.

> Many children are given simple instructions like this and told to 'surf the net'. Watch them. Like surfers, they bounce from wave to wave, they click from page to page. Of course, not a great deal happens, but you can guarantee that a piece of paper will emerge from the printer – containing somebody else's words. There is no research focus, there is no structure or purpose to the learning. We ought to be thinking in terms of 'mining the net', i.e. really getting below the surface with a purpose in mind, equipped with correct and appropriate tools.
>
> (Barker, 1998, p. 3)

> **Four-block model: block 2**
> In writing, students must write to become better readers; learn to write when given daily opportunities to see others write; have frequent opportunities to write without standards to make progress in the process of composition.

> ICT resources may include word processors, **word banks** in **onscreen keyboards** or on **overlay keyboards**, **symbol software**, **talking word processors**, **predictors**, **spell checkers**, **laptops** or **palm tops**, and **planners**.

The Internet provides many opportunities to write for different audiences and purposes through the use of **electronic mail**.

> **Four-block model: block 3**
> In self-selected reading, students must have daily opportunities to read easy books that they select to become better readers. They enjoy reading more when they can talk about and share books they read.

> ICT resources to support this may include **talking books** and texts written by other learners on **talking word processors**, **symbol software** and the **world wide web**.

Jeffrey (1996, p. 7) reported the opinions of an 11-year-old boy with specific learning difficulties and a reading level of 8 years. He had used a **talking book** alternated with the paper-based version of the same story for a number of teaching sessions. This is what he said:

(1)   It's got something to think about – a lot to understand.
(2)   When it's more fun you think it is easier. When it's boring then you don't want to read and you get stuck.
(3)   You learn more when it's fun and on a computer you think about it more.
(4)   Once you take more interest in the story line you understand the story better.
(5)   It is rewarding because you like it more, it's more fun and you take more interest and you just learn more if you take more interest.
(6)   I would like to look at it again because it's fun, a normal book is boring but on a computer it is fun and I want to do it over and over again even if it's the same.
(7)   I think my friends would like to work on the computer – they don't like reading books either – but they would like this.

It may be argued that this learner would have made a similar comparison if he had been asked if he preferred the video cartoon version rather than the book, and that he would say it was good because of the novelty effect. However, he may have been provided with enough support to be able to engage with a text rather than be frustrated by it. Jeffrey suggests that 'curling up' with a good book is a vital experience for someone learning to read. The talking book might be helping this boy to do this by providing scaffolding which looked after lower-level decoding skills so that he was able to think ahead and engage with the possible meanings of the text.

Four-block model: block 4
In working with words, analogic phonics are critical to the processes of reading and writing. Students must be taught what to do when they find a word they don't know. Traditional phonics instruction focuses on rules that describe how the letter sound system works, not how to use it.

The emphasis on the active application of these phonic skills in support of meaning-making is laudable. However, the ability to use speech synthesis (see **speech outputs**) and **voice activated software** plus the presentation of media in different modalities may mean that learners can circumvent these critical processes in reading and writing.

ICT resources that may support this are appropriate **word game** software that teaches phonics in relation to meaning, and **cloze procedure** with poems that have strong rhymes or alliteration.

Pen portraits

(You may wish to consider the pen portrait of Claire in Chapter 5 in this context. All names used in the pen portraits are fictitious.)

Pen-portrait: Eve
Eve is 10 and attends a mainstream school. On standardized tests administered by the school Eve is slightly above average in verbal and non-verbal ability but has difficulties with reading and spelling which are below her chronological age level. Her handwriting is poor and she has difficulty producing the drawings and diagrams required in different subject areas. Her writing includes reversals of letters and parts of words.

Eve's class uses the four-block literacy approach in which she has support for some activities from a classroom assistant who adds subject words to **selection sets** on an **onscreen keyboard** for use with a talking word processor for writing activities. In the shared reading activities she uses word games based upon words she has used in her writing and uses a talking book version of the class text.

She is also using a simple spreadsheet to produce tables and charts in her maths and geography work. Eventually, she may be allocated a laptop computer.

Points to consider:

(1)   Eve can manage the standard keyboard so it may be worth using a **typing tutor** to increase her familiarity with letter patterns. If she had significantly more

difficulties in using the keyboard some of the alternatives described by Lesley Rahamim in Chapter 7 should be considered.

(2)   To avoid distracting others in the class Eve uses headphones with the talking word processor.

(3)   If a laptop is considered later it will need to have appropriate software. Eve may not need all the facilities she is using now or she may need different facilities such as a **predictor**.

Pen portrait: Jean Paul

Jean Paul is 28 and studying for a degree in Psychology at university. He has had an assessment for dyslexia by an educational psychologist which stated that his reading and spelling skills were well below his verbal abilities. The psychologist also noted that he had a short-term memory deficit compared to his peers. Jean Paul had always struggled at school and left to work in a shoe factory for a few years. Eventually he restarted his studies at night school which, with support from college staff, led to his current course. Jean Paul has had the patience to train **voice activated software** which he uses on his desktop computer alongside synthetic speech to read and review his writing. Jean Paul is supported in seeking out visual resources for his subject on the **Internet** by his tutor who also has begun to publish some of his lectures notes and OHP presentations on the department's web pages. However, other colleagues are reluctant to do this because they fear it will reduce attendance at their lectures. Jean Paul has gained permission to audiotape their lectures for his personal use. In addition to using a statistical package to produce charts that visualize trends in data, Jean Paul uses a **planner** to organize his essays and project work in conjunction with voice recognition because he feels he is very disorganized.

Points to consider:

(1)   The lecturer's intellectual rights to the knowledge they impart in lectures is carefully handled in consultation with the tutor.

(2)   Will the university allow the use of IT in the examinations they set or does the course employ alternative methods of assessment? Would a scribe be allowed instead?

(3)   Would access to a scanner in the library be possible so that articles can be scanned in to be read back by the talking word processor on Jean Paul's desktop? Would this infringe copyright?

Conclusion

Information and communications technology can be used to support or ameliorate the achievement of traditional concepts of what it is to be print literate. Alternatively, it can be used to enable engagement with meanings that can be created and published in a wide range of modalities of which print is only one.

The National Council of Educational Technology (NCET) noted the importance of IT within the development of literacy in that:

used at its best, it is a collaborative medium; texts can be written collaboratively, and, with a computer screen, reading can be easily shared

it is interactive in nature

it broadens the concept of critical literacy

it is all-pervasive

it is a dynamic medium, always shifting and developing new forms.

(*Source*: http://www.ncet.org.uk/projects/cits/english/intro.html)

If schools concentrate on traditional print literacy many learners will be disadvantaged in the short and longer term.

Alternatively, we can use high technology to solve the educational problems of today and tomorrow but can we justify its use in solving the problems of yesterday?

Part II

Enabling Socialization

In the following three chapters we consider how learners can be enabled to engage with their peers in worthwhile learning activities. In each case it is clear that enabling technology needs to be facilitated by people who are at ease with the technology and who can empower others who may be less confident. In Chapter 4 , Sally Paveley considers how some people with learning difficulties are finding a voice through their use of technology.

Colin Hardy in Chapter 5 considers that ghostly tautology 'self-esteem' which has recently been linked with the development of empathy, social understanding and interpersonal skills (Goleman, 1995).

In Chapter 6 Richard Walter considers how communication and social interaction can be supported through the use of ICT by learners who have cognitive difficulties alongside physical disabilities.

A framework for action

The Theory of Mind (e.g. Astington,1993; Baron-Cohen, 1996) is an awareness of the mental world of beliefs and desires. Most young children naturally develop this awareness into an understanding that other people can have beliefs and desires and that people can have false beliefs.

Dennet (1996) suggests that minds can work at different levels to interpret their world:

- The physical stance, where the world is predicted by physical laws, e.g. dropping a stone.
- The design stance, which works with designed things including nature, e.g. press a button and the light goes on or plant a seed and it might grow.
- The intentional stance, where complex things have goals and desires. We use the intentional stance for people and animals, and sometimes we even apply it to photocopiers.

It is through meaningful interaction with older peers or adults that children develop cultural or social understandings. This may be seen as a consolidation or refining of the intentional stance which is akin to Feuerstein's (1976) 'mediation of meaning' (see **early learning**). These interactions may be linked with a refining of attentional styles which support social and cognitive functioning, i.e. the ability to focus, sustain, re-direct and share attention so that individuals can interact with their environment. Progress in the development of skills in sharing attention has been outlined by Reynell *et al.* (1978) and provides a context to understand what a learner is gaining from the use of technology to aid **early learning**.

A note on autism

Colin Hardy in Chapter 5 briefly notes that ICT may be useful in encouraging social interaction amongst learners within the autistic spectrum. Individuals with autism and Asperger Syndrome have different degrees of difficulties in understanding social interaction and the intentions of others. They need support in applying the intentional stance. The capability of ICT to be a visual medium may be of help in structuring and representing their environment, making implicit understandings more explicit. The visual-based approaches of Linda Hodgon (1995), Brenda Smith Myles with Richard Sampson (1998) and Carol Gray's *New Social Story Book* (1994a) and *Comic Strip Conversations* (1994b) may be readily transferred to take advantage of ICT. The editor is currently examining the potential of digital video as a means of facilitating social skills and understanding amongst learners with these difficulties.

Consider **early learning software, pictorial microworlds,** floor **robots, talking word processors, multimedia authoring, symbol software, planners, virtual reality,** but not facilitated communication. A discussion of which is beyond the scope of this book but see Twachman-Cullen's, 1997 highly authorative and critical assessment of facilitated communication as used with people with autism.

4

Advocacy and Self-Advocacy

Sally Paveley

Introduction

In 1983 I was a student in my final year of teacher training and I chose to write a dissertation entitled 'An Examination of the Use of Microcomputers in Severe Learning Difficulty Schools'. This choice was made for two reasons: first, I had read and been inspired by a booklet by Green *et al.* (1982), *Microcomputers and Special Education*. Second, final year students were not going to be admitted into the college's newly refurbished 'Micro Lab' – unless of course they were going to write a dissertation on 'Using Microcomputers . . .'! Green *et al.* convinced me that the 'micro revolution' was going to be important and exciting for the students I was going to teach. They suggested that two of the areas of difficulty that may be helped by computer use would be in generalizing from observations and transferring what was learnt in one situation to another (the metacognitive skills of sorting and grouping and then finding similarities between old and new problems). My subsequent experiences with the 'microcomputers' behind the locked doors of the laboratory showed me that this wasn't going to be as easy as I had thought because of the limitations of the educational technology of that time.

Fifteen years later I still feel the same way about both the inspiration and vision of people like Green, who have defined and developed the technology, and about the computers with which I continue to have 'interesting experiences'. Last week I worked with a group of sixth form students who attend a school for learners with 'severe learning difficulties'. They had used a digital camera to take photographs of the area around their school to send to their 'penpals' in another school many miles away. With the aid of an **overlay keyboard** they wrote symbol (see **symbol software**) enhanced letters describing their city neighbourhood and asking what it was like to live in a small town. Last night I read an **email** from a woman with learning difficulties telling others on the list about a new web site for self-advocates becoming empowered.

The label 'learning difficulties' can be confusing because it is used, and is therefore interpreted, in a number of different ways as noted by Mike Blamires in the opening chapter. When used in schools in the UK, it is qualified into types of difficulty, e.g. specific learning difficulty, and into degrees of difficulty, e.g. mild, moderate and severe including profound and multiple. The label 'learning difficulties' has been adopted by self-advocacy groups such as People First and rejected by many Social Services Departments in favour of the term 'learning disabilities'. The people I am referring to in this chapter probably attend or attended schools for students with severe learning difficulties (SLD) and I will use the label 'learning difficulties' because people who have learning difficulties have chosen to use it.

This chapter focuses on people with learning difficulties and the contribution ICT can make to their lives. It not just about learning; it is about becoming a member of society. It is about advocacy and enabling self-advocacy and not just about curriculum delivery. It is about the quality of life that a person can achieve at any stage of their development through the range of real choices that they can make. Ultimately it is about ICT enabling people to take control of their own lives and extending the possibilities open to them. It is not just about the technology in front of them but, more importantly, the support behind them. An interesting perspective on support is contained in the following excerpts from an email written by Jim Quist to the 'Usupport' mailing list.

> I am the friend of an individual who lives in a group home type of institution. What I do is honor my friend's initiative at every chance, but I offer very little choice.
>
> Self-direction is a 24-hour-a-day, moment-to-moment enterprise under the control of the individual. This can't be faked or planned for. People living real lives are not a snapshot frozen in time on a piece of paper – 'Tamera wants this, Tamera doesn't like that'. Such an approach is useful if it can lead to a better life, but it is not enough. With supported living, staff members often take control of a person's life with exactly the opposite in mind. For example, it is easy to get hung up on choice. In a group home setting, choice may come to represent the agenda and preoccupation of the staff, not of the person stuck there.
>
> Life requires spontaneity and serendipity. When a person is valued as an equal and listened to, they will start to speak up and take charge of their life. 'Tamera will make choices as it suits Tamera', a process quite different from the structured choices of a staff person wanting to help.
>
> 'A person is not a thing, but a process . . . a form of motion . . . not a noun but a verb'
> (Kelly, 1955, p. 83).

If we are to look at the contribution ICT can make to the empowerment of people with learning difficulties then we must begin by defining what we mean by empowerment. It is a term that is used widely and means, I suspect, different things to different people. Using electronic mail I put the question 'What does empowerment mean to you?' to 'Usupport', a mailing list for self-advocates and supporters. Bob Mercer, President of People First of Newfoundland and Labrador, Canada wrote: 'I believe empowerment is the ability to make one's own decisions. I am presently in my second term as President. . . . I wouldn't be able to run it if I wasn't empowered to do so. I still need help from time to time making difficult decisions, everyone does.' John Jacobs, another member of the list wrote: 'Empowerment to me means being able to take control of my own life including being able to use my computer.'

Nancy Pellegrino's reply illustrates the empowering effect of using ICT:

> I'm a Self-Advocate of People First of Massachusetts. Working with computers is a lot of fun and we can all learn from our own mistakes, we can all learn from computers, it's so easy to use it. I talk to people all over the world and learn from them as well. When I get upset I have people on line to make me feel good. We have people from all over to talk to and it's great.

Empowerment is about being, and more importantly feeling, in control of your life. It involves being supported by others when you need support and being supported in a way that helps you to remain in control. Information and communications technology can support this process by helping children and young people to develop the skills they will need to take their place as adult citizens in their community and the wider world. We will look at some ways in which this can be achieved later in this chapter.

We could start from a traditional special needs perspective which tends to define people in terms of what they cannot do. For example:

Some children with learning difficulties will be identified before school age and the great majority should be identified very early in their school careers. Their general level of academic attainment will be significantly below that of their peers. In most cases, they will have difficulty acquiring basic literacy and numeracy skills and many will have significant speech and language difficulties. Some may also have poor social skills and may show signs of emotional and behavioural difficulties.

(Code of Practice, 1994, p. 54)

However, to recognize a learning characteristic does not mean that it is fixed for ever and not susceptible to change (Norwich, 1996). Sitko and Sitko (1996) propose that ICT can provide the scaffolding (structured support) that enables the learner to engage with new learning tasks that they would not otherwise have been able to do. The focus moves from deficit to potential asset.

The TTA model of ICT outlined in Chapter 1 suggests a number of ways in which ICT can support learning. We can consider their implications within this discussion.

- *Provisionality*: delete and undo options allow mistakes to be corrected with relative ease.
- *Accuracy*: feedback can be provided as frequently as required in a manner meaningful to the user.
- *Presentation*: ideas can be presented in a wide range of formats including sound, video, music, pictures and graphics. A multi-sensory approach can be used or a preferred modality used.
- *Communication*: technology can aid the process of communication. Work can be published to a wide audience electronically in a range of formats.
- *Speed*: laborious aspects of work can be eliminated such as letter formation and the duplication or movement of text, images and sound. Whole words can be recognized, listened to and entered.
- *Information*: a wide range of information from CDs and the web is available which may be used to engage the interest of the learner.

Preschool

Learning difficulties can arise from a wide variety of causes some of which are identifiable from birth, for example, Down's Syndrome. People can also acquire learning difficulties at any time in their lives, for example, as a consequence of accident or illness. There are also many people who have learning difficulties for no easily identifiable reason.

For some children, a condition that manifests learning difficulties as one of its characteristics is diagnosed at birth. For other families the first indicators that their child may have a learning difficulty appear gradually as the motor and communication milestones common to all infants are reached much more slowly than in the child's peer group or are not reached at all during infancy.

It is important to point out that, whilst the likelihood of a child having a learning difficulty may be identified at an early stage, the extent to which this will affect the child's learning ability cannot be predicted. Many children will, with appropriate extra help and encouragement from their parents or carers, and possibly support from professionals such as speech and language therapists and teachers, achieve the early milestones albeit later than their peers.

Where a child's learning difficulty is compounded with a severe physical disability and/or a sensory impairment, then a much greater degree of professional support is needed by the parent or carer in order to provide the child with appropriate strategies and experiences to cope with this additional barrier to learning. Richard Walter in Chapter 6 writes about his experiences with children and young people who have physical disabilities and sensory impairments in addition to learning difficulties.

What is the role of ICT in early years?

In the preschool years ICT can be used to extend opportunities for learning through interaction and exploration. It can be used to support the mediation of meaning between infant and parent or carer providing stimuli for the shared attention that underpins the development of communication skills. For example, **talking books** and other **early learning** software provide the child with the added stimuli of sound, animation and opportunities to control onscreen events. These features can extend concentration and motivation as the child and adult interact with the software and have fun together providing quality shared attention.

For children who have additional physical disabilities ICT can be used to provide them with opportunities to control toys and other devices via **switches**. For some children this may be their only means of making something happen independently! For more detail about this type of ICT application see Richard Walter's contribution in Chapter 6.

The school years

Inclusion in the state education system and the provision it makes is particularly important to the parents and teachers of children who have learning difficulties. The response of teachers of children with severe learning difficulties to the English and Welsh National Curriculum indicated that inclusion was important. Prior to the Education (Handicapped Children) Act 1970 children who were labelled 'mentally handicapped' were considered 'ineducable' and provision was made for them by the health authorities. They were excluded from schools and placed in 'training centres' which had a 'custodial' or 'caring' ethos. In 1971 local education authorities assumed responsibility for them. Today the majority of children and young people with (severe) learning difficulties will be educated in special schools a small minority will attend mainstream schools. In England and Wales, the Department of Education and Science (DES) stated in 1989 that 'All pupils share the same statutory right to a broad and balanced curriculum, including access to the National Curriculum.' Peter Mittler (1991) reiterates this commitment to this statement when he writes in the foreword of *Literacy for All*, 'There can be no doubt about the strong commitment (by teachers of children with severe learning difficulties) to ensure that all pupils are entitled to a "broad, balanced and relevant curriculum".' *Literacy for All*, Ackerman (1991) was one of a series of books exploring ways in which students with learning difficulties could be included in the National Curriculum of England and Wales. The concept of 'entitlement' to a common curriculum was a stimulus and challenge for inclusive practices.

What is the role of ICT in the school years?

The National Curriculum entitles all students to develop 'IT capability'. In addition to this, schools are expected to use ICT in the steps they take to meet special educational needs. 'For pupils with learning difficulties, IT can provide cognitive access (to the curriculum). IT enables us to present the curriculum in a variety of ways, thereby encouraging the pupil who has difficulty grasping the concepts, skills and knowledge required of him' (Day, 1995, p. 4).

There is a great deal of anecdotal evidence that ICT can have benefits for children with learning difficulties. The opportunity to use an **overlay keyboard** and onscreen **selection sets** containing symbols linked to a talking symbol (see **symbol software**) processor has enabled many students to develop literacy skills that would have been beyond their reach a generation ago. **Talking books** enable students to experience and interact with literature in a multi-sensory manner without needing to decode the printed text themselves. Technology facilitates the learner obtaining swift feedback with a range of modalities. Controlling a floor **robot** enables students to develop thinking skills and mathematical concepts (Haigh, 1990). This moves learning into three-dimensional space related to the perspective of self and/or through body movements. Multimedia authoring can be used by students to combine familiar sounds and images in presentations that reflect and validate their own experiences.

Adulthood

If one of the purposes of education is to prepare the child for life as an adult then adulthood should be the culmination of this process in a life that is chosen and controlled by the individual in question. Adults with learning difficulties, as discussed above, like all people, need varying degrees of support depending on their individual circumstances. Historically, adults with learning difficulties have been marginalized and stigmatized. They have been placed in large institutions far from their families; they have been given degrading labels; they have been the subject of both fear and ridicule from the general populace; they have been politically voiceless and powerless (e.g. Foucault, 1967).

The work of Barton (1998) and Armstrong (1998) suggests that this was not always the case. Whereas agricultural communities could and did utilize the wide range of abilities of people, the Industrial Revolution created new demands for workers who could handle machinery for long periods of time. Those who could not work in these conditions had to find work elsewhere or were condemned to the workhouse or asylum as surplus to requirements.

Information and communications technology can be the means of bringing marginalized people back into their communities. More recently there have been initiatives that are leading this change. In the UK the closure of institutions and the move towards providing care in the community was a first step in the process of including people with learning difficulties in society rather than expelling them from it. While this book is probably not the right place to go into detail about the issues arising from changes in government legislation that affect people with learning difficulties, perhaps the most exciting consequence of the change in the political climate, from rejection to a form of acceptance, has been the rise of the self-advocacy movement.

The following statement, taken from the Northamptonshire People First web site, illustrates the power of self-advocacy when combined with the Internet. It also sums up how some people feel about how they have been treated.

Who are we?

We are run and controlled by people with learning difficulties.

We work to improve the lives of all people with learning difficulties.

In the past we used to be called labels like mentally handicapped, mentally retarded, intellectually handicapped, or mentally subnormal.

We didn't like these labels as they kept us down. We choose to use 'learning difficulties' ourselves. It is a label which doesn't hurt us as much as those above.

Jars should be labelled not people!

We know what it is like not to have much power in our lives.

To be treated differently from other people because we have learning difficulties.

To have other people make decisions for us.

We are here to speak up for all people with learning difficulties.

What is the role of ICT in the adult years?

As adults in the UK we live in an 'information rich', some may say 'information saturated' age or even an 'info. glut'? We use ICT in our homes, for our work, for our leisure and for our learning. We use ICT because it makes some things easier or quicker to do and we use ICT because we choose to. We use ICT because it is available to us but some of us choose not to use ICT. Some of us do not have or cannot afford access to ICT. Some of us don't know how to use ICT. Adults with learning difficulties will use or not use ICT for similar reasons, but they do face additional difficulties. At a minimum, they will need powerful machines that can use multimedia efficiently to provide swift feedback in an appropriate way and alternative input devices.

The issues here are about cost, opportunity and access. If by ICT we are talking about the latest and fastest computer technology then we can expect to find it in the homes of people who have a reasonably high income. While you now get many more 'bytes for your buck' than you did ten years ago, the cost of an average home computer system seems to remain fairly static. People with learning difficulties do not generally have a reasonably high income. For many the only opportunity to use ICT will be outside the home in the community services they use. These may be day centres, colleges and other establishments that make special provision. Here the way in which ICT is used is likely to be decided by the service providers rather than the users themselves. Finally, ICT resources that are made available to the general public in places like libraries and supermarkets are often inaccessible to people with learning difficulties because they are set up with an assumption that users will be able to read and follow onscreen instructions.

Historical use of IT leading to key approaches and principles

When computers were first introduced into SLD schools on a wide scale they were met with a variety of responses from teachers. There were a few teachers who rose enthusiastically to the challenge of shaping this new technology to meet the needs of their students; there were many more who were simply bewildered. In 1981 I carried out a case study in an SLD school for the dissertation mentioned at the beginning of this chapter. Here is an excerpt from the diary I kept:

> My visit began in the staffroom where I was waiting for the teacher with responsibility for the computer to finish a PE lesson. I spoke with several teachers as they took their coffee break explaining that I had come to do some work on a report about computers. I asked how they felt about the computer and the general response was that they wouldn't have a clue how to use it and couldn't really see the point of having it. I did not speak to one teacher who believed it would be of value.

The feelings of many teachers at that time can be summed up in this response to a questionnaire I sent out to twenty schools for children with severe learning difficulties as another part of my dissertation:

> Although the DTI (Department of Trade and Industry) scheme to help with the cost of computers was inviting we have not been convinced of their value in our school and felt we would find more appropriate ways of spending our money . . . Perhaps you will come up with some interesting answers and conclusions to the use of computers in SLD schools. We are still open to being, (perhaps hoping to be) convinced.

These responses were hardly surprising. Computers were seen by most people at that time as highly complex machines that required a great deal of expertise to use and most teachers did not see themselves as 'computer experts'. Furthermore the cognitive leap required to comprehend just how such technology could be of benefit to students who had learning difficulties was simply too great for many teachers. The concept of the personal desktop computer that could be used by everyone was only just beginning to emerge and is still developing as the practice of **universal design** becomes more widespread.

While there was a general antipathy on the part of teachers towards this new technology there was also a growing vision of its power as a tool that could change people's lives. Evangelical claims were even made for it! Seagrave (1983) suggested in a talk at that time that 'Technology gives the power to perform biblical miracles'. Maddison (1982, p. 5) stated that the computer is 'Possibly the most significant new educational tool since the printed book'. Sheingold, Kane and Endreweit (1983, p. 141) added a note of caution when they wrote, 'But a piece of equipment does not a revolution make'.

The role of ICT within the curriculum has evolved from an optional extra that teachers could choose to either utilize or ignore, to an entitlement for students that teachers are under a statutory obligation to provide. The National Curriculum for England and Wales has placed ICT within each of the subject areas and has acknowledged its role in the support of students who have special educational needs.

Some of the ICT tools that have been developed to support students with learning difficulties have indeed made a significant contribution to their lives. In the 'early' days access to ICT was hampered by a scarcity of software that was suitable. The need to use a keyboard to interact with a computer presented another barrier to the students. These difficulties were overcome as alternative input devices such as **overlay keyboards** became available and software developed that presented graphics and sound cues to the user rather than just text.

Much of the early software for students with learning difficulties was focused on the development of basic skills. This could be described as an extension of the 'Teaching Machine' concept developed in the 1930s. Activities ranged from pressing a **switch** to make something happen (cause and effect software) to simple matching and sorting tasks that give a reward when you get it right (drill and practice). These programs were, and still are, often the easiest for teachers to use because the content is predetermined by the programmer and the teacher just follows the onscreen instructions. Such software has its uses but one would hardly classify it as 'revolutionary'.

The advent of **symbol software** which adds symbols to words as they are written, however, is an example of how ICT can change teaching practices and learning opportunities in ways that are revolutionary. Students for whom the development of literacy was a distant dream are now reading and writing with symbols. Some go on to develop traditional orthographic skills, others will remain 'symbol literate' – a concept that challenges traditional definitions of what it means to be literate. The 'symbols revolution' that began in schools is now present throughout services provided for adults with learning difficulties. Service providers are under pressure to provide information that is accessible and the use of symbols may be one way by which this can be achieved.

The 'symbols revolution' is not without controversy. There are issues about which symbol system should be used, the lack of standardization between symbol systems and 'ownership' of the symbols (see also Chapter 9). There are members of the self-advocacy movement who perceive symbols as yet another device imposed on people with learning difficulties by professionals and resent the fact that end-users were not involved in the process of developing the systems. It is important to recognize that adults should be consumers of symbols not consumed by them.

Furthermore not everyone is able to decode symbols. For some people they are too abstract. Another issue is the readability of the text that is written. The act of adding symbols to a piece of text does not make it automatically accessible to somebody who can read symbols. For example, a tenancy agreement written in complex legal jargon will be no more accessible with symbols than without them.

Mary Hope (1986) made a distinction between 'content specific' and 'framework' software. Software like the basic skills programs mentioned above generally fall into the content-specific category. The programmer defines the content and the user is meant to do what the programmer had in mind. Framework software, on the other hand, provides a framework for the user to work within. The advantage of this type of software lies in the opportunities it affords the user to determine the content. A word processor is a good example: the programmer provides a tool to write with but the user decides what to write. A symbol processor combined with symbols on an **overlay keyboard** or **onscreen keyboard** is a good example of framework software that is particularly useful to students with learning difficulties.

Framework software can enable teachers to customize ICT to suit the requirements of their students. These applications can enable students to explore and extend their creativity as well as their cognitive and communication skills. Framework software encourages teachers and students to become active consumers of technology rather than passive recipients. It is often through framework software that users can exploit the power of ICT to achieve results that otherwise would be extremely difficult if not unattainable for them. Art and design programs enable many people to draw a perfect circle or square, or experiment quickly and easily with different colour combinations in a design task. Controlling a **floor robot** engages the user in a task involving the higher order skills of hypothesizing and problem-solving but in a context that is tangible.

The distinction made between content-specific and framework software has been recognized as one of the key principles of universal design for learning. This is the desirability of multiple representation to suit different perceptual and learning styles. A content-specific program has its content bound up in its structure. A vital potential of the **world wide web** is that structure and content can be separate. The temptation to structure content should not preclude others from applying a different structure of part or the whole of the content for a different audience. The NCET (1997) reports on subject groups of software often noted that this was a problem with many collections whether they be historical documents, photographs, poems or gallery collections.

There are some ICT applications that were simply not possible when the first computers were placed in SLD schools. The arrival of the 'multimedia' computer system with its high-quality graphics and sound capability has improved considerably the visual appearance of software, a fact in itself that is of tremendous importance when the computer is being used by someone who may have a visual perceptual difficulty. The replacement of the rather tinny noises that the early computers were capable of making with digitized sound was a great improvement, particularly for users who have difficulties with auditory discrimination. These features mean that people can be valued in terms of their preferred modality of operation. The possibility of using a **multimedia authoring package** to combine photographs the students have taken with sound the students have recorded into a presentation that they have created is exciting. The opportunity to use the Internet to broadcast that presentation to the world is mind blowing! Children and adults who were largely invisible and without a voice a generation ago can now become players on a world stage.

Supporting teacher development of ICT skills

Whilst the possibilities offered by ICT are truly inspiring to those who have chosen to embrace the technology, there are still many parents, carers, teachers and others who lack the skills and enthusiasm that are necessary to exploit these possibilities. The prospect of creating a multimedia presentation and publishing it on the Internet would probably leave the majority of teachers rushing to the staffroom for a stiff cup of coffee and stress counselling. Becoming a competent and confident user of ICT takes time, commitment and access to a computer. The odd half-hour on your class computer between the students going home and the next curriculum development meeting is hardly ideal especially when something goes wrong and the IT co-ordinator is on the phone to a distressed parent. A computer in a quiet room at home and a reassuring voice on the end of a telephone when you need it is likely to be far more conducive to becoming computer literate and confident. The gap between the enthusiastic proponents of ICT and those who are reluctant users remains. It is a gap that does a disservice to the children and adults who stand to benefit from the opportunities that ICT can afford them. As I stated earlier in this chapter, it is not the technology in front of them but the support behind them that matters.

Pen portrait 1 – a timetable for John

John was 3 years old. He had been coming into the nursery on a part-time basis for some time and was about to start school on a full-time basis. While he seemed to enjoy most of the nursery activities once they got started, he found the transition between activities difficult to cope with. Sue, his teacher, was concerned that an increase in these changes that would come as a consequence of full-time attendance would overwhelm him. She wanted to find a way to prepare him for what was going to happen throughout the day.

Sue had enrolled on a two-day 'Introduction to Multimedia' course and on the first day she was asked to produce a presentation for the second day later in the term. She decided to create a multimedia timetable for John and asked me to help her. John liked the computer and Sue felt that this would be an ideal medium for preparing John for the day ahead.

We began by using a digital camera to take photographs of John at different times. For example, John coming into school, John having his lunch, John in the playground, John doing activities in the classroom. We then recorded Sue's voice describing what John was doing. Finally, we combined the photographs and sound samples into sequences of pages for each day of the week. The end product was also printed out to make a book for John to use when he didn't have access to the computer.

Sue then used the presentation and the book with John on a regular basis and reported that in her opinion it had worked extremely well. John has now settled into the nursery routine and still loves using the computer.

Pen portrait: making books with a reception class

I had been working with a reception class using a painting program with a touch screen when the class teacher suggested that we might put the children's work into a book. The program came with some drawings that could be coloured in using a fill tool so we began be asking each child to choose a picture of something they liked. This choice was, of course, restricted to the pictures on offer. In the first session each child chose a picture then chose some colours to paint it with. These were saved and printed out.

We had decided that each child would contribute a page that contained their photograph with their name, a 'like' symbol and the word 'likes' followed by their chosen picture. As photographs of the children were already on the computer I suggested that we create a multimedia book as well as a paper one. In the second session each child used a microphone to record their voice and we added the recording to their photograph.

In the final session a 'like' symbol and the pictures the children had coloured were added to the multimedia book and each child recorded the name of their chosen picture. They then all used the touch screen to make the computer read out their pages.

The pages were printed out and the teacher laminated them and spiral bound them into a book for the whole class. He also made individual books for each child with their name on the first page followed by 'likes' on the second page and their picture on the last page. These were books that all the children in the class were able to read themselves.

Pen portrait: talking books with Anna

Anna is a lively 9-year-old with lots of problems; she displays many challenging behaviours which prevent her from making the educational progress that she is clearly capable of. Anna can be affectionate and engaging, when she is calm she is delightful to work with but she is easily distracted into disruptive and anti-social behaviour.

Anna likes using the class computer and was very motivated to use the talking books that the school had just acquired. The first few times I worked with Anna and the talking stories she responded extremely well. She would talk about what was happening in the pictures and could answer questions about the story. She is able to use a mouse competently and was soon accessing the stories independently.

Later in the term I returned to work with Anna. By this time she had developed a fixation on one of the stories and refused to let me run any of the others. She was no longer talking about what was happening in the story preferring to repeat certain phrases over and over again. The need to be in control of the story and to use it for what had become her own agenda had taken over from the interest and exploration that had been a feature of our earlier sessions. She has now done similar things with other programs.

Anna is motivated to use the computer and the fact that it is a medium that she can control is enabling her to act out something that she needs to act out, but it is increasingly difficult to progress the use of ICT beyond Anna's own agenda. Information and communications technology is not going to solve everyone's problems.

The pen portrait of Anna illustrates several points. The first of these is that we as teachers have an agenda when we teach. We have a purpose in mind that relates to learning. We like to assume that our students will follow the same agenda and validate our teaching by learning what we expect them to learn. When we used the talking book my agenda was to extend Anna's literacy skills and the early indicators were that I was being successful. Anna talked about the pictures and was able to discuss the content of the stories. Anna's agenda was different. She was prepared to go along with my agenda until she had learned to control the book sufficiently well to use it to satisfy her own needs. These clearly did not include the development of literacy skills.

A second point that Anna illustrates relates to who is in control of the technology. Anna, like many other students, is able to start up the computer and use the mouse to start up and shut down applications. Anna has used these skills to develop ritualistic ways of using a variety of programs. There is no easy answer to the question of whether or not this is desirable for Anna but I have found that where students have been given free access to a computer, problems for the teacher can arise when she or he then decides to assume control and turn what the student regards as a toy for playing their favourite game into a teaching tool.

Pen portrait: the zebra crossing (Pedestrian Crossing)

The art teacher had been working with a small group of students aged 12–13 on recognizing black and white. This was to complement work they were doing on road safety and her objective was to produce a zebra crossing using various techniques including printing on various materials and taking rubbings. Some of the lessons involved the students going off the school premises and using different media such as charcoal and candle wax to make rubbings of artefacts such as drain covers, paving stones and plaques that were then taken back to class and painted on with contrasting paint. They also practised using a zebra crossing.

To make a record of this work and to extend it I suggested that we take photographs with the digital camera and build these into a multimedia presentation. We added a session with the computer to the end of each lesson. The day's photographs were downloaded and this provided the students with an opportunity to talk about what they had done. We used a microphone to record their comments and added these to the photographs. Some of the students needed a lot of support to articulate their comments but the photographs helped them to remain on task. They all enjoyed using the touch screen to play back their contributions.

Finally, a menu page designed to look like a zebra crossing with symbols on each of the stripes completed the presentation. This work helped the students by providing them with an additional medium through which to experience the concepts of black and white and road safety, a vehicle to extend their language, an *aide-mémoire* and a means of validating their experiences. It also helped the teacher to appreciate how ICT could contribute to her work.

Adult pen portrait: writing with symbols

Reg attends a day centre that took part in a project which was exploring how symbols could help people to become more independent. The project worked with a group of people to develop and facilitate their ideas rather than to teach a specific set of skills. The project aimed to examine how symbols could be used to make information more accessible and as a way of recording and expressing written information. Reg was not able to read or write and, prior to the project, had shown little interest in doing so. He chose to take part in the project because he liked computers.

Some months into the project Reg said he would like to write an article for the centre magazine. He told his supporter what he wanted to say and this was typed into a word processor that placed symbols above the words. Where the symbols helped Reg they were left in the document and if a symbol confused Reg it was removed. When the article was finished the computer 'read' it back and it was printed out. Reg was very proud of his work.

In the weeks that followed Reg and I read the article together many times. I would read the words without symbols and pause while Reg read the symbols. This gave him a great deal of pleasure but it was not until the final editorial meeting that the full extent of Reg's achievement became apparent. In response to a rather tactless question from another member of the group who asked 'Why can't Reg read?', Reg replied 'I can read, I can read the symbols', and proceeded to read his entire article unaided.

Reg has gone on to write more articles. His self-confidence and the perception others have of his ability have risen considerably. Reg now sees himself as somebody who can read, a skill that is valued highly and one that he was aware he didn't possess prior to the project.

The pen portrait of Reg writing with symbols provides a powerful example of empowerment through ICT by helping people to develop the skills needed to take their place as citizens in the community and the wider world.

There are different ways of supporting a person who is using symbols to write. **Overlay keyboards** and onscreen **selection sets** containing symbols give people independent access to a limited vocabulary and sometimes these provide the best support. Similarly some people will find an overlay keyboard easier to use, others will prefer onscreen word banks. For Reg dictating what he wanted to say to a supporter was the most appropriate solution.

The most important aspects of writing with symbols are that the writers are able to write what they want to write and, furthermore, that the writers have opportunities to read and understand what they have written.

Adult pen portrait: an on-line community

People with learning difficulties are using the Internet to speak up for themselves. They are discovering that there are people around the world who have similar life experiences and are providing support for each other. Using facilities like email, on-line chat and video conferencing, people are making friendships and learning about the world. The following extracts from the 4th International People First Conference web site provide an insight into what is now possible.

ANCHORAGE, April 22 1998 – More than 900 people from around the world have begun to arrive in Anchorage for the 4th International People First Conference April 23–25, the largest meeting of its kind ever to be held in the US.

From: Kristin Ryan
Date: 3/23/98
We would like to welcome you to the People First chat room. If you have any specific questions about this forum or comments please respond! This page is set up for conference participants to communicate with others not able to attend and for ongoing discussions about important self-advocacy issues. Please participate!

From: The On-Line Connection Committee
Date: 3/28/98
We are a group of Self Advocates around the world who are working to support other Self Advocates to connect with the International Self Advocacy movement and the People First International Conference at Anchorage.

We are determined that the Internet be 'Accessible to All' and that this includes people with learning difficulties. We are determined to help people who cannot come to Anchorage so that they can share in the spirit of Self Advocacy.

We have been working together for up to 5 years and we know how to help people regardless of disability or access to resources.

We welcome your involvement. We respond quickly, with kindness, respect, determination and good humor to everyone.

Gracias Arigato Merci Ef charisto Dunkashern Toda rahbah Suchrum Thanks Cheers The On-Line Connection Committee

From: Don OCallaghan
Date: 4/26/98
Self Advocacy is a 365 day a year thing.

The people who are working on the on-line connection will continue to meet through the year. The video conferencing we demonstrated at the conference will continue and there will be on-line presentations, meetings and social gatherings.

We now have some very effective ways to communicate whenever we want with all Self Advocacy organizations around the world. This has never been possible before. Next year it will be ordinary.

The On-Line Connection Committee will continue to work to support 'Access to the Internet for All'. We are learning at an incredibly fast rate and are very good at including all people, regardless of disability or access to resources. This does take work, but we know how to do this and we can teach anybody.

The rewards, and the potential of this is huge. There are risks, but these risks are the same risks that have always existed. We know how to manage them.

Take the International Challenge.

The pen portrait of an on-line community speaks for itself. People with learning difficulties have been marginalized and isolated. The Internet can provide opportunities for that to change by enabling people to communicate with one another. This will not be a solution for everyone. Many people do not have access to the Internet, others do not have the skills or support that would enable them to make full use of the facilities that are currently available. At present much of the information on the Internet is text-based and this excludes people who cannot read. Search engines assume literacy skills. Electronic mail currently requires literacy skills. These obstacles have yet to be overcome but the will is there, it is just a matter of time before the solutions are found.

Key conclusions

The three pen portraits, 'A timetable for John', 'Making books' and 'The zebra crossing', illustrate the flexibility and versatility of multimedia applications. One major advantage of this type of application lies in its ability to enable students and those supporting them to create onscreen **microworlds** that reflect and validate the experiences of the users.

Each activity was part of a larger agenda and this is another important consideration when planning for the use of ICT. In each case ICT enhanced the activity by adding a dimension that could not be achieved in any other way.

It is also important to acknowledge that ICT may not always provide a suitable way of enhancing or extending an activity. I still clearly remember my daughter, then aged 5, saying 'But I don't want to use the computer Mummy, I want to use felt tips and paper!' I gave her the felt tips.

Key software

The software in this list is described in the References at the end of this book.

- Symbol software.
- Multimedia authoring software.
- Software to support literacy and numeracy.
- Software that allows students to consolidate skills in ways that are fun and rewarding. Teachers need to check for ambiguity in the presentation of tasks. I did have one student who was meant to count the flowers but started counting the petals instead! Students can often use these programs independently; some keep a record of what the student has done which can be useful. These programs can also

be used with groups of students, then discussion can take place. Most of these programs can be easy to use, you just start them up and follow the instructions.

- **Painting and drawing** software: look for painting and drawing software that can be customized so you don't have to have lots of tool buttons available if you don't want them, as these can confuse students. Symmetry tools and other effect tools can enable students to create very pleasing pictures. Stamps are fun but can be overused. Introduce the tools one at a time; many users will simply whiz around the screen without realizing which tool they are using unless this is drawn to their attention. Painting and drawing software can be a good way of helping students to develop mouse control. Use a mouse port switch adaptor (see below) to avoid unwanted mouse presses that can have alarming consequences. Painting and drawing software is easy to use. You just click on a tool and see what it does.
- Overlay keyboard software: this will allow you to create selection sets to use with your **overlay keyboard**. You should also be able to print these out. The overlay keyboard is most useful for supporting writing. I select sets of symbols in black and white on A4 size paper and use a photocopier to expand them to A3 size for my overlay keyboard. I also make an A4 copy for each of the students and we discuss these before we work on the computer. For other uses of overlay keyboard software see 'Key hardware; overlay keyboards' and the References.
- **Onscreen keyboard** software: this allows you to create selection sets including pictures, symbols and sound. The selection sets can usually be 'nested' so you can have a fairly long list displayed in manageable chunks. I have found these most useful with more able students when writing with symbols. If the student needs big symbols then the screen soon gets cluttered and it becomes difficult to discriminate between the symbols in the bank and those that have been written. Creating selection sets does require some thought and effort from the teacher, particularly if you are going to make multilayered or 'nested' banks.
- Talking books.

Key hardware

- Overlay keyboards: overlay keyboards are most commonly used to enable students to write. They can also be used to enter information and control other applications such as databases and spreadsheets. There are graphing programs that allow the user to enter information from an overlay keyboard in order to build up a pictogram. It is also possible to set up an overlay keyboard to access the Internet by creating an overlay file with web site addresses and other tools that the user may need like 'Back' and 'Forward' buttons.
- Touch screens: many students with learning difficulties find it difficult to use a mouse and manage far better if they can interact directly with the screen.
- Mouse port adaptor for switches: I have found this a useful device when using a CD-ROM with a group of students. I just pass the **switch** to the student whose turn it is to make something happen and they press it. This prevents the disruption of the student coming to the computer preventing the rest of the group from seeing the screen.
- Serial port extension lead. This lets you plug in your overlay keyboard or digital camera without having to get at the back of your computer.

5

Raising Self-Esteem

Colin Hardy

Introduction

The benefits of ICT for students who have various types of special educational needs produces a surprising degree of agreement between popular opinion, legislators and researchers, and is a consistent theme in recent DfEE pronouncements. The English and Welsh Green Paper (DfEE, 1997, 42.6) states: 'New technology can help improve access to the curriculum and limit pupils' communication difficulties'. More specifically, improved motivation and self-esteem are frequently identified as resulting from the use of computer technology. Strack, for example, states:

> The interactive nature of IT can improve concentration, motivation, independence and self-esteem as well as developing problem solving, thinking and communication skills. . . . In some cases it could be important to ensure that access to different forms of IT is written into pupils' statements (IEP in US) to ensure access to the curriculum.
>
> (Strack, 1995, pp. 9–26)

Experience of real classroom situations sadly indicates that 'access to different forms of IT' is only the start. Curriculum engagement is equally dependent upon empowering those people who will be expected to use the software and hardware; pupils, parents, learning support assistants, teachers, and so on. It is an exploration of the generic principles underlying this later area that is the main focus of the descriptions and practical examples in this chapter.

The aims of the chapter are to

- sketch out the commonly agreed features of 'self-esteem'
- explore some of the 'special qualities' ascribed to ICT and hypothesize how these might be focused on the raising of self-esteem
- suggest 'generic principles' to apply to the 'real world situation' to help parents and others maximize the enabling potential of any ICT usage.

Why study self-esteem?

A review of the literature confirms the common-sense view that a pupil's performance on school tasks is closely linked to their self-esteem. A number of authors, Margerison (1996) for example, go on to establish the link between emotional and behavioural difficulties and low self-steem. Lawrence (1996) describes the 'happy circle' of improved self-esteem leading to success at school tasks such as reading and this in turn further boosting self-esteem and so on (Figure 5.1). Many Special Educational Needs Co-ordinators can regretfully report the contrasting 'vicious circle', of a pupil whose failures at school tasks have led to lowering of self-esteem which in turn reduces performance.

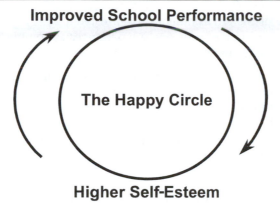

Improved School Performance

The Happy Circle

Higher Self-Esteem

Figure 5.1   The 'happy circle'
Source: Lawrence (1996).

What is self-esteem?

Definitions within the literature on this subject invariably begin with a disclaimer along the lines of Curry and Johnson (1989–1990), 'SELF-ESTEEM IS NOT A WELL-DEFINED CONCEPT. It is, rather, an intuitive notion that has stimulated and variously guided research and practice.' There does, however, appear to be sufficient consensus to suggest the following:

- Self-esteem is multifaceted; it is possible for a child to have high self-esteem and confidence in one situation and low self-esteem in another.
- 'Global self-esteem', that is one's overall feeling of self-worth, need not be affected by feelings of low self-esteem in any one area as long as the individual is able to avoid those situations. So, for example, my tone deafness need not affect my self-esteem as long as I avoid any situations involving prowess at singing, music, etc. An important caution is offered here by Lawrence (1996): 'It is worth reflecting on how children cannot escape school subjects which is why failure in school so easily generalizes to the global self-esteem.'
- Perceptions of what others think or say about us are important contributors to self-esteem. In this respect children are particularly vulnerable as they are very impressionable and they have much less prior experience than adults upon which to base their judgements.
- Developmental differences must be taken into account in relation to children. Ward and Ward (1993), for example, identify:

  (1) Early childhood, with 'self' distinguished on the basis of physical appearance and activity.
  (2) Eight years on – beginning to see self as separate from body parts and realize the influence of subjective thoughts, feelings and behaviour.
  (3) Later adolescence – more abstract understanding underlying dimensions of the self is conceived to influence behaviour.

- There are various methods of assessing self-esteem but Ward and Ward (1993, p. 18) comment that, 'There is minimal consideration of situation-specific behaviours or the influence of the environment on self-esteem.' They go on to state, 'If one believes that no one understands one's experiences as completely as oneself, then the best source of information is the individual.'

This final comment parallels the model of learning outlined by Mike Blamires in Chapter 1. The primary focus on 'deficits' within the individual student is rejected. Any consideration of the role of ICT in relation to raising self-esteem must clearly take account of the broader environmental factors or 'external variables' as Blamires calls them. The second part of this chapter will try to take account of this by considering various ICT applications in context using a series of pen portraits.

How can information and communication technology help raise self-esteem?

Age 5–7 pen portrait: 'She used to tear up her work'
In the past Claire had been described as 'clumsy', her fingers were plump and she had always found holding a pencil difficult, and her statement of special educational need stated that her 'hand-eye co-ordination was very poor'. Her efforts at writing soon distinguished her from her peers in their total unintelligibility both to herself and those around her. Despite the suggestion that Claire 'had learning difficulties' she was quick to comprehend that others saw her as a failure in the literate world. Her response was to rush from one written task to the next, destroying all evidence as she went and claiming that she had 'finished'. As both her parents and the class teacher pointed out that she enjoyed working on the computer, it was suggested that she be given an 'IT assessment'.

The assessment was a formative process spread over several months. The early stages were devoted to building up a working partnership between myself, the child, her parents, the support teacher and the learning support assistant (LSA). An initial visit to an IT resource centre was used to identify a range of devices that *might* be helpful: a colourful 'Big Keys' simplified keyboard, a metal **key guard**, an **overlay keyboard**, a **talking word processor** and two or three stimulating early years programs. Their use was viewed as experimental. The feedback on their usefulness in improving curriculum access came from the practitioners themselves, teachers, parents and LSA, as they were the experts on the curriculum and on Claire's learning styles. As the IT specialist I only visited once a week and this was vital evidence in building up a picture for me of the 'real world' situation in which Claire operated. It informed my decisions in fine-tuning the IT offer. It also spread ownership of the assessment process to all those involved.

An extract from my diary gives a flavour of how things were going early on:

This week although she still made mistakes she was clearly better. She again typed in 2–3 phrases. She needs to be guided away from just typing random words or letters (which she likes doing). 'T' (*the LSA*) helps by encouraging her to read back her own work, or reminding her of the topic that we are talking about. Again after about 15 minutes Claire felt that she had finished and was raring to delete all the work and start something new. Fortunately we were one step ahead of her and had already pressed the 'PRINT' key. When she saw the hard copy of her work she beamed all over and wanted to show it to everybody and to take it home to show to her Dad.

When I last saw Claire she and her support teacher had produced a 6–8 page book with her word-processed description of a class outing pasted alongside some photographs of the trip. This she had proudly displayed at 'showing time' to the whole school. She brought this book to the next annual review. We felt confident in adding 'goals' for the use of ICT to her individual education plan (IEP) in the knowledge that they would be meaningful to Claire and those who worked with her.

Key software

- The enlarged text and audible feedback of a simple talking word processor is important for students with poor handwriting as it allows them to see and accept where a mistake has been made. In addition the ease of correction allows improvements in accuracy and appearance of work. This is important where pupils have been demotivated by the quality and quantity of their pencil and paper skills. The Teacher Training Agency (1998, 14.c) talks of 'provisionality – the function of ICT which allows changes to be made easily'. But these dividends are not at first apparent to the child and, early on, the situation has to be heavily structured to prevent the switching off of the machine or deleting of work. For self-esteem to be boosted it is essential that the child gets the reward at the end of the task, an attractive printout of their story. This is highly motivating and over time should divert the student's attention from the 'off switch' to the printer tray.
- For younger children who lack motivation or who have a short concentration span it is important to choose programs that take advantage of what the Teacher Training Agency (1998, 14.d) describes as 'interactivity – the functions of ICT which enable rapid and dynamic feedback and responses, as appropriate to the subject(s) and age of pupils.' This may take the form of simple cause and effect software to build up a child's awareness and confidence that their actions can have an impact on the world. Simple switch programs which encourage cause and effect fall into this category as do talking stories and **early learning** software.

Key hardware

- This is where the **multimedia** qualities of the modern computer should be taken full advantage of. For younger students who have already experienced frustration it is important to keep everything as simple and reliable as possible. A large colour screen and good sound facilities are helpful as 'quality feedback' to the student is the first step to success.
- Alternative input and output devices may well be necessary. There is a vast range of sizes, shapes and colours of commercial switches available, some of which can themselves be programmed. In addition there are a number of small companies who will custom-make a **switch. Overlay keyboards**, **ergonomic** and **expanded keyboards** and **keyguards** should be considered.

Hardware is expensive and equipment needs can change. A number of agencies have advocated the setting up of resource banks so that short-term loans can be made to schools to try devices out before committing resources. This is in line with the view of assessment as 'experimental' and best pursued where the curriculum is being engaged, that is in the classroom.

Age 7–11 pen portrait: 'The student helper/expert'

Philip was a quiet shy pupil, apprehensive about any participation in group work. He was said to be over-dependent upon adult help and in need of a more independent learning style. He had some difficulties with both fine and gross motor control and as a result his handwriting was poor. His spelling was also weak but reading was a strong point. He was reluctant to take the risk of putting pen to paper for fear of making mistakes.

His father was a regular visitor to the school and the learning support teacher set up a meeting with the Special Educational Needs Co-ordinator and included Philip. A discussion of his home computer, a Commodore 64, proved a good way of breaking the ice and revealed that Philip appeared to have quite a high level of keyboard and computer skills. A suggestion by the support teacher that Philip do some of his recording using the class computer and a word processor was received enthusiastically by Philip and his father. The class teacher was not so sure, as she did not feel at ease with information technology.

Three to four INSET sessions were set up, not for the class teacher, but for Philip. It was then his job to help other pupils if they got stuck. The intention was to boost Philip's confidence in an area where he already felt at ease and to use his skills to involve him in more interaction with other members of the class. His increased knowledge of five or six popular programs (a spelling program and a visual **microword**, etc.) and his confidence on the word processor made him a useful source of support for his peers. For creative writing he was put in a mixed ability group with some able writers, but Philip's typing skills and ability on the word processor gave him an important role and he could not help but respond when the group discussed their stories. The computer provided a non-threatening centre of attention for small group work of various kinds.

Transition was an issue as Philip was in Year 6 aged eleven. His improved computer skills allowed for the issue of a portable word processor more compatible with the secondary/high school setting. More important, though, was the fact that through the computer he had improved his confidence to access the curriculum and to work in group situations and was now more independent in his approach to tasks.

Key hardware

- Whatever the hardware there is the opportunity to train the student in its use (or value an existing skill), and in this way ensure there is at least one classroom activity in which the student can experience success. A number of writers comment on the use of 'student helper or experts', see for example Olson (1988, p. 52): 'Steve, a student, who although less able at his work, gains some status both from staff and students by his ability on the computer.' Teachers may depend on student helpers in the absence of any other support. There are implications for teaching styles and classroom organization which requires a reduction in authoritative style in favour of more collaborative work with students.

Key software

- There is a range or 'continuum' of software. At one end are the 'didactic' rote-learning programs such as spelling or phonics software. They teach very specific skills, but this can be helpful where a student needs to build up and practise a 'tool kit of basic skills' which can later hopefully become automatic in their use (Underwood and Underwood, 1990, p. 20). The specific and easily defined nature of this skill area leads to it often being used for goals in the individual's education plan, ('increase sight vocabulary by . . .'), etc. As long as the goals are 'achievable' this can be motivating as the student can clearly see the progress that they are making.

- Equally beneficial are the more open-ended programs, like word processors. Again the 'provisionality' of word-processing, particularly the ease of editing, makes the word processor 'forgiving' of mistakes and encourages students to become more risk-taking in recording work.

- Choose software that facilitates or encourages small group work. The computer is a less threatening centre of attention. Some children, particularly those on the autistic spectrum, are unable or unwilling to rely upon socially and verbally mediated learning and so computer-presented activities may be particularly helpful. Murray (1997) found that the major gain from computer use with autistic students was in greater social interaction.

- Murray also noted that the use of games software, although often frowned upon in school, may have its place for provoking social interaction. Simulation and educational adventure programs can attract students like bees round a honey-pot and even the most reticent student finds it hard to resist comment or participation.

Age 11–13 pen portrait: 'An after-school keyboard club'

It has increasingly become the practice in the secondary school setting to issue portable word processors to students having specific learning difficulties. Currently a popular model is the Dream-Writer, but models change frequently. What does not change is that the issue of the machine alone, without due consideration of the circumstances in which it is intended to be used and the intended users, may well result in increased frustration rather than a magic wand to solve all ills.

A colleague, Deborah Dickinson, and myself had noticed that after the 'honeymoon period' had worn off the novelty of the machine soon waned and it could end up gathering dust in the SEN store cupboard or worse still used as an additional 'avoidance technique', 'the computer's lost my work!' We decided to start an after-school 'keyboard club' ostensibly to improve the technical skills of the students. What surprised us was that although skills did improve there were other areas in which progress proved more worth while:

- First, students would often bring along their school class work assignments or homework. They together could give each other help or ask us. In particular we were able to explore with them the full range of facilities offered by a word processor in improving access to the curriculum with tasks that were meaningful to them.

- Second, the club was run after school on informal lines; drinks and biscuits were available. Students felt at ease to discuss their common problems and the club assumed a therapeutic and supportive role. Computer programs and some educational games were ostensibly the reasons for attendance but in the case of some students this may have been a face-saving way to get in contact with like-minded peers. Staff who supported the students were encouraged to attend to learn about the software and again the students often found themselves in the role of helper/expert. Parents came early to pick up students and could get a cup of tea and chat to each other, to us and to students.
- Finally, as students relaxed they felt able to discuss the 'real world' issues that they were facing in schools. Two students brought up the issue of security and the problem of other students 'bothering' them because they had a computer. Soon others were chipping in with, 'don't let them know you have games on it', 'hide it in your bag when you go home', 'sit near to the teacher', 'hand the computer in to the office when you're not using it'. At other times problems of staff who did not allow portables to be used in their lessons or did not allow homework to be word-processed were discussed. If 'technology' is one side of the *enabling* coin then the flip side is just these practical everyday issues of use.

Key hardware

- Have as good a ratio of computers to pupils as you can. Pupils often worked in pairs. Some pupils appreciated working on their own for the privacy to make mistakes unobserved.
- Encourage students to bring their own portables and to share problems and solutions.
- We had a computer equipped with a modem and Internet software. This proved very popular but searching the world wide web can be frustrating unless the student is shown 'how to search for information, including using key words and strings' (Teacher Training Agency, 1998, 13. b.2). An ideal example of use was one student who had a clear idea of what she wanted to search for – information for a project on the Kobe earthquake in Japan. A group of us worked with her to find information and then cut and paste it into her report. The 'enabling' qualities of ICT are experienced at their best where there is engagement with real-life situations or genuine curriculum tasks.
- A CD drive enabled us to show another student how to search a multimedia encyclopaedia for pictures and information on Henry VIII for a history project. In this way students learnt search procedures in the context of concrete curriculum assignments and hopefully became empowered to use these skills in school and at home.
- Obtain the fastest CD drive and modem you can. For those with low motivation or memory problems, 'Immediacy of feedback may have proved particularly important as answers could be provided before attention strayed and memories of questions under review faded' (Underwood and Underwood, 1990, p. 21).

Key software

- For many pupils improving keyboard skills from the 'hunting and pecking' at print will be the main goal. If in addition motivation is a problem, go for some of the programs that combine fun and structured tutoring. We found that having a range of programs was good as what suited one student may not suit another. See **typing tutors**.

- Have a good word processor, something that alerts you to errors and can be customized to correct common errors (**autocorrect**). Learning how to become competent on this was a real liberating factor for two or three students and the procedures for saving, printing and editing are simple and becoming standardized across a range of commercial word processors. Choosing a 'standard' word processor is important to achieve *transfer of knowledge to* home, school and, later on, the sixth form college. The degree of control that the students were able to exercise over the word processor and learning programs was often far greater than they had experienced with traditional pencil and paper work in class. The 'control hypothesis' is a theory that increased motivation results from this ability to control the technology.

- **Predictors** and **voice activated software** may be worth investigating though the latter currently requires a very motivated pupil willing to invest considerable time learning how to get the most out of it.

Age 14–19 pen portrait: 'What colour shoes do you wear?'
From GCSE 'Food Technology' to GNVQ level 1 'Media Studies', few students today have escaped the requirement to devise a questionnaire, administer it and write up the results.

Fazila, a 14-year-old with Down's syndrome, did have learning difficulties but was not bad at reading. Hand-eye co-ordination problems severely limited her speed and accuracy at writing and drawing. Socially she was very confident but she had very negative responses to most recording tasks. We usually managed to put together two or three questions on the word processor and she would quite enjoy going round and asking her friends what type of desert they liked or the colour of their eyes. The problem came when we had to collate all the forms, count the little ticks, add up totals and try to produce something resembling graphs and charts.

Fazila was able to enter most of the data via a computer keyboard. We began with a simple database on an Acorn computer but later graduated to the spreadsheet 'Excel' on a personal computer. Both proved easy to use and it was easy to produce a range of attractive graphs. At first I invested a lot of time showing her *how* to use the programs. I viewed it as a 'generic' activity that would pay dividends as she would be more independent on future occasions and she was.

Fazila was really pleased with herself and excited when for the first time she was able to produce quality graphs and charts that compared favourably with those of the other students. And to this day she still gets a kick from watching a perfect colour pie chart slowly emerge from the printer (and so do I)! We always have to do three or four copies – one for her tutor, one to show friends in class, one for Mum and Dad and one for her brother.

Key software

- **Databases** and **spreadsheets** allow us to remove what Underwood and Underwood (1990) call 'inauthentic labour', that is pointless laborious tasks that distract a student's attention from the questions that they should be investigating. The Teacher Training Agency (1998, 14.a) refers to the automatic functions of ICT 'which enable routine tasks to be completed and repeated quickly, allowing the user to concentrate on higher order thinking and tasks'. These are powerful features for a student with poor motivation or limited memory.
- Commercially available products can be very 'user friendly'. They have the advantage over specifically educational software in that as well as being used in schools they are also frequently available in colleges and businesses. To maximize the pay-off from investing time building up 'generic procedures' in a pupil you need to be sure that the software will be around for a few years and will be widespread in its use.

Key hardware

- Databases in particular can use large chunks of memory so a good size hard disc and as much memory as you can afford are in order. Searching, sorting and collating data can be time-consuming procedures so, again, where immediacy of feedback is important to a student a faster processor can be important.

6

Developing Social Communication

Richard Walter

Introduction

Developing communication and enabling social understanding is a major focus at Meldreth Manor school. Most of the learners are alternative or augmentative communication (AAC) users and rely on devices to help them interact and communicate in social situations. For students ICT also plays a major role in providing access to communication aids which vary in complexity from a single switch message to complex multiple linked dynamic selection sets.

Social understanding and communication are mainly developed through social interaction with other people, and ICT can play a part in this development by encouraging the necessary skills of shared attention, discussion, negotiation and purposeful communication through pointing, eye gaze and body orientation. Information and communications technology can help learners interact with their environment to become players in the world, responding to others, making requests and developing appropriate responses.

Information and communication technology can be used to help learners explore social situations through interactive stories and multimedia simulations which can be used to develop social understanding in a controlled environment such as a **virtual reality** microworld. For example, the skills necessary for shopping or mobility may be practised or consolidated.

The pen portraits in this chapter illustrate how ICT can support and develop social understanding and communication with learners who have profound and complex physical and learning needs. As the use of multimedia by people with these special educational needs poses many problems, these will be considered in the second part of the chapter.

The pen portraits exemplify some of the ways in which ICT can help to develop social and communication skills from early social awareness to more advanced social understanding. At a fundamental level a prerequisite of developing social understanding is the knowledge of oneself as an effective individual who can impact upon the world. Information and communications technology can help develop learners' self-awareness and knowledge of themselves as effective individuals through simple cause-and-effect access programs.

ICT can help to develop the beginnings of social awareness through developing an understanding of cause and effect

Pen portrait 1
Adele has a single switch access to a multimedia computer. She is using a program that responds to each switch press with a simple large graphic and

61

sound. By monitoring her body orientation, head movement, eye gaze and vocalizations one can infer that she realizes for part of the time that she's having an effect on the computer but that her realization is not yet consistent nor permanent.

Points to consider:

(1)   Adele may just be responding to the stimuli unconnected to her previous switch press. It might be that her use of the switch may need to be reinforced through rewarding even approximate moves toward the switch and attributing a meaning to her actions through a commentary (e.g. Jordan and Powell, 1995).
(2)   Adele is positioned in a dark quiet room or corner to maximize her concentration on the computer. She has a large bright single switch optimally positioned for her own use and which has previously been assessed as the most successful input method for her to use with computers. She uses a number of single input programs that respond to her switch presses with bright and noisy animation. She is using a mixture of commercial cause-and-effect software and software written specifically for her with sounds and graphics she responds especially well to, and which can all be controlled from her single switch.
(3)   Although Adele is placed in a low stimulation setting she is not being socially isolated as a teacher or assistant will be monitoring and intervening to engage her in the activity.
(4)   Communication with Adele is all about practical choice at a real and fundamental level, allowing her to anticipate experiences and to exercise choice. Music and tactile cues are used to help her orientate herself during the day. For example, classroom activities are introduced with a set music theme, and before she goes horse-riding she is given a piece of horse tack to feel and smell. Technology plays an important role in her development since it is one of the few external realities that is totally under her control responding only to her specific input.

See also **early learning** and compare with the pen portrait of Matthew in Chapter 7.

Activities for developing social awareness in small group activities using ICT

Information and communications technology can be used to develop collaborative working, turn-taking and social awareness where learners must respond to other people through making requests, interacting and negotiating.

Pen portrait 2
Kulvinder is developing awareness and communication with his peers through turn-taking activities using ICT. Using the computer, he is sharing switch input to a progressive cause-and-effect program that responds to each switch press with a clear graphic and sound. A big red switch is passed between him and his partner and his participation is enhanced and prompted by physical contact when it is his turn. He is encouraged to respond to questions and comments about whose turn it is through eye gaze, physical orientation and vocalization.

Point to consider:

(1) Kulvinder's recognition and understanding of his role in the social activity of turn-taking is being facilitated with ICT.

Pen portrait 3
Tony and Sarah are using the computer to develop turn-taking using separate switches to access a program that requires alternate switch presses to build a series of pictures. The program only responds to one switch at a time corresponding to whose turn it is. The learners are required to co-ordinate their activity and co-operate in taking turns to press their own switch. They are developing skills of social interaction, basic negotiation and communication. When Tony and Sarah are engaged in this activity Tony will often prompt Sarah that it is her turn, at times even physically reaching across to press her switch.

Pen portrait 4
A group of learners are joining in telling and creating a story. They each use a communication aid which is appropriate for their physical and cognitive skills. The story has a recurring chorus that is recorded on to their personal communication aid. The narrator starts the story and lets the learners know when they have to join in. Some of the learners learn when it is their cue and start to join in independently.

Point to consider:

(1) Group communication can be developed in social activities such as story-telling and drama. ICT can help learners to join in group communication activities.

Pen portrait 5
In a class setting a group of learners have simple commands recorded on to their communication aids. They are giving instructions to their teacher. One learner has the command 'sit down', another 'stand up', etc. The teacher or a chosen individual has to carry out the learners' commands thus providing a possibly rare opportunity for learners to become active controllers of their environment.

Point to consider:

(1) If the learners are using a communication system augmented with speech, this approach may reinforce their understanding of the vocabulary available on their communication system.

ICT can be used to aid social understanding and communication in different settings

Pen portrait 6

Jacob is using different messages on his communication aid to interact with peers and staff. He is using a simple communication aid which allows him to take part in class language activities and to interact with his helpers to ask for things to meet his personal needs. His communication aid is set with relevant messages for different activities and situations. He uses it for turn-taking, joining in with simple language games, and simple interactions requesting and responding. He is learning how to take part in basic social activities. He also uses a simple communication board with three symbols for making familiar choices, accessing it through touch and focus of eye gaze. The approach used in 'Pen portrait 5' may help Jacob learn the meaning of his symbols.

Jacob also uses ICT and multimedia programs with a small group of classmates, jointly constructing simple multimedia slide-shows by choosing pictures and sounds to create pages in an interactive slide-show. Skills of turn-taking, awareness of others' choices and collaboration are being developed in this activity.

Pen portrait 7

Maurice is a more able learner who communicates at an advanced level using rebus symbols. He has independent control of his own mobility using switch control of his electric chair through a number of head switches. Maurice has a rebus board of approximately eighty symbols divided into colour boxes. He first eye-points to the box and then chooses the colour to indicate the line within the box which contains the symbol he wants. He then confirms the correct symbol by vocalizing. His rebus board is supplemented by an extensive rebus file for accessing a wider vocabulary. With this system Maurice can communicate most of his needs, ask and answer questions, and take part in social interactions as long as he has a facilitator with him.

Maurice is also using a laptop **communication aid** with multiple linked selection sets. This gives him access to independent verbal communication.

Maurice is using **electronic mail** and the **Internet** to communicate with people all over the world, sending and replying to letters. He constructs his messages using his symbolic communication system which are transferred by a facilitator on to the computer into **symbol software**. He then checks the symbolic message before it is sent as text file via email. When he receives an email it is transferred into symbols by exporting the text into symbol software which he can then read.

Maurice is using multimedia and ICT as tools to develop his own resources. He is engaged in creating a record of his school life to go in his Record of Achievement. He is choosing and recording the pictures, text, symbols and sounds to go on his pages and he will present his pages at the next leavers' assembly. The construction of his multimedia Record of Achievement book has led Maurice to research into his time at school, interviewing his past teachers and collecting photographs of his activities. This has helped Maurice to develop greater awareness of himself and his life history as well as extending his skills of communication through information gathering.

Points to consider:

(1)   Maurice is using both high- and low-technology communication systems which ensures he has a 'backup' system when the high-technology system is inconvenient or unavailable.
(2)   Maurice is engaged in social activities that have meaning and support his growing role as a person who has a point of view to be heard.
(3)   The letters he receives may need slight modification in consultation with Maurice so that they can be represented by symbols.

How ICT can help support inclusion within a wider community

Pen portrait 8
Many learners contributed to the development of the school web site which is easily accessible to most learners using adapted switch access. They choose and construct information about themselves, the school and school activities. This has developed links with other special schools and encouraged email contacts with groups and individuals in the global community. It has enabled some of the learners to experience themselves as being part of a wider social community in addition to developing a sense of pride and identity as a result of publishing information about their own lives and achievements.

Students were involved in creating the web site when Jack helped choose pictures and information about his class activities and constructed pages about how computers are made. He can access these pages on the world wide web from the site's index pages using independent switch access. These web pages also allow learners independently to show visitors and parents about their life at school. Many email contacts with the students have been developed from people viewing the web site and then contacting them.

These pen portraits have demonstrated how ICT can be used to develop social understanding and communication with learners who have a wide range of physical and cognitive learning needs as a result of increased opportunities for interaction.

Using multimedia stories to aid communication and social understanding.

Talking books can present social situations in an appealing and entertaining way. They can give learners experience of different scenarios and their effect on people. For example, the Sherston Naughty Stories provide a number of multimedia stories exploring different social scenarios demonstrating a variety of social interactions and their consequences.

Multimedia can be a more powerful, motivating and accessible media for learners with special educational needs than just listening to the story from a book. It engages the learners on more levels and it can be independently accessed by non-readers. It can be an excellent stimulus for group discussion, questions and answers, and exploring social contexts within the microworld created on the computer.

One of the major advantages of using multimedia is the flexibility it offers for enabling learners to engage with a learning task. Certain modalities can be emphasized to suit preferences (e.g. sound for a person with a visual impairment) and the tasks can be simplified or structured in more appropriate ways using selection sets controlled by alternative mice, **switches** or **overlay keyboards**. Just like Shakespeare at his best, different learners can engage with the same story at their own level (see **universal design** for learning, Chapter 1).

Just as a story does not in any way replace real experiences, neither do multimedia talking books, but they can be valid and active social experiences in themselves.

Developing access to multimedia microworlds

Currently a major format for multimedia on the computer is the **CD-ROM**, although the Internet will eventually play an increasingly important role if it becomes more capable of delivering large amounts of data at speed. A way forward might be for schools and their community to develop their own networks with selected resources from the Internet or developed locally and stored locally so that it can be accessed at speed (an **intranet**).

Multimedia operates mainly through hyperlinks or **hotspots** accessed by positional mouse clicks. (Positional mouse clicks are where the user moves the mouse to a specific part of the screen and then clicks the mouse button, i.e. standard mouse operations such as clicking on a button displayed on the screen.) This is a very skilled input method and it is a major difficulty for people who have physical and/or learning difficulties and who cannot move a mouse into position. The next section will consider some of the difficulties and possible solutions to the use of multimedia by people who find these skills difficult or impossible to understand or physically accomplish.

Enabling engagement with multimedia software

There are a number of ways in which positional mouse clicks can be made more accessible or circumvented.

Software adaptations

Using the customizing features of the operating system, the speed of the mouse pointer and the speed of click and double-click can be adjusted. The size, colour and animation of the pointer can also be changed to increase visibility (see Chapter 8).

Software and hardware adaptations

Selectively turning off mouse buttons can help people who may be confused by their different functions, so that only one mouse button is functional.

Hardware adaptations

Using different sized **mice**, **trackballs** or **joysticks** can help people who find control of standard mice difficult. **Arm supports** and **wrist rests** can help people who can move a mouse but who experience pain or fatigue.

Using an external switch with a **mouse port switch adaptor**, the learner only has to control the movement with one hand and can use the switch to mouse click.

Adaptations to enable access via the keyboard to mouse functions

Keyboard access to mouse movement uses the accessibility option or utility known as mouse keys (see **mice** and Chapter 7).

Full switch access to mouse pointer movement can be achieved by **scanning** a selection set that controls mouse movement. Alternatively some programs use a rotating pointer to give switch users control of the mouse functions.

To indirectly control mouse functions by scanning with a switch is a very difficult skill for people with cognitive difficulties in addition to physical impairments. Consequently, it is often more productive to use a direct access switch method for group work on communication and social interaction for these learners. A direct switch access method could be a switch operating one function such as page-turning.

Enabling group switch access to talking books using switches connected to a switch assisted mouse or mouse switch adaptor

Aims

- The development of shared attention, participation and turn-taking skills.
- The development of language and reading skills, text decoding and meaning, and word recognition.
- The development of an understanding of a social situation and the consequences of social interactions using the plot of the story.

Equipment

- A switch is attached to emulate the operation of the mouse button.
- A book of the story (or a big book).
- Supplementary materials: pictures, rebus and words to reinforce the text.

Activity

The class focus can either be on the text in the book or on the multimedia on the computer. The mouse pointer is moved to the active region (**hotspot**) on the screen to allow learners to control the media using their switches to emulate the mouse button. Learners can listen to the story, participate in turn-taking to control the switch, and practise word recognition and text decoding skills. They may also develop social and communication skills of anticipation and prediction.

Any program that uses mouse clicks can be used by switch users in this way. It does require someone who can control a mouse to enable group access. It has the advantage that the teacher can control the pace of the session, highlighting and emphasizing any points. The disadvantage is that it does not enable completely independent use.

To enable independent switch access to multimedia you need software which allows the switches to directly generate or emulate positional mouse clicks. This can be achieved by scanning through a selection set of **hotspots** or by direct control where a switch press activates a particular hotspot. Direct access to hotspots is usually more successful for learners with severe and profound learning difficulties.

Direct access to hotspots can in some cases be achieved by using keyboard **short cuts** which are in turn generated by a switch press using hotspot software. This results in the page being turned or the text being spoken when a switch is pressed.

Some overlay keyboard creation software will enable hotspots to be allocated to areas of the overlay keyboard as part of a **selection set** (see Figure 6.1). In Figure 6.2 one switch reads the story while another turns the page.

Figure 6.1 A selection set

Figure 6.2 Choice of two switches

Example 1: enabling independent switch use of a multimedia story 'The fish who could wish' by Oxford Multimedia using hotspot software

This is a story especially useful for developing the idea of personal wishes, e.g. 'If you could wish for anything what would it be?' It can also be used to examine the social consequences of choosing certain wishes.

The CD can be set to read through the story from beginning to end or the learners can choose one of the fish's wishes to explore. The program uses move, point and click for learner interaction which, as we have seen, is not independently accessible to people who cannot use a mouse.

Using the software you can set any key on the keyboard or any area on the overlay keyboard to directly activate a hotspot. Depending upon the switch interface, two to four switches can be connected to activate separate hotspots as allocated by the software.

In the story, the fish has eight wishes so there can only be direct switch access to the first four wishes from the fish-wish page. The four switches can be set to control the next four wishes on the same page by using another facility in the software which allows separate access sets on a single page. Direct access to the next four wishes is therefore achieved by a facilitator pressing the Space Bar in the fish-wish page which then branches to a second access set allowing direct access to the second four wishes (see Figures 6.3a and 6.3b). Figure 6.4 shows the choices available when the fish wishes for a horse and Figure 6.5, when the fish wishes for a submarine.

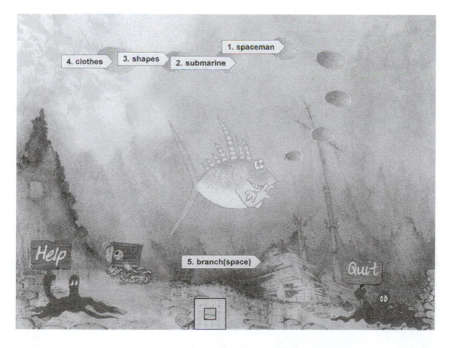

Figure 6.3a   Four switches and space bar access to additional choices

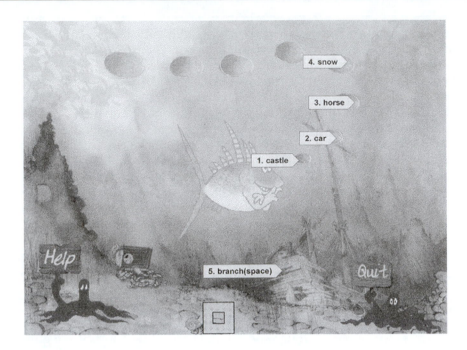

Figure 6.3b   An alternative selection set in the same story

Figure 6.4   Choices available when the fish wishes for a horse

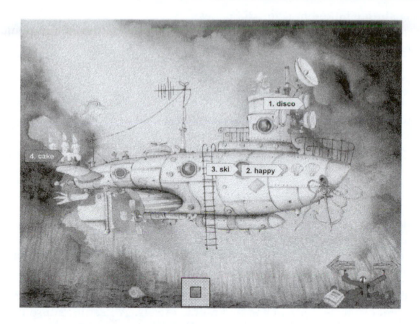

Figure 6.5   Choices available when the fish wishes for a submarine

The story has been used successfully with a group of non-readers. They chose which wish they wanted to explore from labelled switches. They then explored their chosen wish using direct access mixed with supplementary switching using a mouse switch adaptor. They are currently adding their own pages to the story and making up their own wishes.

Another method of making multimedia software accessible to switch users is by providing switch input to specially written multimedia programs made with **multimedia authoring** software. An advantage of this method is that the program can be tailored to the specific interests of the learner. Very simple full page multimedia presentations can be made with any of the multimedia authoring programs. Some of these can be converted into web pages which can then be used by anyone who has access to the Internet. This offers exciting possibilities for publishing.

Example 2: the creation of multimedia presentations operated with a single switch

Resources

- Mouse switch adaptor or keyboard switch adaptor.
- Multimedia authoring software.
- Digital camera, scanner, clip art.
- Microphone, tape recorder.
- Paper and pencil.

Making simple linked multimedia pages

Since many of our learners find it difficult to move the mouse, the presentation consists of a linear set of linked full pages that can be controlled by a switch which sends a mouse click. Everything has to work from a single switch press and each page has to be visually clear and simple.

Overview: Make a series of linked pages. Make each page separately and link them together sequentially and add a sound file to each page. Use clipart or scanned/digital photographs relevant to the learner. Sounds can be recorded by the learners or chosen by them from other sources (tapes, CDs, etc.). These pages can then be displayed in turn by single switch presses.

For example:

- By using **on-screen keyboard** software to create a sequence of selection sets which each take up the entire screen and consist of an image, animation and/ or sound which are displayed in sequence after each switch press.
- By using multimedia authoring software to create a sequence of full-page graphics with a transitional sound set for each page.

Additional hotspots or buttons can be added to the story-line containing pictures, symbols, texts, video clips or graphic effects. A useful feature in some software of this type is the **dwell** facility which allows access to links simply by positioning the mouse over an active area. This can enable access for learners who can control the mouse directions (perhaps using a **joystick** or **trackball**) but have difficulty in using a mouse button or switch to produce a mouse click.

In this way learners can construct multimedia books, or personal records of achievement that are relevant and personalized on topics of their choosing.

Learners with multiple or profound difficulties can have very restricted opportunities for developing social skills and communication. We have seen some of the ways in which ICT provides a means of allowing them to participate and communicate in a variety of social situations and to develop social understanding, which might not be possible with other educational technologies.

Part III

Enabling
Physical Engagement

In the following chapters we consider how learners can be included as a result of taking advantage of the variety of control methods that are available and the versatility of ICT to represent information in different sensory modalities. Lesley Rahamim, in Chapter 7, outlines the ways that learners with a physical disability can be enabled by technology and extends the ideas of Richard Walter in the previous chapter. In Chapter 8 John Lodge compares and contrasts ICT resources for blind learners and those with visual impairments. The impact of graphical computer environments has been highly disabling for many people with these difficulties but John Lodge locates a number of promising developments. Ann McDevitt describes in Chapter 9 the approaches using ICT which can facilitate language and concept development amongst learners with hearing impairments or who are deaf.

7

Scaling Physical Barriers

Lesley Rahamim

The range and form of physical disability has changed over recent decades. Medical advances have greatly reduced the occurrence of disabilities caused by poliomyelitis and spina bifida, but the increasing survival rate of pre-term babies can lead to different forms of disability including dyspraxia and multiple disabilities.

> A child's physical disabilities may be the result of an illness or injury, which might have short or long-term consequences, or may arise from a congenital condition. Such difficulties may, without action by the school or the LEA, limit the child's access to the full curriculum. Some children with physical disabilities may also have sensory impairments, neurological problems and learning difficulties.
>
> (DfEE, 1994, p. 61)

The role of ICT in supporting learners with physical disabilities

For some students with physical impairments, ICT can provide physical access to the curriculum and facilitate involvement with their peers.

Pen portrait 1

Moira is now 15 years old. She was born with cerebral palsy, mainly affecting her upper limbs. She has a tremor and her large sweeping movements make handwriting difficult. As a baby she was encouraged to crawl about and explore her environment. Her parents read her books, taught her rhymes, and developed a rich oral environment even though her speech was sometimes difficult to understand. As a result she entered school with many positive experiences. She found controlling a pencil difficult and tiring so throughout her school career she was given access to a keyboard to supplement her handwriting. Gradually, because of her need to produce greater amounts of writing, she has moved away from handwriting as her main means of recording. She is currently using a portable version of the computers used in her school, supplementing the word-processing software with a **predictor** to speed up her text production and reduce effort. She is considered by her teachers in her mainstream secondary school to be a student with exceptional abilities. She intends to be a journalist or lawyer after university.

Moira's successes in the education process have been built on the rich early experiences provided by her parents, particularly in the area of language. Children with speech difficulties need exposure to stories, rhymes, etc. to develop phonemic awareness and other basic literacy skills. As soon as she entered school she had access to appropriate ICT provision and has been able to demonstrate her high abilities by minimizing the physical barriers presented by her disability.

Points to consider:

(1)   The role of the parents was vital. They had high expectations for her.
(2)   Since starting school Moira was included in mainstream education and was exposed to a range of peer role models of achievement.
(3)   Moira herself has been involved in the reviews of her technology provision which have taken place at frequent stages of her education to ensure its use remained appropriate. For example, she has recently given up using word-prediction because she felt it influenced her style of writing too much by suggesting words and phrases from her past vocabulary rather than encouraging innovation.

Pen portrait 2

Matthew is also 15 years old. He has a rare progressive condition that prevents him moving independently. Recently he lost most of his eyesight. He has missed much of his school life through illness and has significant learning difficulties. His individual education plan focuses on developing his knowledge that an action can cause an effect, and ICT is one of the tools used to help achieve this.

Matthew's teachers have noticed that he reacts positively to music so a system has been set up to enable him to work towards taking control of a tape recorder. The tape recorder is connected to a mains controller, an electrical interface that enables low voltage electrical appliances to be operated by an external **switch**. It is set to operate for a chosen length of time when the switch is pressed but will then stop until it is pressed again. A simple metal switch was chosen because it gives sensory and auditory feedback – it is cold to the touch and makes an audible click when activated. A facilitator helps Matthew press the switch to turn the music on, repeating the activity when the timer stops the music. Each time the facilitator is looking for an indication that Matthew is intending to activate the switch himself. Sometimes they work alone but at other times they use the set-up as part of a social activity, providing snatches of music for a game of Musical Chairs.

Hopefully ICT can assist Matthew in developing the understanding that his actions can have an effect, and give him an element of control over his world. The technology may provide access to a world of communication and learning that has been closed up until this time.

Points to consider:

(1)   Matthew is being facilitated in pressing the switch. If he can learn cause and effect in this context he may learn to press the switch himself.
(2)   What activities does Matthew enjoy? It is important that the reward for a switch press is at a level that he understands. The observations and knowledge of parents and carers is important here.
(3)   The use of ICT may increase the quality of Matthew's life by enabling him to exert some control over his environment.

The importance of early intervention

Children whose physical disabilities are evident from birth need early intervention to overcome barriers. Technology may not always be the most appropriate solution. Restricted mobility can lead to reduced opportunities for exploring the environment, so it is important for the young child to be given the means of independent mobility as soon as possible. If not, their perceptions and concepts of space and distance may be impaired, as well as diminishing their natural curiosity about their environment (e.g. Tingle, 1990; Ware, 1994). Some children may have difficulties controlling the muscles that they need to develop understandable speech, and lack of interaction with adults and peers can compound their speech and language difficulties.

For these children an enriched spoken and social environment is crucial to developing language and literacy. Information and Communications Technology may be able to give improved access to the curriculum, but in order to maximize its effect, children with disabilities will need the same opportunities to develop through play during the pre-school years as their peers. Play enables the development of understanding about the world through the sharing and clarification of meanings. This is supported by pointing, direction of eye gaze, tone of voice and facial expression. If ICT is to have a role in early intervention it is to support these types of interaction between a child and her peers or adults.

See also the *early intervention* section in the References and Chapter 4, and compare the pen portrait of Matthew with that of Adele in Chapter 6.

The development of educational technology for physical access

Historically, one of the areas in which technology has been most successful is that of physical access. From the earliest electric typewriters, which could be operated with a lighter touch than a manual model, people with physical disabilities and those working with them have exploited technology to overcome barriers (e.g. Ridgeway and McKears, 1985). Early portable communication aids were developed to relay simple messages by displaying typed words on a small display screen, or by selecting a pre-recorded message with a switch.

When the first microcomputers became accessible to education, programs were written by enthusiasts to address the needs of learners with physical disabilities. Computers are particularly appropriate for these users because they can be operated with a variety of inputs, the usual ones being the keyboard and mouse. If appropriate adaptations cannot be made to the keyboard or mouse then the learner may be able to use a **touch screen**, an **overlay keyboard**, a microphone or a **switch**.

Ways of speeding up text input were developed. Overlay keyboards could be set up with whole words and phrases assigned to areas of the board so that the writer could enter chunks of text with a single press. Switch-operated word processors were designed that incorporated word banks, again enabling the writer to avoid entering every letter individually. Speech synthesizers were added to read out what had been written, giving a voice to those with no verbal communication, even though in the early years the only voice available was often that of an American male.

With the advent of battery-operated portable computers, users could move away from the mains electricity outlet and work where they wanted. Inclusion of learners with disabilities in ordinary secondary schools became more attainable because they could now move their equipment with them.

More powerful computers have brought disadvantages as well as advantages. The widespread introduction of graphical user interfaces such as Apple Macintosh and Microsoft Windows have placed greater emphasis on selection by pointing devices such as the mouse which can be difficult for some users with disabilities. See John Lodge's Chapter 8 on the difficulties people who are blind have, for example. However, pressure from disabled users themselves resulting in US federal legislation (IDEA, 1990) has led to keyboard alternatives being incorporated into operating systems. Solutions developed by other sources such as the military, mobile phone technology and business worlds have also been adopted as alternatives to the mouse and keyboard. The **trackerball** and **voice activated software** are examples of this.

The ability of modern computers to run more than one program at a time (multitasking) has led to the use of add-ons to make ordinary programs accessible to those with physical disabilities. They no longer have to use different programs, specially written for them in order to use an alternative input (device). For example, some writers may prefer to use a mouse to input text rather than a keyboard because they may not have enough strength to use a keyboard, or perhaps they have problems continually changing their gaze between the vertical screen and the horizontal keyboard. These users can run an **on-screen keyboard** alongside their word processor and write by clicking on the letters with the mouse.

Key devices

Keyboards

The standard keyboard consists of the letter and numeral keys which are usually laid out in QWERTY array, plus other keys which perform functions such as navigation, selection and deletion.

Problems and solutions
- If the keyboard is too big, change to a smaller one
  - use a portable computer – **palm tops** have particularly small keyboards
  - change the keyboard for a **miniature keyboard**.
- If the keyboard is too small, change to a bigger one
  - use an **expanded keyboard**
  - use an **overlay keyboard** with a QWERTY overlay.
- If the user can only activate one key at a time
  - switch on **sticky keys**.
- If the user keeps hitting the wrong keys
  - use a **keyguard**
  - switch on the **input filter keys**.
- If the user needs support while typing
  - use a **wrist rest** – a piece of wood, plastic or foam that supports the user's wrists while typing; most portable computers have areas in front of the keys where the wrists can rest
  - use a keyguard – as well as preventing unwanted key presses the keyguard can be used to support the hands.
- If the keys keep repeating because the user cannot remove their fingers from the keys quickly enough

- in the control panel of the computer set a long character repeat delay and a slow repeat rate.
- If the user cannot use a keyboard at all
  - use a different input method such as a mouse or switch with an **on-screen keyboard**, or **voice activated software**.

Mouse

The mouse has become increasingly important in accessing computers because graphical user interfaces display icons on screen. The user must navigate an on-screen pointer by moving the mouse around and pressing buttons on the mouse to 'click on' an icon or select text.

Problems and solutions
- If the mouse is difficult to control
  - in the control panel set a slow pointer speed
  - replace the mouse with a **trackerball**.
- If the user cannot click-and-drag (hold the mouse button down at the same time as moving the mouse)
  - use a latching trackerball and lock the button down while moving the ball.
- If the user cannot double-click (selecting by pressing the mouse button twice within a pre-set interval)
  - in the control panel set the double-click speed to slow
  - use a programmable trackerball as this has an extra button that can be set to perform the double-click (or a range of other actions) with one button press.
- If the user cannot use a mouse at all
  - use the keyboard – **mouse keys** (see **mice**) alternatives in the accessibility options which allows the numeric keypad to control the pointer and perform button actions
  - use an **overlay keyboard** – selection sets can be made for overlay keyboards with areas that perform the function of the mouse in simple programs
  - use switches – with an **on-screen keyboard** that includes mouse control or **hotspot** software.

Overlay keyboards

Overlay keyboards are flat boards covered with a touch-sensitive membrane and connect to the computer via the serial or PS2 keyboard ports. A printed overlay is laid on top of the board and choices are made by pressing areas.

Problems and solutions
- The user hits the wrong area by mistake
  - fit a keyguard over the board to define the cells more clearly
  - edit the selection set to make null areas around each key, thus avoiding close proximity of sensitive areas.
- The user does not have the control to make a single definite press
  - use the board's own access utilities to customize the way the board reacts, e.g. set a delay so that the user can move around before settling on the required key, or set it to ignore repeated key presses.

Switches

Switches can be used as an input if the user can understand the task and can also hit a switch and release it. The simplest use is for cause-and-effect activities where the user presses a single switch to make something happen. It might be attached to a mains controller, a simple communication aid or a simple switch program on the computer. Switches are connected to the computer through the serial or keyboard ports using a switch interface or **mouse port switch adaptor**.

Pen portrait 3

Anne is 4 years old. She has little intelligible speech and does not have sufficient motor control to use a keyboard or mouse. She likes to use a yellow button switch to access a variety of activities. Sometimes her switch is connected to a BigMack communication aid, set up with real messages to deliver to the school secretary. ('Can we have the register please?') At other times it is connected to early years software which can be operated by switch access.

Points to consider:

(1)   Anne is developing her switch use in real-life settings.
(2)   She is developing switch skills that may lead on to her use of scanning software or she may develop enough motor control to use an alternative keyboard or mouse.
(3)   The communication aid supports home–school links because messages can be recorded by staff and parents so that Anne can press her switch in response to the questions, 'What did you do at school?' and 'What did you do at home?'
(4)   Children who can use two switches can control the scanning by using the first switch to drive the highlight and the second to select. Once scanning has been learned the child may move on to faster, more complicated methods such as row-column scan (see **scanning**).
(5)   Some software has switch access programmed in so that the teacher just has to choose it as an input. If not, a scanning utility must be used to fix **hotspots** to it which can then be scanned.

Pen portrait 4

Amira is 7 years old. She has a little intelligible speech but uses a portable hand-held communication aid to augment it, particularly for telling stories, which she loves. Pre-recording messages to match a story is quick and simple, so when her teacher reads out the phrase'What's the time, Mr Wolf?' in the story of the same name, Amira can join in by pressing her communication aid. She has many different overlays, each one with twenty different message areas labelled with icons. Amira attends a special school for two days a week and her local ordinary school for three. She uses her communication aid at home as well as at both schools and her parents co-ordinate the recording of messages. She is beginning to reach the stage when her current provision is not keeping up with her needs so a more powerful machine is being considered.

Points to consider:

(1)   Amira's communication messages are not just related to physical needs.

(2)   Her needs are changing as she develops so there is periodic reassessment.
(3)   The overlays are for different settings. One set is for messages which she uses with her grandmother.
(4)   Amira has a dual placement in a special and mainstream school. It is important that she has overlays that support her communication needs in each setting.
(5)   Currently, her parents record their voice into the communication aid. Would the ability to record a child of similar age and background, be more suitable and convenient?
(6)   Would the use of synthetic speech be something to consider next as many phrases could be produced easily?
(7)   How would the use of synthetic speech affect the use of Amira's communcation aid in Arabic language settings?

Voice recognition

Voice recognition software converts the spoken word into text and has been a long sought after alternative input device for many. It has been used by people with physical disabilities for several years but its cost, and that of the hardware needed to run it, has prevented more widespread use until recently. The cost of the software has plummeted and modern computers now have high enough specifications to run the systems. Continuous development of the software has resulted in more accurate recognition, a shorter initial training for new users, and the ability to recognize continuous speech rather than diction. However, there are some accents and voices which are less successful than others, the young child will need a high level of support during the initial learning period, and the systems assume a reasonable level of both literacy and IT capability. See **voice activated software**.

Pen portrait 5

Rajik is 9 years old. He has cerebral palsy with associated perceptual difficulties. He finds writing by hand very difficult because of his motor difficulties and he is very slow when using a keyboard. He holds his pen so tightly it exhausts him and makes him tense. In addition he has problems with even the simplest spelling. This is causing frustration because the only way he can get his many interesting ideas down on paper at a reasonable speed is to dictate to a scribe. Rajik has clear speech and he reads well, so speech recognition is being considered for him. He has had an initial training session, with promising results, but there are concerns that need to be addressed. Rajik is quite adamant that he does not want to use it in his mainstream primary classroom because of the attention it will draw to him. It is also difficult to see how the system would cope in the classroom either. He is willing to consider using it for homework, and his family have a computer that will run the software. But his parents have concerns about their ability to train him in the system. Rajik has decided to wait until his final year at primary school before trying again.

Points to consider:

(1)   Rajik and his parents are involved in making decisions about whether a solution is appropriate for him.

(2)   A software solution is only a solution if it solves a problem for the user.
(3)   It may be that the software could be introduced as a resource for the rest of the class to use so it is then accepted as part of the classroom resources and not unusual, but each user must use their own voice settings which can take up a lot of storage space on the computer.
(4)   Will Rajik be able to work through the long training procedures required by the voice recognition software?
(5)   Will he have the motivation to correct errors in recognition while using it in his work?

Key software

Onscreen keyboard software

Selection sets containing word banks can be run alongside a word processor or other applications so that whole words can be entered with a single key press, switch or mouse click. Some word processors include integral word banks. Word banks can be used on overlay keyboards or as an onscreen keyboard. They may contain subject vocabulary and key words.

Predictors

These also run alongside other programs, offering word banks that can reduce key presses and speed up writing by providing alternative guesses for the next words and phrases to be typed. They can reduce fatigue and increase accuracy in typing.

Symbol software

This may be appropriate for some learners who cannot read text or who need the support of graphics to clarify meaning.

Typing tutors

Typing tutors aim to teach the writer to type using standard fingering. This might not be achievable for many children with physical disabilities, but writers with dyspraxia may find it a useful skill to acquire.

Making provision

In the first place a child's school might reasonably be asked to give a child with disabilities an appropriate means of access to the curriculum. If the school is rich in ICT provision and competency this goal is often achievable. However, if the child's needs are such that they cannot be met from within the school's own resources then an external agency will need to be consulted for specialist advice. That agency might be a specialist service set up by the local education authority (LEA) or one of the national assessment services. Whenever the needs of a child with a physical disability are being considered the potential of technology should also be considered and appropriate resources sought out. Aims and targets for use should be included in a resultant individual education planning including training and awareness for parents and members of staff involved.

8

Developing Curriculum Access Based on Sensory Approaches: Partial Sight and Blindness

John Lodge

Visual impairment is rare in children. Out of an estimated one million blind and partially sighted people in the UK today, only about 25,000 of them are between the ages of 0 and 15 years (Bruce *et al.*, 1991). About half of these children have another disability in addition to their visual impairment. This makes visual impairment a low incidence disability in schools, so few teachers will have experience of a blind or partially sighted child in their class. For this reason, the partnership between experts in partial sight or blindness, the learner, the educational establishment and parents is vital if the learner is to be successfully included in the learning opportunities on offer.

Most blind learners, for instance, use their own reading and writing system – a system which few people outside visual impairment circles are able to understand. Special pedagogical approaches and new resources need to be mastered if the learner is to make effective progress in learning. This chapter focuses on the current ICT resources available to assist learners and provides information and guidance in its selection and management.

What is visual impairment?

Visual impairment covers a wide range of visual conditions sometimes grouped under the categories of blind and partially sighted. However, these terms – although they have legal definitions – do not always convey the functional vision of an individual. One learner who is registered blind may have no light perception at all, whilst another – also registered blind – may be able to negotiate his way confidently around school using visual clues only.

Two key measures of vision are 'acuity' and 'field'. Acuity describes how clearly an object is seen and includes the notions of distance vision and near vision. A normal field of vision permits an individual to see horizontally over approximately 170°, almost in line with each shoulder (Best, 1992). There is no correlation between these two measures although certain eye diseases result in predictable outcomes. For example, a visually impaired learner may have good acuity but a very small field of vision, e.g. a learner with retinitis pigmentosa (RP). Alternatively, macula degeneration results in the opposite effect, with central vision being first affected. Other eye conditions, e.g. a squint or nystagmus, will have a direct bearing on a learner's work in class. Both of these conditions can cause eye fatigue and headaches if a learner undertakes extended reading from a book or screen.

The conclusion one can draw from these observations is that a learner's eye condition is therefore quite specific. This means that an individual solution to accessing the curriculum needs to be devised. It is for this reason that ICT resources, which can provide such flexibility in some situations, are often excellent tools for visually impaired learners to work with. However, the appropriate ICT solution is not always obvious. The aim of this chapter is to explore the resources available and comment on their suitability.

How can ICT help?

Visually impaired learners face at least three sets of difficulties in their day-to-day education:

(1) *Access to information*: although there is a strong shift to visual and audio channels, much of the world's 'educational' information is still formally recorded in print format. Without intervention of some kind, print is inaccessible to many visually impaired learners.
(2) *Access to the curriculum*: as well as the print issue, a learner has to use equipment, interpret pictures and diagrams, read notes from the blackboard, and so on. Many of these activities are impossible for visually impaired learners to undertake without special intervention of some kind.
(3) *Personal communication*: many visually impaired learners write in Braille – a code which few sighted people are able to understand. Others may write by hand but their handwriting is wobbly and difficult to decipher. Both sets of writers need tools to help them communicate with people in the sighted world.

The potential of ICT

Information technology is an excellent tool for presenting information in a range of forms. It can switch information between one sensory channel and another, e.g. print displayed on a visual display unit (VDU) can be turned into synthetic speech output and listened to through a speaker. These presentational and transformational ICT functions are powerful and significant for users (a principal of universal design). But despite this flexibility, there still remain serious barriers to access.

One of the most significant of these is the **graphical user interface** (GUI) used by most modern computer operating systems (see References). It is assumed the user can see the objects on the screen and has sufficient hand-eye co-ordination to carry out certain manipulative tasks. But what happens when a learner cannot see the screen?

As you can well imagine, the GUI metaphor for interaction breaks down in the case of a blind user. Fortunately, blind people do have an ally in the shape of the American disability laws (IDEA, 1990). These require all software to be accessible to disabled people. They have influenced the designers of operating systems who have now include speech 'hooks' to enable developers to produce screen readers for blind computer users. The result has had a positive outcome and blind learners are able to access GUIs with some measure of success. In particular, most companies now allow software actions to be accomplished by pressing certain keyboard equivalents or **short cuts**. If these combinations can be learnt, a blind person can operate independently.

Besides the GUI, there is another real access challenge for blind learners. This relates to the form in which information is laid out – or formatted – on a page. Modern desktop publishing and web page creation software enables images and text to be mixed freely on a page or computer screen. Text which is displayed in columns or buried in graphical elements on the page or screen can often be very challenging for a **screen reader** or **scanner** to make sense of. As a result, blind learners are effectively barred from all sorts of information – and that includes many pages on the **world wide web**.

Yet for all the current problems, ICT has proved to be a powerful tool in helping to meet many of the communication and access needs of visually impaired learners. I propose to explore the contribution of ICT using a framework based on three of the main channels of communication, i.e. vision, speech and touch.

Enhancing the visual sense: ICT helping partially sighted users

Paper versus screen

In considering computer use by partially sighted learners, it is important to bear in mind some of the fundamental differences between paper and screen. These media differ in several significant ways that affect legibility – particularly with respect to size, resolution and display features. These differences are summarized in Table 8.1. Note that the comparisons are for desktop monitors rather than the LCD displays of laptop computers. In general, although they are improving in quality, liquid-crystal display (LCD) screens tend to have inferior display qualities compared to standard (CRT) computer monitors although the gap between the two technologies is narrowing quickly.

Improving onscreen legibility: lessons from the paper medium

Legibility of print is a crucial matter for all readers but especially so for partially sighted learners. Arditi (1998) lists some basic guidelines for designing legible text in print. Although not made specifically for the computer screen, they do provide a useful framework for discussing how to present text on the monitor. General suggestions of this kind are useful, but their application is limited because visually impaired learners are so individual in their needs. Consequently, the needs of some learners will diverge widely from the preferences listed here.

Contrast
Text should be printed with the highest possible contrast. In most cases light coloured letters on a dark background will be the most readable combination, e.g. white or yellow text on a black background. The computer's operating system – or, frequently, the software application – will let you change text and background colours (Lodge, 1998b). Note that some operating systems, e.g. Windows 95, will let you reverse foreground and background colours with a key press combination.

Besides computers, colour CCTVs offer the user a range of preferences for foreground and background colour. These colours can be set at the touch of a button or two.

Table 8.1   Differences between paper and screen

	Paper	Screen
Size	• Paper is available in a wide range of sizes *e.g. A5–A3 plus all the others used in the publishing industry for books.*	• Smaller range of sizes. The 14-inch display is the most common desktop screen size. But you can purchase larger options, e.g. 15, 17 and 21 inches. *Screens greater than 17 inches are expensive and can be uncomfortable for partially sighted learners to use because of the large amount of head movement required to scan the screen.*
	• Average text density (print to white space) is around 50%. This makes paper a compact medium for reading. Example: *Children's books average around 200 words per page.* *Engineering handbooks contain around 1500 words per page plus diagrams.* *Windows Help screen display holds about 50 to 100 words* (Horton, 1991).	• Reading long documents on screen is not comfortable at all. Designers tend to break up a large document into 'chunks'. As a result, content per screen is smaller and the reader has to undertake a lot of scrolling as well as scanning. This can be tiring work.
Resolution	• Excellent. Typeset documents have a resolution of 1,250 dots per inch (dpi). Laser printouts are around 600 dpi. *These documents retain their crispness when magnified using a low vision aid (LVA) or closed circuit television (CCTV).*	• Poor. Most screens have a resolution of 70–100 dpi. *On magnification, the quality of the text breaks up, significantly reducing its legibility. Special font smoothing techniques are used by magnification software in order to maintain the clarity of onscreen text.*
Display features	• Can cause glare if glossy paper is used, although many qualities of paper have a matt finish.	• Causes much glare and steps need to be taken to minimize this, *e.g. use an anti-glare filter. On the other hand, a screen display is a light source and – in the right environment – it can be easier for some partially sighted learners to read.*
	• Text can be printed out in a range of font sizes – but changes are laborious.	• The size of the display can be magnified at the touch of a button or the press of a key.
	• Highlighting features are available, *e.g. bold, italics.*	• Offers more highlighting features including blinking text, etc.
	• Commercial texts use colour – but this is expensive.	• Most screens have colour as standard and so it can be used quite readily, where deemed appropriate. This can be very helpful to many partially sighted learners who often have specific preferences relating to colour and contrast.

Point size

Many partially sighted learners prefer to use large fonts but by no means all of them. Readers with tunnel vision, for example, often prefer to work with small point sizes since magnification reduces significantly the amount of text they can see on the screen. Magnification would make it more difficult to read a text, since it greatly increases the need for scrolling.

Most software applications allow the font size of the text editing area to be changed. But if the learner is unable to read the system font – because it is too small – then this will need to be enlarged separately. There are two ways to effect this:

- change the system font settings from within the operating system
- magnify the whole screen desktop.

Changing the system font in Windows 95 is straightforward. Perform a search using the term 'system font' in the Windows 95 on-line help and you will be given instructions on how to make the changes. Do be aware that enlarging the system font can produce unwelcome side-effects, e.g. some dialogue boxes become too large to fit on the screen. You will need to experiment a little until you get the appropriate size for a learner.

The other way to increase text size is to enlarge the whole screen using magnification software. This can be a very effective way of giving screen access to some partially sighted users and magnification levels of sixteen times and above are readily achievable. These programs are reasonably intelligent. They can track the mouse pointer and force any pop-up dialogue boxes to appear within the field of vision. The software performs font-smoothing at larger magnifications, thus maintaining the legibility of the text. But magnification does brings its own difficulties. Since the screen is enlarged, the user cannot display all of it. In order to read the text, the user is obliged to scroll constantly from side to side. Some users find this irritating.

Closed circuit televisions offer a great range of magnification and since they are using a superior display technology to the computer, the clarity of the image is better at higher magnifications. To help with scrolling, CCTVs have a base table on which to place the book or object being viewed. The table moves from side to side on rails and is an effective accessory.

Leading
Leading is the vertical distance between lines of text. In general, this should be around 25 to 30 per cent of the point size. A sensible space between lines makes it easier for a low-vision learner to locate the start of the next line when reading. Modern word processors allow the user to adjust the leading of the text. A comfortable leading can be set up for a learner and then stored in the basic document template. Every time a new document is opened subsequently, the correct leading will be in place.

Closed circuit televisions cannot adjust the leading of a text but they do have other features which help with reading. For instance, the user can place two 'tram lines' on the screen – one above a line of text and the other below it. These serve as a guide to the reader – and, in some cases, prove to be very helpful. Windowing is another feature of most CCTVs. This is similar to the tram-lines feature. But here all text on the screen is blanked out except for the line being read.

Font style
Current thinking is that sans serif fonts are more readable than serif ones. This appears to be true for both printed text on paper, as well as onscreen text. Arial and Lucida are recommended for good legibility (Horton, 1991). Interestingly, a new font has been developed to make it easier for low-vision users to read subtitles on digital

television (Silver *et al.*, 1998). Note that highlighting techniques such as italics and underlining reduce readability, so use them sparingly. It is best to avoid decorative fonts which are complicated and not easy to make out.

Letter spacing
Close letter spacing can be difficult for some readers to distinguish, so avoid condensed fonts. For certain learners with central visual defects it can help to use a monospaced typeface in preference to a proportional one. Some word processors let you control the amount of space between individual letters.

Margins
Extra wide margins allow the user to hold a book flat – helpful if the learner is using an LVA or a CCTV. But there is no need for a wide margin around a computer screen, since the window adequately frames the display.

Colour
For those with no colour blindness, the use of colour has a useful signposting or labelling function. It can, for example, be difficult for low-vision users to locate a book when it is buried among similar publications. Often a highly coloured cover will help locate it more easily. This principle can be used on a computer screen. A judicious use of colour can help pick out the menu bar or a mouse pointer on a busy graphical display (Lodge, 1998c).

Using the auditory sense: access through speech

Visually impaired learners depend heavily on their sense of hearing to communicate with others. There have been a number of significant ICT developments in the auditory communication channel which have benefited visually impaired users – especially blind users.

Synthetic speech (see **speech output**) production is arguably the most significant of these developments. A screen reading program selects text from a computer screen and sends it to a synthesizer. The latter converts the text into signals which can be heard from a speaker or set of headphones. The screen reader has to be intelligent and to make sensible guesses about what text displayed on the screen the user wants to hear. But we are seeing steady improvement in the quality of these readers, particularly in interpreting GUI screens.

Synthetic speech is available for most computer platforms. However, it is important to realize that not all software – or indeed all modules within a program – are accessible to speech. Some programs are written in such a way that a screen reader is unable to access the screen text. Other software demands a manipulative strategy such as mouse selection and no keyboard equivalents are provided. In both these situations a blind user will be stumped.

Hardware speech synthesizers are efficient but are expensive to purchase. They are available in several formats: as an external unit which connects to the serial port; as an internal card which is installed inside a desktop computer; or as a PC card which inserts into a laptop computer. More recently, screen readers have been developed which use standard sound cards for speech instead of the specialist synthesizer. This has resulted in significant savings. The latest development in speech synthesizers is to eliminate hardware entirely and create the speech synthesis in software only. There are now several programs on the market which do just this and the savings are substantial. A software synthesizer is a convenient option to install into a laptop computer since it reduces the amount of clutter needed to be carried around.

But not all text is available in electronic form – far from it. Most text appears in printed form. To meet the challenge of turning print into speech, reading machines have been developed. To use a reading machine you lay the page of a book or a sheet of text face down on the glass surface of a scanner and press the start button. The device scans the page and, using optical character recognition (OCR), deciphers the page and reads it out using speech synthesis. You can purchase a dedicated reading machine or attach a standard **scanner** to a computer and use OCR software to perform the same task. Optical character recognition has made great strides in recent years and accuracy has really improved.

In addition to computers and reading machines, there are several specialist speech output devices which are useful in helping blind learners access different areas of the curriculum, e.g. talking calculators, compasses, colour testers, multi-meters, dictionaries and teletext adaptors. These devices have limited application but they do help access some difficult parts of the curriculum.

One of the most commonly used speech devices is considered fairly low-tech these days. I'm referring to the cassette player or dictaphone. Visually impaired learners employ them a lot. A teacher or helper can record a chapter from a text book on tape and pass it to the learner for reading later. This is an effective way of undertaking background reading, because reading Braille is much slower than reading print and listening to a cassette certainly speeds up the process. Some learners like to make notes into their dictaphone – this can be particularly helpful for learners with dyslexia. There are one or two cassette models on the market specially adapted for visually impaired users. They support variable play speed and indexing during recording. Both features can be very useful.

Finally, it is worth mentioning **voice activated software** which uses speech recognition technology (SR) to turn talk into text on a computer screen. These systems are especially useful for learners who cannot record using either print or Braille or who have writing difficulties. Computer speech recognition has recently made real progress and is now a serious tool in schools. Some SR products permit hands-free operation which can be necessary for use by some blind learners.

Gaining access to information using the sense of touch

The Braille code

Many blind learners use their sense of touch to read and write in Braille. The Braille code is physically presented as raised points, usually arranged in cells of six dots. Braille writing devices have six main keys for this reason. In the basic Braille code (grade 1) each cell corresponds to a single letter (Figure 8.1). Contracted Braille (grade 2) – which is used by most blind learners – is a shorter form which makes reading and writing much faster.

Writing Braille

The most popular device for writing Braille by hand is the Perkins Brailler. It is robust and reliable and is used widely. There exist several electronic additions to the Perkins.

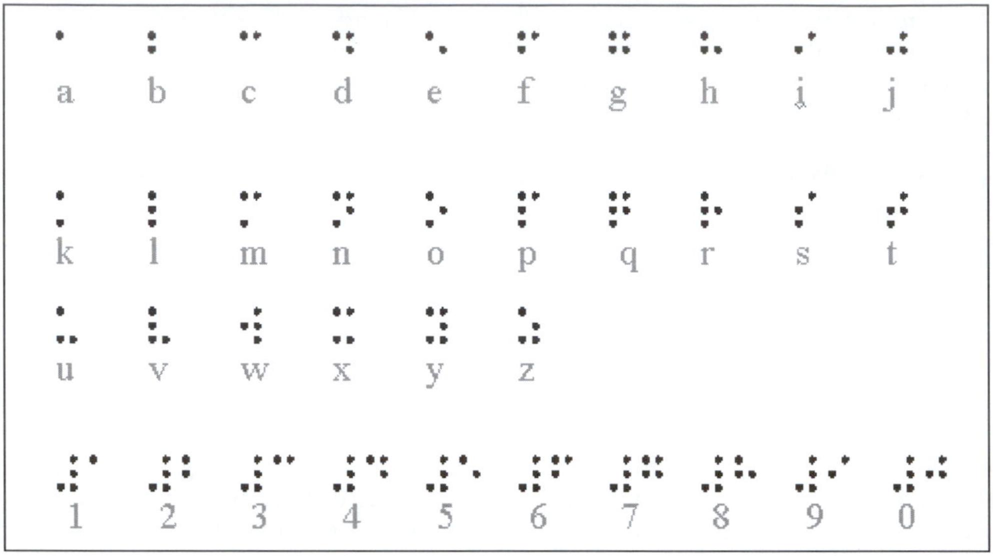

a	b	c	d	e	f	g	h	i	j
k	l	m	n	o	p	q	r	s	t
u	v	w	x	y	z				
1	2	3	4	5	6	7	8	9	0

Figure 8.1   Grade 1 Braille

The Mountbatten Brailler, for instance, is a multipurpose machine which requires only a light pressure on the keys to produce the Braille. This can be of great value to some learners who are unable to operate the stiffer keys of a Perkins. Or one can add an electronic module – called a Braille'n Print – to the base of the Perkins. As its name suggests, this allows the Perkins to be connected to a printer. Both of these devices can be very useful in mainstream school settings because a blind learner is able to produce print as well as Braille. This reduces isolation by making the learner's work accessible to the teacher and to fellow learners.

The Braille note-taker

However, Perkins-type devices are heavy to carry about and are unable to offer the features of a modern computer. In response to this need, a number of Braille-based electronic portable computers, called **note-takers**, have been developed (Figure 8.2).

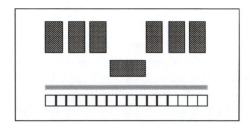

Figure 8.2   Braille note-taker with refreshable Braille display

The note-taker's battery life between charges is long compared to that of a laptop computer. A single charge, for example, can be sufficient for a learner to work with for two or three days. Since relatively few keys are needed to produce Braille, a note-taker is small. It fits comfortably into a school bag or even a large pocket. These features make the note-taker very suitable for learners on the move (Thoms, 1998).

Portable technology: an issue at transition to secondary school

Portable technology becomes a specially important issue to blind learners on transition from primary to secondary school. Learners have the choice between two different technologies, i.e. a Braille note-taker or a laptop computer fitted (usually) with speech software. So which of these solutions is better? The answer to this question is not always obvious and a careful assessment of a learner's technology needs will have to be undertaken. However, a review of the two technologies will be helpful in arriving at an informed solution for an individual learner (see Tables 8.2 and 8.3).

Table 8.2 Comparing specifications

	Braille note-taker	Laptop computer
Keyboard	Full-size Braille keyboard No need to learn touch-typing	QWERTY keyboard Touch-typing needed for effective use
Screen type	None supplied	LCD screen. Of little personal use to Braillist, but allows others to see work
Screen size	N/A	12.1 inches on entry level machines
Weight	1 kg approx.	3.5 kg
Size	A5 footprint approx.	A4 footprint
Output	Speech with an integral Braille line option Full access to all software applications	Speech usually. Braille display available but this is expensive Access to software applications is far from complete but usually sufficient for many key tasks
Battery life between charges	24 hours	2–4 hours
File storage capacity	4 Mb approx.	2 Gb
CD-ROM	N/A	Standard or option
Modem	Option on some models	Option
Cost	£1,200 (speech only) £3,000 (speech and integral Braille line)	£2,000 (speech only) £7,000 (speech and Braille display)

Several observations can be drawn from the information in Tables 8.2 and 8.3.

The note-taker
- Since a note-taker has a Braille keyboard, a Braillist without touch-typing skills can begin to use it immediately.
- Writing in grade 2 Braille is fast since it is a contracted code. This gives the note-taker an edge for taking down notes in class.
- The note-taker is flexible and well adapted for portable use, so it is suited to situations where a learner moves around for lessons, e.g. secondary school or college.

Table 8.3   Comparing functionality

	Braille note-taker	Laptop computer
Powering up	Ready for immediate use. Just switch on and go	Resume feature available but not always reliable. Usually learners will have to load up the operating system and then the software application. This can cause an irritating two or three minute delay in starting work
Battery life	Typically 24 hours between charges Learner is largely independent of the need for mains electricity in school	Short battery life of 2–4 hours. Learner may need regularly to connect the computer to mains electricity. Can be an inconvenience in class
Portability	Excellent. Goes into any school bag and is light to carry around	Rather heavy. It is tiring to carry for more than short periods
Robustness	Designed from tough plastic. Because it is light this makes for a very robust product Can be successfully used in a range of environments – in class and out in the field	Strong but because of its heavy weight it is prone to damage if dropped. Trailing mains cable makes it vulnerable to passers-by
Software	Narrow choice. Usually a word processor and some office-related productivity programs	Full range of software
Internet access	An option on newer models	Standard option

- A note-taker can help a learner maintain good Braille reading and writing skills.

But . . .

- The note-taker can be expensive to purchase.
- Because it is specialist technology, a learner in an integrated setting is unlikely to find any on-site technical support for the note-taker.
- A note-taker uses a small range of proprietary software, so a learner will have to use other school ICT resources to complete certain areas of the curriculum.
- Since the note-taker has no screen (usually), learner progress is not visible to the teacher or to fellow learners in class. This can be isolating.
- Braille technology is not mainstream. Some learners – especially adolescents – are sensitive to this and will refuse to use non-standard equipment in the presence of their peers.

The laptop computer
- Being a mainstream product, the full range of software is available on a laptop.
- Using a laptop helps to develop a learner's ICT knowledge and skills as defined in the National Curriculum.
- A laptop is usually much cheaper to buy than a note-taker.
- Having your own laptop is 'cool'. You can play games on it, for instance.

But . . .

- A blind learner needs to be able to touch-type in order to use a laptop.
- A laptop is heavy to carry about; it is also less robust.

- A learner may need to change position occasionally in class in order to sit by a mains electricity socket. This can be socially disruptive.
- Speech software helps a learner to use computer applications. But the quality of the access is not always satisfactory, thereby reducing the learner's productivity and independence.

Conclusion

Getting the appropriate portable technology for a student is most important. But specifying the right equipment is not enough. Training and support need to be put in place also. In the case of a note-taker, it will be necessary for a support teacher to spend time with the learner introducing him to the basic features. In the case of a laptop, similar arrangements will need to be put in hand. In particular, time needs to be spent setting up the machine so that it suits the needs of the learner (Lodge, 1998a).

Refreshable Braille display

Although in widespread use in Europe, until recently **refreshable Braille displays** (Figure 8.3) were rare in UK schools. The reason for this is probably financial – Braille displays cost a lot of money. However with the emergence of Braille output note-takers, we are seeing more and more of them.

Figure 8.3   Refreshable Braille display with twenty cells

Printing out Braille with a computer

A special Braille printer – called an embosser – can be used to turn electronic text into paper Braille. A note-taker is already designed to do this, but a computer requires Braille translation software in order to Braille out a text file. The quality of the Braille produced varies according to the subject-matter of the text and the Braille translation software used. Equipping a learner to print out Braille will cost around £1,500.

Moon: an alternative to Braille

For some people, Braille is too difficult to master and so an alternative tactile code called **Moon** may be used (Figure 8.4).

A computer can be used to create Moon also.

(1)   Write some text in your favourite word processor.
(2)   Highlight it and then change its font to Moon using the RNIB TrueType font for Windows.
(3)   Print out the Moon text on paper and photocopy it on to a separate sheet of Minolta-type paper.
(4)   Pass this photocopy through a swell paper machine and the symbols become raised.

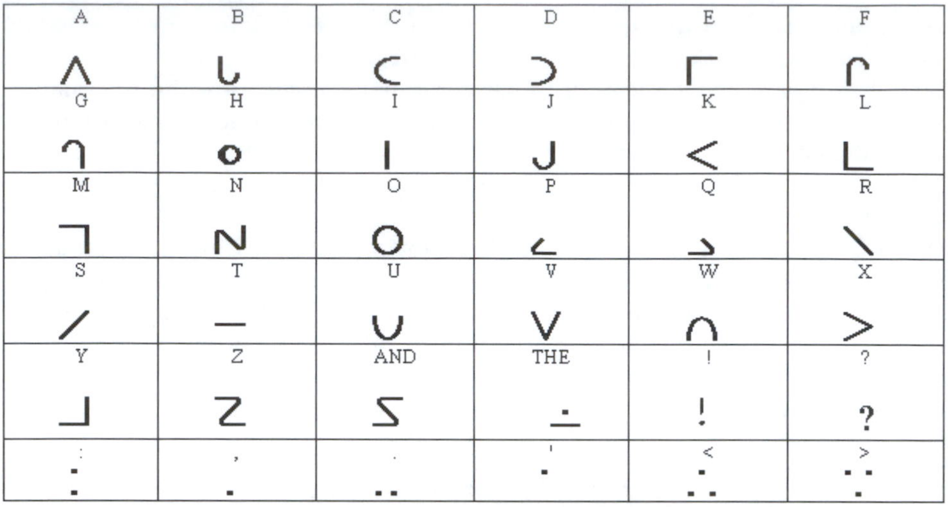

A	B	C	D	E	F
∧	∪	C	⊃	⌐	∩
G	**H**	**I**	**J**	**K**	**L**
∩	o	I	J	<	L
M	**N**	**O**	**P**	**Q**	**R**
⌐	N	O	∠	→	\
S	**T**	**U**	**V**	**W**	**X**
/	—	U	V	∩	>
Y	**Z**	**AND**	**THE**	**!**	**?**
⌐	Z	S	∴	!	?
:	,	.	'	<	>

Figure 8.4   Moon

The RNIB can supply lots of resources for making Moon.

Pen portrait: using a Braille note-taker in lessons

George is 15 years old and attends a residential special school. Although he is a touch typist, he has opted to use a BrailleLite note-taker in preference to a laptop computer. This note-taker has a Braille keyboard, a refreshable forty-cell Braille line and speech output, if wanted. It can be connected directly to a printer or embosser for hard copy. Using a disc drive which connects to the BrailleLite, George backs up his files on floppy disc.

He uses the note-taker for writing in most of his lessons. It is ready for immediate use once the 'on' switch is pressed and this is appropriate in lessons where there is little time to waste getting started. He finds it light and convenient to carry around, which means he is rarely without it.

George has been assessed as having dyslexia and appreciates the editing functions of the onboard word processor. In particular, he finds it easy to locate the position of the cursor using the Braille line. He complains that editing is something you cannot do on the standard Perkins Brailler. However, with his note-taker he can spell-check his writing. In practice, he finds that the BrailleLite spell-checker vocabulary is quite small and of limited value. So he saves his writing to disc, loads it into a computer and spell-checks it in MS Word! This gives much better results.

Points to consider:

(1)   The note-taker is not a suitable recording tool in all subjects. George finds many mathematics activities are unsuitable, e.g. exercises involving fractions or graph-plotting are much simpler using the Perkins Brailler. Music has its own Braille code and again George has been unable as yet to use the BrailleLite successfully in this subject. He would like to use the BrailleLite for French but

for this he would need to purchase an additional French language chip for the machine.

(2) By and large the note-taker has proved a successful writing tool in lessons. Its range of features have made it a practical device for the school situation. Its small size and use of Braille output mean that it can be used quite unobtrusively in class.

Future developments

The Internet represents an enormous source of information for blind people and already many are using it on a daily basis. In the short and medium term it will be crucial to influence standards bodies to ensure that information is available in formats that do not bar access for blind people.

The CD-ROM – or digital video disc (DVD), its likely replacement – is also a key information medium with many reference works and curriculum materials already being issued in this format. It will be of key importance to influence publishers to ensure that information stored in this medium is not locked away from blind users.

Speech recognition technology holds out much promise for all visually impaired learners. The SR software is improving apace and, with the power of desktop computers continuing its inexorable rise, we can look forward to good results within the next decade. A speech-based human-computer interface is likely to be a more productive one than the present GUI.

9

Developing Visual Approaches: Hearing Impairment and Deafness

Ann McDevitt

The visual and interactive nature of technology can also provide support for learners with hearing impairment to ensure that they engage with the topics being covered. Similarly, supportive word processors with wordlists and planners can support their understanding.

Outline and assessment of developmental educational needs

It is widely recognized (e.g. Webster, 1989; Wells, 1987) that any significant degree of hearing loss may be highly detrimental to language development and cognitive development. Without appropriate intervention and support, educational achievement and personal development may be restricted. As a consequence, children with hearing impairments may often be labelled as 'egocentric', 'concrete', 'impulsive', 'poor at dealing with questions'. However, as suggested by Pester (1993), these may be secondary consequences rather than inevitable effects of hearing loss.

It has been suggested that a learner's understanding of the world, which is reflected in their receptive and expressive use of language, is a product of the 'joint construction' of understanding by the child with more expert members of his culture, Feuerstien (1976). Vygotsky's concept termed the 'zone of proximal development', considered earlier in this book, underpins the work of those supporting all children with special needs, but especially the deaf whose engagement with language is predominantly via supporting adults.

Hall (1987) considers that children's development of language occurs through the attempt to engage in communication, both as producer and receiver. However, studies of young child–adult interaction show that it is usually the child who initiates and terminates the action, not the adult. Adults are considered by Wells (1987) to be intuitively aware that the responsibility for mastering language lies with the child and that their role is essentially one of encouraging the child's self-activated learning. For children with hearing impairment, Webster (1989) stresses the importance for teachers of seizing all the opportunities presented in school, across the subject boundaries, where children are involved in communication whether by talking or signing. He considers that

> The most effective learning experiences are those which impel the child to use language in situations which are meaningful to themselves and their lives . . . Good teachers begin with a clear understanding of children's existing understanding . . . the greatest impact is often achieved through real-life visits or participatory experiences . . . more remote subject matter . . . can be brought to life with photographs, artefacts, tools or implements,

archive material, recordings, video, role play, stories, poems and printed evidence such as news reports.

(Webster, 1989, pp. 83–4)

At the time of his writing, computers were only just being introduced into schools but he was enthusiastic of the benefits that they offered to deaf students:

material is presented visually; children find (micro) computers non-threatening, non-judgmental, stimulating and highly motivating; learning steps can be individually paced and controlled by the child; children can take risks and make mistakes; there is opportunity for repetition and overlearning for children who have difficulty in retaining ideas and forming concepts, linked with immediate feedback . . .

(Webster, 1989, p. 90)

Webster encouraged teachers to look beyond the fact that deaf children may be unable to hear sounds in words, have visual-perceptual problems or less well-developed vocabularies, syntax and semantic awareness. He argued that if children were not expected to enquire, initiate questions, seek out rules and reconstruct their own models of how language works, then they would be poorly prepared for actively reading for meaning. Although teaching must address the additional problems for deaf children, he considered that it should aim to move them towards independence in learning, aware of how to go about their own study, learning how to learn. This chapter attempts to show how the use of ICT can play a vital part in this process.

Historical use of IT leading to key approaches and principles

When computers were being introduced, teachers of the deaf were quick to seize the opportunities that IT appeared to offer their students. Although use was made of the same software as other children, their application was slanted towards the needs of the deaf. For example, the **scenario programs** enabled students to explore language within a **microworld** that encouraged correct sentence construction – if the sentence was not correct, the action did not happen! The scenario programs encouraged a learner to complete a scene by typing instructions. For example, 'Put a table in the kitchen'.

In addition, software was produced by teachers of the deaf, or by specialist university departments and organizations, aimed at addressing areas of need particular to the deaf. Unsurprisingly, these were predominantly aimed at language development. Like most software of that time, these programs tended to be judgemental but provided exciting, non-threatening opportunities for repetition, overlearning, etc. However, unlike other software, the presentation and rewards were visual and could include familiar signs, rather than more usual Rebus symbols.

Specialized applications also included the use of computers, with additional hardware, to encourage and refine vocalization. The more complex and expensive applications were more commonly used by speech therapists, rather than teachers, to refine articulation. However, the latter were able to make creative use of simpler devices, such as **MicroMike**, to assist students with their speech programmes using cause-and-effect games.

The **overlay keyboard** was found to be particularly useful in enabling deaf students to access mainstream software such as word processors, scenarios (a pictorial microworld controlled by written language) or **Logo**. Teachers could produce selection sets on the overlay keyboard for students with explanatory pictures and/or signs to accompany words on the paper grid. In this way, the barrier to learning imposed by vocabulary limitations was removed. One of the most exciting aspects of the use of overlay keyboards was in the exploration of **Logo microworlds**. Using purely visual overlays, students could control the movements of a turtle, either on the floor or on screen, to solve problems, estimate distances, and predict results. As their language and confidence developed, these overlays could increase in complexity, as well as offer transition to the use of the standard keyboard.

Word-processing was found to be a very powerful application of IT for the deaf. The ability to edit work enabled students to write freely without worrying about maintaining correct grammar and spelling, which was particularly appealing to students and their teachers. Writing that might in the past have appeared unintelligible could be split into its two- or three-word sentences and the story revealed.

> Neil was 8 years old and had very poor communication skills. Using a word processor he wrote a 75 word piece about a picture story of a birthday. At first sight, this is a mere jumble of words. Nevertheless, it was produced independently, confidently and with pride. It starts:

> **Birthday   look girl   walk tree   laugh man   and mummy letters   postman . . .**

> Looking carefully, it was possible to see extra spaces between 'sentences' and alongside the pictures. The following structure can be deduced and a possible interpretation made.

> Birthday   title
> look girl   'A girl is looking'
> walk tree   'a man is walking by the tree'
> laugh man   'the man is laughing'
> and mummy letters   'Mummy takes the letters'

> (Holdsworth, 1991, p. 8)

Word-processing was found to reach a wider audience when it was used in conjunction with an overlay keyboard. In the early stages, a selection set with pictures and words could help students to write confidently and quickly about everyday events (Figure 9.1). Later the selection set could provide a bank of unusual or specialist

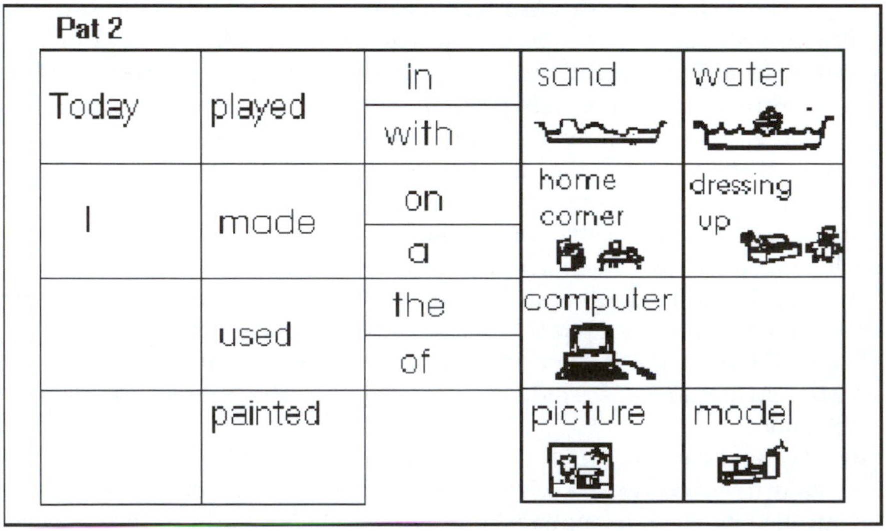

Figure 9.1   A selection set for an overlay keyboard for writing about early learning activities

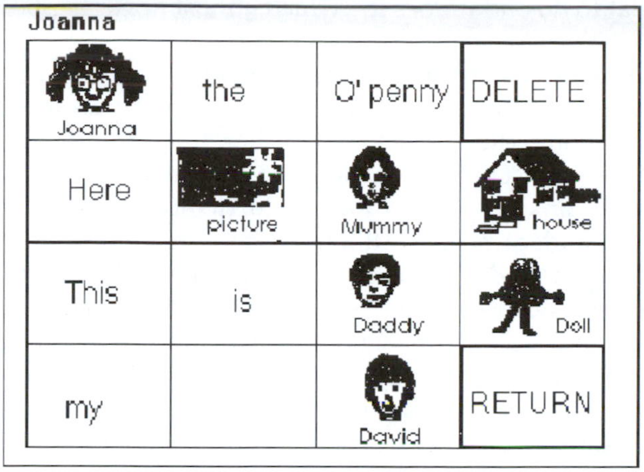

Figure 9.2   A selection set for an overlay keyboard to support a language development activity

subject vocabulary. When appropriate, these could also be used as a part of structured language development programs (Figure 9.2).

Webster's anticipation that the computer could be used to explore language visually was exploited by a hypertext dictionary that was developed through the collaboration of a teacher of the deaf and a programmer (Word Web by Janet Holdsworth and Rik Leedale). By today's standards the pictures appeared simplistic but using this software, children were able to visually explore components of sentences associated with common experiences such as their home, a farm and the zoo.

Pen portrait: age 5–6

Amy is profoundly deaf and attends a local infant school that has an attached unit for hearing impaired students. Like many young deaf children, she has limited communication with both children and adults. These communication difficulties have, in turn, reduced her experience of making choices and of living with the results of decisions. The use of ICT could be a powerful way of assisting Amy to access the curriculum. Like any other young child, Amy is encouraged to forge relationships with both adults and children but she is also learning that the computer can be 'a friend' too. To foster this concept, Amy has been introduced to simple cause-and-effect software, at first within the unit situation. Here, the computers are equipped with a greater range of input devices, such as touch screens or switches that can be used by students who find difficulty with keys or mouse. The software has been chosen for its simple bright images and sound effects that can be used, when appropriate, but which do not provide cues or rewards. Amy was introduced to the computer with another young child in the unit. Having established the way that the initial program operated, the children were able to take turns, experiment, communicate, often in a mixture of sign and gesture, and have fun! Staff unobtrusively monitored the children's progress and the activities offered are changed to meet students' needs. Amy now feels that the computer is one of her friends. It helps her in school, she can also 'tell' it what to do and it does it – which almost never happens in the rest of her life!

The confidence she has in the use of IT makes it easier for staff to use the computer to help her to access the curriculum both within the unit and in her integration classroom. She spends part of her time within the unit and part integrated into a mainstream classroom. In the latter situation, computer activities are closely linked to the National Curriculum with software chosen to meet a range of student needs. Although she is unable to appreciate the full range of sound effects and 'speech' facilities of some of the programs used, Amy now has the confidence to join in these class activities. Like many young children, Amy likes to draw pictures and has learnt to use a simple painting program on the computer. Within the school's literacy hour, the class has been reading a simple story and retelling it in a variety of ways. Amy 'retold' the story as a series of pictures, which her teacher has linked into a slide show that can be shown on the class computer and also saved to disc to take home and show Mum and Dad. Later, it is hoped to develop this idea and for Amy, with adult help, to add a few simple words as captions to her pictures.

Key issues

- If the computer is to help a child, then it must be perceived, from the outset, as helpful, interesting and non-threatening, i.e. user-friendly.
- Careful choice of software and task ensures that the child enjoys success but subtle changes can be made, when appropriate, to move them into their 'proximal zone'.
- When using the computer, Amy feels she is 'in control'. The computer is a friend who does what she tells it, though sometimes this may not be what she intended!
- Confidence gained in private (the unit) enables Amy to be more confident in a more public setting (mainstream classroom).

Key software

Although there is a wide choice of simple introductory software designed for the early stages, care needs to be taken when selecting suitable material for use with young hearing impaired children. The improvement in computer sound facilities has encouraged software developers to use sound for rewards and instructions. Provided these are duplicated visually, there may be no difficulty; children have a wonderful knack of ignoring what they cannot access – subject to the activity that they *can* access being suitably interesting and appropriate. Some simple switch software is capable of using an adapted microphone as a switch. This apparatus may be helpful to the child who is beginning to vocalize or to encourage those with very quiet voices to produce louder sounds.

Many young children use painting programs; less commonly used, in mainstream schools, is the use of slide-show software to link a series of pictures into a story. This software is sometimes supplied with the painting program itself. More recently, **multimedia authoring** has become available that can be used with any pictures that have been saved in particular formats. When children are ready, simple captions in words and/or signs can be added. This provides a stepping-stone to written communication that can be seen by a wider audience than just the children's own books. It can also be used to raise the self-esteem of children who perhaps do not often experience success.

Pictorial microworlds controlled by a mouse, trackerball or touch screen can help children with a hearing impairment to demonstrate what they understand as the information is presented in a visual form which then has to be reorganized in some way by the learner to demonstrate their understanding. (See also **early learning** in the References, Chapter 4 and Chapter 7.)

Key hardware

Young children enter school with a range of experiences and expertise with IT. Over a period of time, it can be helpful to build up a range of access devices. Computer mice are designed for adult hands and many young children find a **trackerball** much easier to use, as the complex movements required can be split between two hands. Young deaf children, with additional difficulties, may need a much more direct access method, such as a **touch screen**. For these students, it may also be helpful to have access to a switch box and small selection of switches, including a sound switch.

Where children are using colourful **painting and drawing** programs, the provision of a colour printer that will produce good quality results, relatively quickly, can be a boon. It is also necessary to ensure that funds are available for an adequate supply of the necessary inkjet cartridges or ink. Young children tend to draw large pictures, which can quickly deplete ink cartridge stocks! (See also Colin Hardy's pen portrait of Claire in Chapter 5.)

Pen portrait: age 7

Ben started school in a unit for the hearing impaired, first in an integrated hearing-deaf nursery and later in the unit attached to a mainstream infant school. He made excellent progress and now attends his local school. He has support in some lessons and uses a radio aid to help him in class. His class is making a newspaper about themselves using the word processor on the class computer set to write in columns. Their teacher has made a simple on-screen selection set to help the children with the more complex words that they may require. Working in pairs, the children write a few sentences, and perhaps draw a picture to illustrate their 'article' using the painting program. The selection set software enables the hearing children to listen to the words before they choose them. However, Ben would not be able to hear them clearly enough, so sign graphics (pictures of signs) have been added to some of the words in the selection set to help Ben identify them.

Ben also uses the class computer for some free writing, either with or without selection sets. Like many deaf students, he tends to leave out the less important words; when he is enthusiastic about a story, the punctuation can disappear too. However, he can read back his story with a classroom assistant and add the necessary punctuation to split the story into sentences. He can also be helped to use the editing facilities to correct the grammar, to the level appropriate for the task.

Key issues

- The newspaper format can be a powerful way of enabling students, who may only write a sentence or two individually, to put their contributions together and achieve a finished product where the whole is more than the sum of the individual parts. This can improve the self esteem of all the contributors.
- The use of group word-processing fosters communication as well as the higher writing skills of drafting, editing, etc.
- Signing is used with some deaf students to clarify their incomplete hearing and/or lip-reading. Meaningful signs can clarify a student's comprehension of written words and phrases.
- The use of word-processing can help reduce students' reliance on adult help. Mistakes can be corrected independently, to whatever level is appropriate, and are invisible in the final product.

Key software

Selection sets of banks of words and pictures are commonly offered to students as an aid to writing, with either an overlay keyboard or an on-screen keyboard. This type of software can be used with any word processor (or indeed, any other software where instructions need to be given). When used with a word processor, it is most common to just send the word to the writing screen, but it is possible to send a sign (or picture) instead of the word. If both sign and word are needed, it may be most easily achieved using a symbol processor (see **symbol software**). However, these are perhaps less used in the hearing impaired world than might be expected. Unfortunately, symbol processors are usually provided with standard symbol sets, such as rebus or Makaton, not signs. Signs, either as pictures or stylized graphics, are commercially available or can be created using specialist software where the sign graphic is made from pre-drawn parts. It would be better if the symbol/word processor could have a library of signs and that those signs could be linked to phrases. British Sign Language and American Sign Language are true languages but their syntax is not the same as English. Thus a sentence that is in perfectly correct 'sign order' does not produce 'correct English'. This may not matter in the context in which it is being used but mainstream teachers may need to be made aware of these differences. (Just as Braille users may need to have translation software to convert text to and from standard English this is also the case for transcribed sign language.)

The provisionality of a word processor can be particularly powerful for deaf children. They do not have to keep stopping to ask an adult how to spell words. Instead, they can concentrate on communicating their story, confident that all the problems can be sorted out at the end. In this way they are exploring language and moving into the 'proximal zone' between what they can do themselves and what can be achieved with sensitive assistance from a more experienced person or the technology. The extent to which correction is made can be varied according to the child's needs and those of the audience at which the writing is aimed. (See also the four-block model in Chapter 3.)

Key hardware

Large banks of information, including pictures, signs, etc., are currently supplied on CD-ROM and DVD. Multimedia is now standard on new computers. The availability of a sound card plus extras (speakers and/or headphones, microphone, etc.) may not appear essential for hearing impaired students. However, those who are in any way able to access even some of the sounds appear to take great delight in them. If the sound is found to be intrusive to the rest of the class, use headphones or just do not switch on the speakers!

Pen portrait: age 11

Julie is severely deaf and attends a school with a unit for hearing impaired students. She spends part of her time in a mainstream class with adult support and the rest of her time within the unit. In the latter setting, teaching can be more closely focused on her individual needs, particularly in the development of language. The unit has recently obtained a computer and both staff and students are experimenting with the new facilities that it affords. Julie has been using a multimedia CD-ROM dictionary with another Year 6 unit student and adult support. At first they needed to learn how to navigate this CD-ROM, so they took turns to choose words that they would like to see explained or demonstrated by an animation. Having found their chosen word, they were able to click on buttons to move to other related words or subjects. Julie is able to understand more of the sound aspects than her partner, Sophie, who cannot understand any of the speech but greatly enjoys the less sophisticated effects. Like all children, they were fascinated by the animation; their teachers welcomed facilities such as the animated display of several, quite different, dogs which graphically showed that 'dog' was a generic term, thus aiding semantic language development. The girls also discovered that there were games on the CD-ROM. Some of these were less successful as the questions were only 'spoken'. With access to visual clues only, the girls were disappointed to find it was almost impossible to solve the word puzzles without adult help to sign and speak the clues. However, they discovered other games where they could be successful. A particular favourite involved sound discrimination. Staff have been amazed at the ability of some students to discriminate sounds, well beyond that expected from their audiograms. Although this may be idiosyncratic, staff consider that it could prove very helpful to them in making the curriculum meaningful to the children in their care.

Key issues

- Even at the earliest stages, multimedia was recognized to be of particular relevance to deaf students. Webster (1989, p. 91) considered it to have 'incredible potential for education. Essentially this software acts as a database where pictures, maps, statistics, programs and simulations are stored. The materials are then used to foster co-operative learning, problem-solving, research skills, decision-making and creative thinking skills.'

- One of the earliest uses of multimedia in education was the Interactive Video in Schools Project (Jones, 1986–87) that developed exciting, and meaningful, stories for deaf children on 11-inch laser discs. Sadly, the extremely high cost of the necessary hardware precluded use by more than a very few schools. A few years later, when multimedia systems were being introduced into both secondary and primary schools, data compression techniques enabled the use of standard CD-ROMs. However, very few CD-ROMs have been developed which take into account the needs of deaf users apart from signing databases. Instead, schools make creative use of commercially available titles, many of which were developed for the American home market. Evaluators of each of the DfEE CD-ROM in Schools Initiatives (Collins *et al.*, 1995; Nash, Steadman and Eraut, 1992; Sparrowhawk, 1995) commented on this American origin and reported British teachers' requests for material specifically developed for the English and Welsh National Curriculum. However, McDevitt (1998) found that little had changed apart from British/ European versions of some of the most popular American CD-ROM titles. Despite their shortfalls, many schools are successfully using multimedia (CD-ROM) sources of information with their students. Abbott (1995, p. 8) considers that 'the combination of text with sound and pictures can make ideas more accessible. Each element of the multimedia can reinforce the meaning and its multi-sensory nature can help many learners to understand ideas and information that might be too difficult through text alone.' He suggests that students who do not have the necessary search skills to use traditional encyclopaedias can successfully search CD-ROM titles because there are usually alternative pathways to reach the required information. He postulates that accessing information from a CD-ROM requires different skills from traditional information handling. Both Sparrowhawk (1995) and McDevitt (1998) commented on the different ways in which adults and children searched CD-ROMs for information, i.e. students used pictures and icons in preference to text whilst adults used text.

- One difficulty encountered by deaf students is the use made by developers of sound both for effects, such as ambient sound, and for commentary. Even students with small hearing loss, who might normally be able to discern the speech, may find the task impossible where ambient sound has been added. Orford (1995) also discussed the use of sound on CD-ROMs with hearing impaired students. He identified titles where there was an option to remove effects and music whilst retaining 'speech' as being particularly helpful. For students with poor speech discrimination, he considered that onscreen text could support an imperfectly perceived spoken sentence. However, to do this, the text needed to be a verbatim version and presented in synchrony with the speech. He noted that some packages offer a précis of the spoken words or expanded caption of the visual image being presented, neither of which he considered to offer real support for the understanding of speech. This emphasizes the need to accommodate multiple representations of content according to the principles of **universal design** for learning.
- The text on screen can present reading difficulties for language delayed students. Although some CD-ROM titles present text in a larger font, few offer alternative levels of language. Abbott (1995) included a case study of deaf children who were able to 'read' a commercial talking story, where signs had been added to the original. However, few schools would have either the necessary hardware, expertise or time to achieve this level of modification. Most will need to rely on the careful use of standard products. Despite these difficulties, Orford (1995) was convinced that many hearing impaired children depended a great deal on the visual channel for their comprehension of the world around them and that the visual elements of a multimedia package could enable understanding in unique and powerful ways.

Key software

Multimedia software is constantly changing, being upgraded and enhanced so that it is not possible to even suggest any form of definitive list. The previously cited research suggests that most schools use CD-ROMs for either simple-to-use applications such as multimedia **talking books** or as a source of information to supplement, not replace, traditional sources. Information on almost any subject is available on CD-ROM. It remains for those working with students to decide what information is needed, look at the material that is commercially available and make their selection to best fit the needs of their students. Some points worth considering are listed in the References under **compact discs**.

Key hardware

Although some schools will need to continue using older computers that lack multimedia facilities, almost all new computers are multimedia systems. Indeed Heppell suggests that the term 'multimedia' will become redundant in the near future since all computers will be multimedia machines (a view we assume in this book). Despite this, few hearing impaired students will be able to understand the spoken commentaries that accompany the opening of screens on some CD-ROMs, especially if the commentary differs from the written text. However, a surprising number of hearing impaired students seem to take great delight in the sound effects that they can hear, however little. It may therefore be important to provide the best possible access to this facility. Some students find the standard speakers supplied with most computers are not suitable for their use and it may be more appropriate to use headphones, especially the better quality headphones that may be used with other audio equipment. Where this sound quality is insufficient, special adaptors to some radio aids can be obtained.

Some access utilities are provided for deaf users as part of current operating systems to provide some visual feedback to replace existing auditory prompts (see sound-sentry and show-sounds in **visual feedback**).

Finally, it is important for those who control budgets to realize that computer hardware and software are constantly developing. The highest specification of machine is always going to be the most media capable machine and therefore the most versatile. Machines will need to be upgraded or replaced periodically and this needs to be budgeted for. Any reassessment of needs should always take into account changes in technology.

Pen portrait: age 13

Greg and Lee attend a mainstream secondary school. In History and English they are studying the First World War and producing a joint project folder. Students are encouraged to use the resource areas in the school where there are network computers with access to both the Internet and information CD-ROMs. The first time the boys tried to use a CD-ROM encyclopaedia, they typed in 'First World War' and found far too many articles to cope with. With help from their support teacher, they made a short list of key words to use in their search for information. Using the same CD-ROM encyclopaedia, they subsequently found an article on the desired topic that included both photographs and videos. Although they could change to less complex text on this CD-ROM, they still appreciated help from a learning support assistant with the words and phrases that they found difficult to understand.

Subject staff had also encouraged students to search the world wide web to see if they could find better, or different, information, using the same key word(s). As articles on the web could be obtained from around the world, different perspectives on the same event might be discovered. The boys' web search produced 200 articles, some of which might be really helpful, others not – the difficulty for them was to differentiate between them. At first they tried looking at the sites, in order, but realized that this would take far too long. They decided to print out the first article, as it seemed useful, and discuss the problem with their specialist support teacher, later in the day.

Key issues

The pen portrait of Greg and Lee has been included to highlight some of the issues that arise when students try to use large databases of information. It also illustrates some of the differences between searching for information using a published CD-ROM information source and the world wide web.

- Although students now have access to much more information than ever before, it can be difficult to avoid 'information overload'. Students need to learn to refine searches. However, this may require a higher level of language comprehension than has been needed in the past.
- Learning to search a CD-ROM and the web may require different searching techniques. CD-ROMs frequently have idiosyncratic indexing and require individual navigation skills to be taught. However, use can be made of icons, picture indexes, etc. to assist the search process. By contrast, the most popular search engines on the web are most easily accessed using standard 'reference book' search methods using text. This requires correct spelling and syntax.
- The validity of material found on the web can be questionable so it may be more appropriate for students to use web search engines created for education purposes and use links from educational organizations.
- The problem of 'too many articles being found' commonly occurs when students start to use the web. Teachers and support staff are becoming more accustomed to aiding students to generate additional key words in order to refine their search. Successful searching needs to make use of the advanced capacities of search engines but surely it is not the student's role to research everything themselves? However, when a useful web site is found its address can be added to the school's collection of links.

Pen portrait: Key Stage 4, age 15
Kirsty is integrated into a mainstream school and is following six GCSE courses. She has support in some lessons plus time each week with a peripatetic teacher of the deaf, in addition to support from school special needs staff. Kirsty has used a radio aid in class for most of her school career. She works extremely hard but still finds that her school work takes her much longer to complete than it does for her fully hearing peers. This was not so obvious when she was in the

lower part of the school but, as the workload increased, she seemed to be spending more and more time on her work. She has good support at home but staff became concerned that her parents might be over-assisting her. Although this strategy enabled her to complete the set tasks, Kirsty's homework was not always consistent with that produced in class. More importantly, she was not learning to correct her own work and was becoming more reliant on adult support.

During Year 9, students were introduced to the work pattern of note-taking and longer project work that would be used in their GCSE courses. Unlike her fully hearing peers, Kirsty cannot take notes and attend to the teacher at the same time. In order to understand oral information, Kirsty needs to look carefully at teachers in order to lip-read them and clarify the speech that she hears via the radio aid. If she looked down at her book in order to take notes, she found that she was missing parts of the lesson. The role of her support assistant changed to that of a note-taker. From these written notes, and her recall of the lesson, Kirsty found she was better able to tackle homework. However, like many deaf students, she sometimes left out of her written work the small words that she did not hear and made mistakes with grammar. Support staff were able to go through her project work with her and help her to correct at least some of these mistakes. Kirsty would then copy the work out again. Unfortunately staff found that she made further errors – and would then copy the work out yet again. She seemed to become more tired as each week went by; she was losing self-confidence and getting further behind with her work. Both Kirsty and her parents started to seriously consider extra years in school or a transfer to a different school. Her teacher of the deaf consulted colleagues in the LEA SEN support service.

Following an assessment by their IT advisory teacher, Kirsty was provided with a simple laptop word processor. This choice was made to meet both her need for help with note-taking and editing, and her desire for equipment to be as unobtrusive as possible. She was quite self-conscious about using the radio aid and did not want to appear any more 'different' or to carry anything more about school. She knows it is essential for her to sit in class where she can best see the teacher's face and that this is not always in proximity to a power point! The simple laptop had excellent battery life so there was no need to carry either extra batteries or a mains adaptor. This type of simple laptop is used by other students in the school, so Kirsty felt less singular in its use, compared to a portable computer.

In class, the laptop was often used by her support assistant, as Kirsty could not touch-type at speed. The support assistant took notes, just as before, but on the laptop. These notes were printed out in the SEN room and also saved to the memory of the laptop. Kirsty then had the notes to use, either in printed or electronic form, in her homework. She completed her homework on the laptop and was able to use the editing facilities to sort out some of the errors, insert the missing words, etc. The finished work was printed out in school where help was available with filing and storing of the loose paper. When needed for her project, text from the laptop could also be transferred to a desktop PC for further embellishment. This pattern of working was developed during the latter part of Year 9 so she was able to use it confidently in subsequent years and not become overwhelmed by the GCSE workload.

To ensure that staff and examiners were aware of the level of help she had been given, copies of the original notes, Kirsty's first draft and the final result have been kept. Over a period of time, both Kirsty and staff have been delighted with the improvement in her work and the extent to which she was later able to self-correct work. This record helped to remind her of how far she had improved – which has, in turn, boosted her self-confidence. She is aware that she will always have to work harder than her hearing friends but now knows that she can succeed and is planning to go to Further Education College when she leaves school.

Through practice, and need, Kirsty can type at a reasonable speed but realizes that even at college, she will have to rely on a note-taker in class unless she can touch-type at speed. Due to pressure of work, there will be no time for this until she has completed her GCSE work. Instead, she plans to include 'touch-typing' in her college courses.

Key issues

Some of the issues in Kirsty's pen portrait are also indicative of the problems faced by a deaf student following an academic course at a college or university.

- Students with a range of difficulties that result in their frequent recopying of work find that the use of a simple word processor can make a tremendous difference to their workload. Some of the time that was previously spent in recopying work can be used more profitably, e.g. to concentrate on the development of language-related skills.
- If students are to benefit from the use of a keyboard, then they need to be able to type at least as fast as they can write. When this need can be anticipated, students use a **typing tutor** to acquire keyboarding skills before attempting to use key-boarding equipment as their main recording method. This takes time and requires both concentration and determination on the part of the student. In Kirsty's case, this was not possible so a compromise was made to meet her needs, as far as was practical, at that stage of her education.
- Although many students use laptops themselves in class, it is less usual for the equipment to be used by support staff. However, for those who need to concentrate hard on the teacher's speech, the laptop may be better employed in class by the note-taker. (However, the validity of teaching methods which employ a great deal of dictation should be questioned in the longer term. Dictation is a hangover from medieval times when there was a lack of textbooks and lectures were an opportunity for groups of students to make a copy of the lecturer's masterwork.)
- Because mistakes can be seamlessly corrected on a word processor, it is necessary for staff to ensure that students correct most of the work themselves. Although adult help may be needed, it is very easy for well-meaning adults to 'over-correct'. The retention of printouts of the 'first drafts' may be important, not only for examination purposes. It equates to most students' handwritten work in the exercise book; however, in this format, it is possible to see staff (or student) corrections. A **predictor** may support the use of correct grammar and in some cases increase typing speed. **Macros** might also be useful for frequent phrases or long bits of jargon.

- Schools are often keen that word processors used by students on personal equipment are identical to that used on the school desktop computers. However, this can present practical difficulties, usually due to battery life problems. As most word processors operate in the same way, often using the same commands, students who understand the concept of word-processing, as against operation of one software title, can easily move from one word processor to another. As text can be easily transferred from one machine to another, as well as between software, the choice of personal keyboarding equipment can be made on grounds of practicality, rather than the need to replicate network software.
- A planner may be useful for laying out mind maps representing different subjects and for planning essays or projects.

(See also the pen portrait of Jean Paul in Chapter 3.)

The leading edge in developing practice

It is always difficult to predict the way in which ICT will be used in the future. Developments that appear to promise much may not always live up to our expectations. It might be better to confine this section to a few expected developments to current practice which may become both possible and practical in the near future.

It is ironic that the invention of the telephone resulted from Alexander Bell's attempts to improve the hearing of his deaf wife. Unfortunately, his invention presents a barrier to both communication and range of employment for the hearing impaired. Text phones (Minicom) are available but these can only be used where both caller and recipient have this device. Although they may be very useful within the deaf community, it may be necessary to make use of a more commonly used device in order to communicate with a wider community. Almost all schools, businesses and many homes have fax machines, which can provide the hearing impaired with an alternative method of communication. Using a fax, even young children can communicate with students in other schools, friends and family in either pictures or words. Although they cannot be used for 'live conversation', they have been successfully used to develop 'buddy' or mentor systems between students who are deaf and with paired adults in a business (see the BT Fax Buddy Scheme). A similar project was undertaken by Foster (1996) with deaf students in Canada who were encouraged to write to each other using email. This led to the exchange of data for different assignments, collaborative writing, contributing work on a common theme to an on-line conference and the exchange of videos showing the students and their activities. He concluded:

> Telecomunications motivated my students in many ways, and encouraged them to remain on task for extended periods of time. They seemed to acquire a better understanding of themselves and other deaf students in settings quite different from their own. They approached telecommunications activities with confidence and enthusiasm in an effective learning environment that was both exciting and fun.
>
> (Foster, 1996, p. 110)

Changes in communications technology have made the development of videophones and video-conferencing a practical possibility. With a standard telephone connection, the screens are small and the picture quality less than ideal. However, with video-conferencing using higher quality connections, the clarity, quality and size of the pictures on screen are now good enough to conduct a signed conversation, if not to enable lip-reading. Already, use is being made of video-conferencing in some areas of the country for communication between deaf students and their support staff. As this technology becomes available on the mass market and video-conferencing or video-phones move into general use, then the barrier imposed by the standard telephone may, at last, be removed.

The vast increase in the use of the **Internet** means that specialist staff with access can have much easier and ready contact with mainstream colleagues across a number of settings where children with special needs are included. The internet also offers the possibility for communication with others working in the same field or, indeed, the sharing of ideas with colleagues with other areas of expertise, in order to solve problems and enhance the curriculum for their students.

Students, too, are being encouraged to use the world wide web to help them with their studies. However, the language used on standard web pages may be daunting for some hearing impaired students. Already, there are a few specialist web sites where alternative forms of communication are provided. However, additional utilities are being produced which make possible the use of close captions or signed support for most web pages to augment text, speech and video content.

Part IV
Summary

10

Summary Themes

Mike Blamires

This book is not an eighteenth-century deed of trust nor a promissory note with the implication that 'you have not got it now but you will get it eventually' and that something might happen in the future. We have attempted to describe practice as it is now and the concerns that need to be considered for some time to come. Legislation and guidance in different countries have provided principles for practice. Universal design for learning provides a positive framework to challenge our thinking and promote action in response to these principles. We are all having to come to terms with our technological literacy and learn to take some pride in our emerging 'Geekdom', even if it is in the face of reactionary derision. The Egyptian scribes must have known what it felt like.

The message of this book is that technology can enable people to be included within their communities and educational institutions. It can provide a temporary or permanent support for learners to establish their voice and achieve things that they could not have done otherwise. Technology has been a powerful tool for accommodating a series of historical accidents that underpin teaching but it can also have a central role in reshaping the curriculum.

At a time when inclusion is moving up the social agenda, the educational tools for its implementation are coming of age. As Hart suggests, responding to diversity requires innovative thinking. Dorman suggests that similarly, the successful educational use of technology also requires rigorous thought about learning. Universal design for learning is an attractive framework because it builds upon design principles to provide a context for inclusion. Universal design has similarities to aspects of 'differentiation' which was a concept of the early 1990s (e.g. Moore, 1992) and also requires proactive planning.

The English and Welsh Code of Practice (DfEE, 1994) encouraged those involved in individual educational planning to explore the benefits of IT to meet the needs of learners and then secure access to appropriate IT and train all those who are going to be involved in its use.

At the very basic level this means a range of individualized provision:

- Special needs staff must be aware of the potential of IT for different special educational needs.
- The ICT co-ordinator should also have this awareness.
- The classroom assistant needs to be trained in how the software or devices can be used.
- The class teacher needs to be informed how the software or device can be used to support curriculum engagement.

This can be supported when:

- The use of appropriate and flexible software is already available in the school; for example, the learner is encouraged to make use of a word processor to present work.

- ICT is targeted for use by the learner for a specific activity; for example, the learner is encouraged to use a painting program in Art in order to carry out a painting task because of her hand-eye co-ordination difficulties. Most software in schools is flexible and under-used. It may be that software which is employed generally in the school has features able to support the learning needs identified.
- Specialist resources are made available from the school's stock to meet some aspects of the learner's needs; for example, the allocation of a laptop or overlay keyboard to support a child with writing difficulties or a talking word processor for a learner who needs to hear what he or she has typed.
- Specialist software or devices are loaned to support an IEP from outside agencies; for example, the loan of equipment not normally available within the school's resource base.
- Specialist software or devices purchased from devolved or external budget are allocated specifically to the learner.

From work undertaken on individual education planning (Tod, Castle and Blamires, 1998) I tentatively suggest that the following dimensions of activity can aid us in considering the inclusiveness of the enabling technology as well as how technology can be applied to universal design principles for inclusion. They form a basis for proactive planning at a whole-school level.

- *Dimension 1*:

Clarity of what is expected

Figure 10.1   Dimension 1

Are expectations explicit through verbal or visual explanation or demonstration? Does the learner know what the task is, how they have to do it, when they are finished and what they have to do next? Does the learner know the implicit routines of the school and class? Are areas with specific functions clearly marked? Does the learner know 'the way we do things here' and why? Does the child have a personal timetable so they know where they are in the day and during the week?

- *Dimension 2*:

Predictability/novelty

Figure 10.2   Dimension 2

Is the day or lesson structured enough for the child or is it so structured that it is monotonous and boring? Would different activities, groupings and stimuli increase the novelty of the activities? Is enough happening to keep the child involved?

- *Dimension 3*:

Affirmation/criticism (reward system)

Figure 10.3 Dimension 3

Are there opportunities to reward the real effort of an individual? Does the frequency of the reward need to be increased? Are the rewards given credible to the learner? Are opportunities for implied or overt negative criticism avoided (e.g. a request for the child to perform their weakest skill in front of an unsympathetic audience of peers)? Are social rewards part of the system?

- *Dimension 4*:

Interaction/group work

Figure 10.4 Dimension 4

Is flexible grouping in operation which avoids the negative effect of sink groups? Are learners able to work by themselves if required or seek the appropriate support from peers? Are learners encouraged to learn through group discussion and activity?

- *Dimension 5*:

Available time for tasks (workload)

Figure 10.5 Dimension 5

Is the workload appropriate for the learner? Has she too much or too little to do? Is the amount of time available for tasks, including homework, enough? Could the learner increase their work rate using technology?

- *Dimension 6*:

Negotiation/conflict (choice)

Figure 10.6 Dimension 6

Does the learner have choice? Is she supported to develop learning and social skills? Are there opportunities for 'real' negotiation so that serious conflict can be avoided? Is there a flexible and fair system of negotiation available for all learners?

- *Dimension 7*:

Level of work (complexity)

Figure 10.7   Dimension 7

Is the work easy enough for the learner to do? Could it be broken down into smaller constituent tasks? On the other hand, does it set enough challenges? Are links made with other areas?

- *Dimension 8*:

Modality

Figure 10.8   Dimension 8

Are tasks set, undertaken and presented just using spoken language? Can multi-sensory approaches be applied? Can the preferred modality of the learner be emphasized?

- *Dimension 9*:

Language demand

Figure 10.9   Dimension 9

Is the language demanded from the tasks appropriate? Is the readabilty level too difficult? Is the material presented in the user's preferred language, i.e. signs or symbols? Is the page layout of materials cluttered or too busy? Do key words need to be taught?

- *Dimension 10*:

Attention (given or expected)

Figure 10.10   Dimension 10

Does the child require extra monitoring and support by the teacher or support staff in order to keep on task? Is the software capable of providing appropriate levels of feedback? Can self-help skills and independence be developed?

In re-engineering educational systems, Straker's (1986) questions are still apposite even if they need slight rephrasing:

Continuity

(1) What steps have been taken to ensure that ideas for learning and teaching with *ICT* are effectively shared and developed throughout the school?
(2) How do teachers know which software the *'learners'* have used previously?
(3) How do teachers prevent unnecessary repetition of work on computers? (*Or off!*)
(4) Are staff aware of how *other institutions are using ICT?*
(5) What has been done to ensure skills developed by a learner are built on by *the next educational institution?*

Curriculum

(1) In what ways, and to what extent, do teachers feel *ICT* has affected opportunities for the learners to
   (a) take initiative and have some control over their learning
   (b) discuss and share ideas
   (c) collaborate with others towards an agreed end
   (d) pose and find solutions to their own questions
   (e) set up and test hypotheses
   (f) organize and analyse information
   (g) express creative ideas and derive enjoyment from them
   (h) experience different modes of communication?
(2) Do teachers consider that they have used *ICT* to
   (a) increase their professional efficiency
   (b) help them develop more appropriate teaching styles
   (c) help them cope with the varied demands of teaching
   (d) focus on how people learn as well as on what they learn
   (e) give better insight into children's thinking
   (f) meet the needs of individuals over a wide range of ability?

National grids or universal webs

Education is currently developing as a network of shared resources and opportunities alongside government initiatives for centralized 'national grids for learning' where educational fuel is piped into learners from approved providers. At odds with this is a participatory democracy growing where providers, producers and consumers can be in direct contact across continents. These communities are beginning to respond to the 'unfamiliar voices' enabled by technology. As well as a quality mark for the accessibility of educational materials, we may now need a quality mark for adopting and extending universal design for learning principles. The world wide web will not be fully woven until it can ensnare us all. We look forward to working with you on that venture – the realization of enabling technology for inclusion.

Appendix I: Sources

You will be able to obtain full up-to-date details of products and suppliers from the special needs Xplanatory web site:

The Special Needs Xplanatory
www.canterbury.ac.uk/xplanatory/xplan.htm

Other useful web sites

The contributors' web sites

John Lodge
www.jlodge.demon.co.uk/web/home.htm

The Advisory Unit
www.advisory-unit.org.uk/

Meldreth School
www.rmplc.co.uk/eduweb/sites/meldreth

Other sites of note not listed in suppliers (Appendix II)

Alliance for Technology Access
www.marin.org/npop/ata/

British Educational Communications Technology Agency (BECTA)
http.becta.org.uk/index.html

Closing the Gap
www.closingthegapcom/index.html

The Disability Mail
disability.com

EASI (Equal Access to Software and Information)
www.isc.rit.edu/~easi/

Trace Research and Development Centre
www.trace.wisc.edu

CAST: Universal Design Education Project
Http://darkwing.uoregon.edu/~uplan/UDEPweb/MainUDEP.html

Bayha, B. (1998) *The Internet: An Inclusive Magnet for Teaching All Students*, World Institute on Disability, http://www.wid.org/tech/handbook/

Appendix II: List of Suppliers

(Visit the Xplanatory web site (see Appendix I) for more up-to-date lists and links to suppliers in other regions of the world.)

Armrests
QED

Communication aids
Don Johnson
Toby Churchill
Easiaids
Liberator
Mardis
Cambridge Adaptive Communications

Direct scan
Clicker 3 – Cricksoft
Discover Switch
SAW – ACE
Windows Switch – Advisory Unit
Wivik
HandsOFF
Ezkeys

Direct switch control of hotspots
Clikit! – Intellitools
Discover Switch – Don Johnson
Windows Switch – Advisory Unit
Hotspots – Ace Centre

Early learning software
Advisory Unit
Inclusive Technology
SEMERC
TAG
Widget
Sherston

Ergonomic keyboards
Maltron/KCS Ltd
Microsoft
Apple

Expanded keyboards
CAC
SEMERC

Integrated learning systems
SIR
RM

Keyguards
SAS
Inclusive Technology
Don Johnson

Logo
Longman Logotron
Advisory Unit
Valiant Technology
Inclusive Technology

Miniature keyboards
CAC

Multimedia encyclopaedias
My First Amazing Dictionary – Dorling
    Kindersley
TAG
Sherston

Onscreen keyboards and software
Advisory Unit
Don Johnson
Crick Software

Overlay keyboards
KCS
Intellikeys
Don Johnson

Robots
Valiant Technology

Scanners
Aptech
Kurzwiel

Screen readers
Aptech

Software houses
Black Cat
Sherston
SPA

Switch controlled selection sets
Windows Switch – Advisory Unit
Switch Clicker – Cricksoft
Saw – ACE
Discover Switch – Don Johnston
Easikeys – CAC

Switch suppliers
Cambridge Adaptive Technology
Don Johnston
Inclusive Technology
Liberator
Mardis
QED
TFH

Talking word processors
Don Johnson
Iansyst
Longman Logotron
Research Machines

Touch screens
Inclusive Technology UK suppliers

Suppliers' Addresses

ACE Centre Advisor Trust
92 Windmill Road,
Wayneflete Road,
Headington,
Oxford
OX3 7DR
Tel: 01865 763508/759800
Fax: 01865 759810

Advisory Unit for Computers in
   Education
126 Great North Road,
Hatfield, Hertfordshire
AL9 5JZ

Aptech Ltd
Aptach House,
Meadowfield,
Ponteland
Newcastle upon Tyne
NE20 9SD

Blackcat Educational Software
The Barn,
Cwm Camlais,
Brecon,
Powys LD3 8LD
Tel: 01874 636835
Fax: 01874 636858

CALL Centre
4 Buccleauch Place,
Edinburgh
EH8 9LW

Cambridge Adaptive Communications
   (CAC)
The Mount,
Toft,
Cambridge
CB3 7RL

Crick Computing
123 The Drive,
Northampton
NN1 2SW

Don Johnston Special Needs Ltd
18 Clarendon Court,
Calver Road,
Winwick Quay,
Warrington
WA1 8QP

Electrone
Unit 1, Central Park,
Bellfied Road,
High Wycombe
HP12 5HG

FCD Foundation for Communication for
    the Disabled
Beacon House,
Pyford Road,
West Byfleet
KT14 6LD

GUS Communications, Inc
1006 Lonetree Ct,
Bellingham, USA
WA 98226

Iansyst Ltd
The White House,
72 Fen Road,
Cambridge
CB4 1UN

Inclusive Technology Ltd,
Saddleworth Business Centre,
Huddlesfield Road,
Oldham
OL3 5DF

KCS
PO Box 700,
Freepost
SO17 1YA
Tel: 01703 584314

Liberator
Whitegates,
Swinstead
NG33 4PA

Longman Logotron
124 Cambridge Science Park,
Milton Road,
Cambridge
CB4 4ZS

Lorien Systems
Enkalon Business Centre,
25 Randalstown Road,
Antrim
BT41 4LJ

Microsoft
Microsoft Campus,
Thames Valley Park,
Reading
RG6 1WG

P.C.D. Maltron Ltd
15 Orchard Lane,
East Molesey,
Surrey
KT8 0BN

QED Ltd
Ability House,
242 Gosport Road,
Fareham, Hampshire
PO16 0SS

REM (Rickett Educational Media)
Great Western House,
Langport,
Somerset
TA10 9YU

Research Machines
New Mill Road,
183 Milton Park,
Abingdon, Oxford
OX14 4SE

Scottish Council for Educational
    Technology
74 Victoria Crescent Road,
Glasgow
G12 9JN

Sherston Software
Swan Barton,
Sherston,
Malmesbury,
Wiltshire
SN16 0LL
Tel: 01666 840433

Sight & Sound Technology
Quantel House,
Anglia Way,
Moulton Park,
Northampton
NN3 6JA

SIR
Suite 4E
East Mill,
Bridgefoot,
Belper,
Derbyshire
DE56 1XQ
Tel: 01773 820206

SPA
PO Box 59,
Tewkesbury,
Gloucester
GL20 6AB
Tel: 01684 81700

Special Access Systems
4 Benson Place,
Oxford
OX2 6QH

TAG Developments
25 Pelham Road,
Gravesend
DA11 0HU

Tandy Educational Suppliers Intertan
  UK Ltd
Tandy Centre,
Leamore Lane,
Walsall
WS2 7PS

TFH
76 Barracks Road,
Sandy Lane Industrial Estate,
Stourport on Severn,
Worcester
DY13 9QB

Toby Churchill
20 Panton Street,
Cambridge
CB2 1HP

Valiant Technology
Valiant House,
3 Grange Mills,
Wier Road,
London
SW12 0NE
Tel: 0181 673 2233
Fax: 0181 673 6333

Virtual Reality Systems
Unit 8, Farm Business Centre,
East Tytherly Road,
Lockerley,
Romsey, Hampshire
SO51 0LW

Widget Software
102 Radford Road,
Luton
LU1 1TR

Xemplar Education
700 Great Cambridge Road,
Enfield
EN1 3BR

References

A

Abbreviation expansion (see **macros**)

Adventure games (see **modelling**)

Arm supports
These can be attached on to a trolley, table or wheelchair to provide flexible arm support at an appropriate level for users who are quickly fatigued whilst using a keyboard or mouse. They can also provide support for those who have tremors. See **positioning and seating**.

Art
ICT can facilitate a student's knowledge and experience of Art. It can facilitate a student's engagement in art through painting and drawing software possibly controlled by a mouse, specialized input device or graphics tablet. Drawing shapes on the computer can be easier than using traditional drawing tools and in some cases this is only possible when a computer is used. Magnification (zoom) facilities can aid learners with low vision and with physical control difficulties.

Images can be obtained on a computer from these main sources:

- External images and photos either scanned into the computer or transferred from a digital camera, captured from existing sources of digital images, clipart, CD-ROM and the Internet. These can be published as part of a multimedia program or presentation with accompanying sound, as part of a web page on the Internet, as hard copy on to different types of paper, foils and fabric using an appropriate colour or black and white printer, or as textiles using specialized sewing, weaving or knitting machines.
- Imported images can also be used as starting-points for the student's own art work, using painting, drawing or desktop publishing software to process the images. Colours can be changed, patterns, gradients and washes can be applied. Labels and text can be added.
- The **Internet** can be a valuable source of information about the work of artists, which is particularly useful for those whose mobility difficulties restrict their visits to galleries. However, this information may not always be in a format that is readily usable by the learner. See **universal design**.

Points to consider:

(1) Is the use of ICT leading the project or enhancing the possibilities of an existing project?
(2) Is the language used to describe the techniques and approaches used within a piece of software or accompanying a piece of work understood by the learner?

(3)   Does the range of images used include minority cultures as well as people with disability?

(4)   How will the final product be published or displayed?

(5)   Is ICT the only means of working with images? Could other sources and resources be employed to enhance visual and tactile experiences?

(6)   Does the software need to be modified to take into account the learning needs of the child?

(7)   Does the software need to be used in conjunction with an alternative keyboard, mouse or other device?

(8)   Does the hardware have enough memory to process and store the images produced?

(9)   Does the use of ICT enable the learner to explore more approaches and techniques?

(10) Does the use of ICT extend or narrow the range of visual resources the learner has experience of?

(11) To what extent is the image produced an artefact of the software used rather than the result of reflective engagement with a task?

(12) Are effects being applied because they are possible rather than because they are appropriate?

(13) Does the task develop creative skills and insights rather than just technical skills?

(14) How are stages in the production documented for assessment?

See also **painting and drawing**.

Assistive technology

'An Assistive Technology device is: any item, piece of equipment, or product system whether acquired commercially off the shelf, modified or customized that is used to increase, maintain, or improve functional capabilities of individuals with disabilities' (USA, Public Law 100–407, the Technology-Related Assistance for Individuals with Disabilities Act of 1998). You may wish to compare this definition with the definition of access technology in Chapter 1.

Auditory feedback

Toggle keys are an example of an accessibility feature which gives auditory feedback. It generates a high tone when the Num Lock, Scroll Lock or Caps Lock keys are toggled on and a low tone when any of these keys are toggled off. This augments or replaces the visual LED feedback on a standard keyboard and may be useful to a blind or visually impaired user.

Augmentative communication

The use of signing, symbols, pictures and visual prompts and cues alongside speech and gesture can support the development of communication skills. **Communication aids** can support the communication of learners who are non-verbal or who have unintelligible speech.

Microtechnology can support this by:

- facilitating the production of paper-based materials which feature symbols and signs

- teaching learners the meanings of signs and symbols through matching games and activities
- allowing users to use symbols to generate spoken language alongside signs via communication aids
- the use of a **symbol processor** which can provide spoken text augmented by symbols 'translated' from existing text sources on CD or the Internet.

The extent to which augmentative communication systems can help learners achieve functional communication uses is described by Latham and Miles (1997) (see also Table R.1).

Table R.1   Development of functional communication

Pre-intentional	Intentional
0–9 months • likes • dislikes • wants • rejects • distinguishes between familiar and unfamiliar	• draws attention to self • requests • greets • protests and rejects • gives information • responds
9–18 months • existence • disappearance • recurrence • possession • rejection • non-existence	• location • action • agent • object • attributes
18 months–3 years • socialization • requests • gives information • describes • directs • questions • repairs misunderstandings	
3–5 years • gives and shares information • describes • directs • questions • reasons and predicts • plans and evaluates • negotiates • conversation skills • expresses feelings	

Source: Latham and Miles (1997).

Autocorrect

This is a feature within some word processors that can be taught to correct typing errors so that when I type 'impariment' and then press space or a punctuation mark it will automatically change it to 'impairment'. Entries in the list of autocorrections can be added during a spell check and edited or removed by selecting a tools – autocorrect menu option. This is useful for learners who make repeated mistakes and those with disabilities as it saves on key strokes.

See also **abbreviation expansion**.

B

Branching tree databases (see **history**)

Browsers
Software that people can use to obtain information and navigate through web pages on the **Internet**. Web pages contain images and other media as well as links to other pages. The ability to browse (viewing pages on the Internet) is now becoming a feature of other programs such as word processors and desktop publishing.

The principles of **universal design** for learning apply to the creation of web pages. It should not be assumed that all users of web pages can see the images and buttons on the web pages, so these needs should be catered for by using alternative representation and explicit captioning of images and other media.

Web browsers are available now for people with visual impairments or who are blind. These browsers take advantage of the hypertext mark-up language (HTML) coding that underpins standard web pages so that headings, descriptions of content and links can be spoken to aid efficient browsing using speech synthesis.

C

CD-ROM (see **compact discs**)

Chording keyboards
A coded access method usually using five or more keys controlled by the fingers of one hand to generate codes that are interpreted as characters. It can remove repetitive motion as only the thumb needs to be moved from key to key. These tend to be efficient methods as the fingers need only to locate a fraction of the keys of a standard keyboard but they require a high cognitive level to learn the chord shapes required to generate characters. They are mainly used by stenographers.

Cloze procedure
A reading development activity that involves the reconstruction and interpretation of a piece of text which may be hidden or mixed up in some form. It can be used in trivial ways as letter guessing but with sensitive support these activities can provide rich language and reading development opportunities for groups of learners.

Cloze procedure can be over-applied and used to literally 'fill in' time. If the task is about building the meaning of a whole text rather than just guessing the right word, then it can become a worthwhile task. Word processors now allow children to take more risks with their suggestions as what they write in the gap can be changed easily. 'Developing Tray' is a classic example of a cloze procedure on a computer. With it the most frequent letters of a text are replaced by dashes. The task is to reconstruct the meaning of the text by guessing (typing in) words and phrases. **Selection sets** of possible words to fill gaps could be produced on a computer using onscreen keyboard software for use with a **word processor** or Developing Tray (Figure R.1). See also Chapter 3 on literacy.

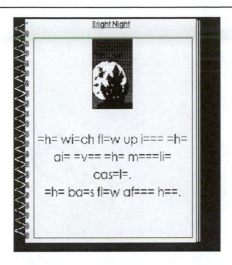

Figure R.1   An example of Developing Tray activity

Coded communication
An example of such a system is Minspeak in which a sequence of items within a selection set of images can have a unique message or action attached to it. For example, the selection of a symbol sequence depicting 'the user', 'a heart' and the symbol for tree could result in the production of the utterance, 'I want to go to the park.'

Communicating ideas
This use of technology is concerned with the best way to get messages across to other people. Our society is media-rich and overloaded with information. This problem or opportunity is caused and ultimately solved by the new technologies. It involves an appreciation of the target audience and the best medium for the presentation of the information (see **publishing**). Because a range of media can be employed with ICT to get the message across, ICT is a valuable tool for **universal design** for learning. This means that words, pictures, sounds, tables and charts can be combined together in different ways to support different learning needs.

Any user of word-processing or multimedia authoring will need to be concerned with the potential audience for the work and its intended function.

Communication aids
People who have difficulty communicating with speech can sometimes be helped by using a communication aid (Figure R.2). These aids vary in cost, size and complexity but they work on the same general principles. The user enters the message by an appropriate method. Some people enter the messages as text, typing the words or perhaps selecting them from a scanned selection set. When the message is selected or entered, the communication aid 'speaks' it out. Some aids use prerecorded spoken messages. At the simplest level one message might be recorded which can be played in response to a switch press to engage a non-speaking learner in a social interaction in a classroom (see **early learning** and Chapter 1). At a more complex level the user might use a switch or switches to choose from a **selection set**. Alternatively this might be achieved by selecting by touch, a joystick or a head pointer. The communication

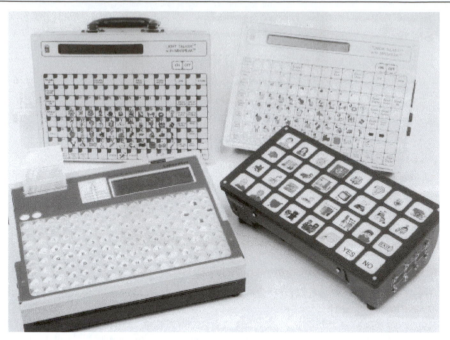

Figure R.2   Examples of communication aids

aid might be a laptop with an inbuilt overlay keyboard if **coded communication** can be used.

There are a number of low-technology augmentative devices which are reliable and robust enough to provide a backup or alternative system (e.g. during a power cut or while bathing). These include transparent eye direction boards, symbol boards, pointer boards and real objects.

Conversation is about social interaction for real purposes. Therefore the choices that the aided communicator can select from should include things that lead to real changes happening. Communication allows us to influence the world around us. Often we ask questions that do not really need answers especially in educational settings. Following Taylor (1992), a list of some of the things that an unaided communicator has to learn and be aware of when conversing with the user of a communication aid can be summarized thus:

- Learn to wait. (The average rate for an aided communicator is only about 12 words a minute. Because this can be frustrating and uncomfortable for people used to standard communication, there is a tendency to jump in and redirect conversation.)
- Respond to all signals, not just the ones the aided communicator makes with the communication aid.
- Time responses. In addition to waiting the speaker needs to respond at the appropriate speed, reinforcing what has been said and allowing the chance of further initiation.
- Follow the non-speaker's lead. A difficult bit of self-control but wait to be guided as to what the aided communicator wants to converse about.

- Think about where you need to be. Where is the best place to be without infringing on personal space?
- Make the communication real.

See also **augmentative communication** and **symbol software**.

Compact discs (CDs or CD-ROMs)
Currently this is the most widely used method of distributing commercial software especially when high-quality images, sound or video are used, but it is quickly being overtaken by digital video discs (DVD) and alternative formats may take over by the time you read this.

Points to consider when evaluating a CD-ROM (or commercial multimedia resource) as suggested by McDevitt (1998):

(1) Does it have additionality, i.e. offer something more than traditional sources? For example, is there
    (a) more information?
    (b) the same information in a more exciting/accessible way?
    (c) a totally new way of presenting information?
    (d) practical demonstrations difficult to replicate in school?
    (e) regularly updated information?
    (f) age-appropriate, developmentally appropriate information?
    (g) unbiased information?
(2) Is the mix of media helpful to the user, or confusing? Is it clear exactly what is seen or heard?
(3) Is it easy to use? Is it navigated using icons, words, or a mixture of both?
(4) Is there an index? Is it age- and/or language-level appropriate?
(5) Is there more than one way to search for information?
(6) Is it easy to retrace your path? Or get back 'home' if you get lost?
(7) Are spoken commentaries identical with the text on screen?
(8) Can the pictures be extracted easily? All? Some? Are they copyright free? Can they be printed? Can they be copied to a word processor?
(9) Can text be extracted easily? All? Selected text? Can it be printed out in age-appropriate size and font? Can it be copied to a word processor?
(10) Is it useful for one aspect of the Curriculum only or a range of subjects? At what ages or Key Stages?

Concept keyboard (see **overlay keyboard**)

Control technology
Control technology occurs widely in our culture but it is largely taken for granted. Electronic kettles, washing machines, automatic doors, heating systems and home entertainment are all examples. Control technology allows learners to use computer control mechanisms and devices in response to sensors placed in an environment. Control technology can enable learners to control and learn about real-world systems. This can provide highly salient problems with immediate tangible feedback. At a simple level a learner might issue a sequence of commands to a floor robot to navigate a path through a maze; alternatively, a wheelchair might be controlled by its user issuing similar commands to direct it around the user's school. With the introduction

of models or robots with sensors there are opportunities for creating control systems which respond to feedback. See also **Logo**, **robots**, **environmental control**.

Convergence of technology (see **digital storage**)

Curriculum
This book views the curriculum as a menu of learning opportunities which can be made relevant and successful with appropriate planning and evaluation. The curriculum also provides a context for social and emotional inclusion. Both the UK principles of differentiation and the US principles of **universal design** for learning can provide frameworks for enabling inclusion within the broad curriculum.

Alternatively, and pessimistically, the curriculum might be seen as a set of hoops to be jumped through, a set of barriers or a mountain of irrelevance. More positively it can be viewed as different contexts to develop and apply knowledge. Irrespective of what the curriculum actually contains, it is the place where most people between the ages of 4 and 18 spend a substantial amount of their time with different degrees of engagement and success. An effective curriculum will take as its starting-point a diversity of learner characteristics which must be taken into account through flexible modes of delivery, variety of activity and assessment. This requires institutional commitment and planning. It is also about the allocation of resources.

Each subject area tends to have software tools that extend and enrich the development of skills and concepts when used appropriately. See the individual subject areas for more detail, but the following questions should be relevant to all these software tools.

(1)   Does the software support or extend the curriculum? Does it develop relevant knowledge and skills? Does it support intended learning outcomes?
(2)   Does the software pitch to the learners at an appropriate level? Does it use appropriate levels of language? Are ideas represented in a variety of ways?
(3)   Does the time available match the time needed to use the software? If not, could it be used in a different way or at a different time?
(4)   Does it support and enhance the approach of the teacher? Can the teacher exploit what it is doing and link it to other areas?
(5)   Does the software or operating system allow customization so that the user can use the software effectively?
(6)   Are the 'Help files' helpful to the learner? Do they explain curriculum terms implicit in the software? If not, do these need to be taught on or off the computer? Is the help at an appropriate level of language? Does the help need to be spoken or presented visually?
(7)   Does the software enable progression as well as customization so that the child can begin with a limited number of features but move on to higher levels of functionality and complexity, and not become stuck at a dead end?
(8)   Is the software going to be readily available when and where it will be needed?
(9)   If the software has to be customized for a learner can the resultant configuration be saved and accessed easily when it is needed again?
(10)   Does the software engage and compel the user?
(11)   Can the software monitor users' progress and offer feedback to them and others at a later date; for example, score sheets in educational programs, records of errors, etc?

(12) Does the software declare the educational theories underlying its design? Are these compatible with the theories underlying the individual education plan or other programs in use?

Customization
Many aspects of the way the computer looks and behaves can be customized to suit the individual needs and working style of the user. For example, the mouse operation and pointer may be altered, superfluous icons can be removed, new ones added to launch **macros** or software, colours and fonts on the desktop may be changed and a stronger screen contrast may be selected. Such customization may be difficult to manage without each user having their own user profile which comes into operation when they 'log on' by inputting their password.

The accessibility options within the control panel on most modern computers can be used to configure:

- **input filtering** via filter keys for the standard keyboard
- **sticky keys**
- serial connection for keyboard/mouse emulation so that an external device such as a communication aid can control the computer
- mousekeys (see **mice**)
- **auditory feedback**
  - toggle keys
- **visual feedback**
  - show-sounds
  - sound-sentry.

See also Chapters 6, 7, 8 and 9.

D

Databases (see **handling information**)

Desktop computers
These are the most widely used computers in education at the moment. Most people are familiar with their components and basic operation, e.g.:

- display – size of screen and quality
- RAM (Random Access Memory) (i.e. working memory) – dictates the ability to make use of a lot of data such as video and audio
- hard disc storage space – the amount of space for storing information and programs
- processor speed – the ability to manipulate complex graphics and data.

Desktops are usually more robust than portables but can lead to the user's isolation because of the mains electricity supply restricting mobility.

Desktop publishing (see **publishing**)

Digital storage
Increasingly now, data is stored in digital form, e.g. video, audio. This is seen as a 'convergence of technology' towards one standard medium. It is potentially very liberating as it can allow the user to capture, manipulate and put to their service a

range of media which are currently imprisoned in the discrete media of books, tapes, films, etc. This enables the principles of **universal design** for learning to become a practical reality.

Digital video
Both moving and still video images can be readily used by current computers. Teachers, parents and, in many cases, the learners themselves can use video cameras to photograph activities and events which can then be transferred to a computer using a cable, disc or infra-red. The images may form part of a word-processed account of the activity or a multimedia presentation. It is particularly useful for recording achievements. See **digital storage**.

Dwell selection
If a user is unable to press a switch to make a selection but is able to move the highlight or pointer, a selection can be made by keeping the pointer or highlight stationary for a preset time. This is termed the dwell select time (Colven and De-theridge, 1990). See also **scanning**.

Dynamic keyboards (see **onscreen keyboards**)

E

Early learning
Mano and Horn (1998) suggest that there are a number of prerequisite skills and concepts which are part of early cognitive development and which can support effective computer use. They are cause and effect, visual and perceptual skills, understanding audio and visual cues, waiting, timing and 'other cognitive skills'. Some children with motor control difficulties may need to be involved in activities within these areas both on and off the computer in order to fully exploit the potential of the computer.

They argue further that

> Developmental theory teaches that children learn through control of their environment and manipulation of objects in their environment. Many researchers (e.g. Ware, 1994; Tingle, 1990) believe that children with disabilities who are unable to control their environment develop learned helplessness, a secondary disability. Provision of Assistive Technology can give these children direct control of toys and their environment.
>
> (Mano and Horn, 1998, p. 3)

The social and emotional aspects of learning at this stage should not be masked by the possibilities of the technology. Feuerstein (1976) and others have emphasized the importance of the interaction between carer, learner and the world in order to build common understandings. Through shared activity the adult or carer can help the child make sense of the world. Feuerstein terms this the mediation of meaning.

Mano and Horn set a key criterion for use:

> Assistive technology should be used in the context of a social activity where children can interact with others and should not replace other social interactions that are necessary for a child's development. Some areas in which we see Assistive Technology used with young children are in the areas of mobility, control of toys and environment, and computer use.
>
> (Mano and Horn, 1998, p. 4)

Schopler and Mesibov (1985, p. 25) suggest that communication can be carried out at different levels of cognitive difficulty based upon their work with learners with autism. An assessment of the preponderant level of communication of a learner might help in selecting suitable assistive technology to augment communication:

(1) motoric level where the child uses or leads the adult to a desired object or place
(2) object level where the child gives an adult an object to signify an activity
(3) picture level where the child gives an adult a picture/photograph of an activity
(4) written level where the child gives written words or a symbol to an adult or writes words for the activity
(5) augmentative aid: the use of a communication board or aid to make a request.
(6) use of speech.

See **overlay keyboards**, **touch screens** and pictorial **microworlds**.

Electronic mail (email)
Messages that can be sent and received by anyone who has access to a computer on the **Internet**. Usually these messages are text-based but other files including video and audio can be attached. However, it is best not to send very large files to people who do not want them because it may take them ages to read if they have a slow telephone link and they may have to pay for this reading time. The text messages can be spoken or composed using **talking word processors** or **symbol software** as well as email software or ordinary word processors.

   If you have access to the Internet you will have an email address (e.g. M.Blamires@canterbury.ac.uk). You can join a discussion list by sending a message to the list stating that you want to join it. You can then send a message to all the members of that list and also receive all the messages that are sent to it. Discussion lists can have hundreds of members so you might end up receiving lots of messages every day. You will need to find out how to leave a list and this usually is given on the web pages associated with the list. There are hundreds of mailing lists on different areas of special needs which provide a forum for service providers, advisors and users to discuss common concerns. The group that contributed to this book are members of a discussion list called SENIT (email: senit@becta.ngfl.gov.uk).

English
Word-processing and **desktop publishing** are two key applications within the English curriculum as they offer opportunities for writing texts for different audiences with different interests. The provisionality of the 'delete' key and 'cut and paste' have enhanced the possibility of writing for many learners. Reluctant writers can produce highly legible results that have a clarity which may have been impossible to achieve previously. The availability of access to **electronic mail** and the world wide web has the potential to extend the diversity of these purposes and audiences much further.

   Multimedia authoring can help pupils to consider how information can be presented in a non-linear manner.

   Cloze procedure using poems and stories may help learners to engage with these texts on a number of levels, considering how the meanings, form and structure of written language interact in building understanding.

   Databases and electronic dictionaries can be useful in researching or classifying words, concepts or texts.

Talking word processors, planners, word banks and **symbol software** may support developing literacy.

The world wide web contains a large range of sources of text in a wide variety of forms. See also Chapter 3 on literacy.

Environmental control

The majority of household appliances are now electronically operated (e.g. kettles, televisions and cookers), or can be made to operate electronically by adding electronic control mechanisms (e.g. curtain controls, door openings). These devices can be switched on or off using technology which displays a suitable selection set the current settings of the device. Concurrent with this control technology is the advent of 'more intelligent' environments. My office lights switch on as I enter the room and switch off when they fail to register movement for ten minutes. There can be problems, though – I now have the responsibility of not falling asleep at my desk when I work at night otherwise my colleague round the corner will be plunged into darkness because the movement sensor does not cover his part of the office.

Ergonomic keyboards (see **keyboards**)

Expanded keyboards (see **keyboards**)

G

Geography

ICT can support the manipulation, interrogation, interpretation and display of information from a variety of sources such as CD or the Internet through the use of databases, spreadsheets and charting. This could include census data, local (from a school weather station) or national weather observations, the results of questionnaires or data from the Internet.

A **planner** or **word processor** can be used to organize a project and display the results.

The Internet can be used to bring the subject 'to life' by obtaining data and information from real places and people through links to schools in other localities and cultures.

Simulations can model geographical phenomena to be investigated which may be difficult to replicate in the classroom, e.g. factors influencing when an earthquake may occur, town planning, etc.

At a simpler level floor **robots** can be used to develop an understanding of direction and alternative perspectives.

Maps and aerial photographs can be compared and contrasted with oblique photographs of the same area to highlight differences and develop map skills. Map-making software can allow learners to explore geographical problems and then suggest alternative solutions.

Satellite images allow the interpretation of habitats, population and industry, using data that is salient to the learner, e.g. their town or area.

Grab bars

A grab bar can be fixed across a table or chair for the user to hold on to with one hand. It can support stabilization of uncontrolled movement. See also **positioning and seating**.

Grammar checkers
These have rarely lived up to their promise although they do appear in some advanced word processors. They tend to provide verbose remedial advice that is frequently less than helpful. One or two word processors now spot homophones and issue warnings, e.g. 'You have used the word "there" meaning a place, are you sure you want to use this word?'

Graphical user interface (GUI)
These are based on a manipulative model of interacting with a computer – the user takes hold of an object on the screen and does something with it. The interface is inherently graphical.

H

Handling information
This is concerned with the retrieval, organization and storage of information. These are skills which are fundamental to learning any subject. The process of gathering data, classifying, sorting and finding exceptions can make learning very relevant with or without a computer. The computer provides a structure with fast and flexible search facilities plus the ability to display relationships and summaries visually through the production of charts. These may be manipulated to highlight trends and exceptions, bringing abstract data to life. Handling information is also closely linked to communicating information because, as you might expect, once you have found out something, you need to consider the best way of presenting it for your intended audience.

History
History teaching can be enhanced through access to written, photographic and pictorial sources to support research and investigation. Simulations can put children in control of factors underlying a historical period which may be more engaging than traditional narrative. Databases can be used to investigate real data and see patterns in past events. Databases including branching tree databases can support classification within the subject.

Time-line software can help students to obtain a sense of self in time as well as the chronology of events as they move along the time line and investigate resources from the documented events. Multimedia authoring can be used by students to present their findings.

Points to consider:

(1) Within a themed collection of resources, are the text resources at an appropriate level and not subject to cultural bias or over-interpretation?
(2) Does the structure of an information archive take into account different educational approaches and outcomes that may be possible with the material?
(3) Is there an emphasis on presentation at the expense of accuracy and detail?
(4) What is the quality of interaction that is supported by the software?
(5) Is the detail in the simulation accurate and does it lead to valid historical understanding?
(6) Do the resources encourage browsing through attractive content or engagement supporting the generation of questions?
(7) Can information from sources be searched by keywords, and type of media, and be bookmarked and grouped for different audiences or purposes?

Hotspots
Hotspots are areas of a screen that, when selected by a mouse click, cause something to happen in a program. Some onscreen keyboard software can enable switch users to mimic the effect of a mouse clicking on hotspots. For example, in a **talking book**, clicking on a button or icon may cause the text to be spoken or the next page to be displayed, while clicking on an object or character might cause an animation.

Selection sets can be created which include hotspots either using overlay keyboard or onscreen keyboard software which supports the inclusion of hotspots. Switch users can then make use of software such as talking books or CDs by scanning.

In some cases hotspots can be activated by pressing a keyboard **short cut** which may have to be researched in the relevant software documentation. See also Chapter 6.

I

Information and communications technology (ICT)
The 'C' in ICT emphasizes that information, once it has been obtained and organized, may need to be communicated to an audience. The form and structure of information is as important as the information itself otherwise it is just kipple (accumulated clutter). The principles of **universal design** for learning acknowledge the need and potential of ICT to cater for the diversity of learner needs.

Information technology (IT)
The range of information resources that are available for handling and manipulating information. Television, satellite, video, telecommunications and fax are part of this technology, as are computer databases.

Input filter
Most input devices allow control over their sensitivity or responsiveness to minimize unintentional switch, key or mouse button activation. Most modern computer operating systems have some control panels that give some control over filtering.

The three main aspects of this responsiveness are:

(1)   Input acceptance filtering. This is the amount of time a key or switch has to be pressed continuously before it is accepted. The delay is called the 'input acceptance time'. This is useful when learners miss-hit keys due to co-ordination difficulties.
(2)   Repeat filtering. This consists of two features: The 'repeat acceptance delay' which is the time a key or switch has to be held down continuously before it starts to repeat, and the 'repeat time' which is the interval between each repeat. Without adjusting the repeat filter some learners, who may have difficulty releasing the key after a key press, will get 'WWWWWWWWWWWWWWW' instead of 'W'.
(3)   Post-acceptance filtering. The 'post-acceptance delay' is how long new switch or key presses are ignored after an accepted switch or key press. This is useful also when a user might miss-hit adjacent keys or the same switch when releasing the key or switch.

Integrated learning systems
Description:

   An integrated learning system (ILS) is a computer-based system that manages the delivery of curriculum materials to pupils so that they are presented with individual programmes of work over a number of weeks or months. The materials are often computer-based but not exclusively so. The system provides feedback to pupils as they work and detailed records which support the pupil and teacher.

(National Council for Educational Technology, 1998, p. 9)

The typical model of usage has a room of computers timetabled on a regular basis with one-to-one use with different levels of supervision, from a technician or ancillary teacher to a full-time teacher, supporting and intervening when technical or educational problems arise. The National Council for Educational Technology (1998) suggests a minimum time of three half-hour sessions per week is needed for pupils to benefit and the quality of supervision and intervention by teachers appears to be important if learners are to develop higher order reading or numeracy skills. (So for the foreseeable future it appears teachers will not lose jobs because of these systems.)

The National Council for Educational Technology suggests the following checklist of ILS features:

System features:
- Help features – does the system offer pupils a help button to explain tasks?
- Feedback – do pupils get feedback on performance?
- Pupil access to profile – is this available for specific modules and overall progress?
- (National) Curriculum – are there useful links within the software or through support documentation?
- Curriculum support materials – can worksheets be printed off, matched to individual needs or are there photocopiable worksheets on general themes?

Management system features:
- Topic routes – can the teacher select units according to the topics which will be covered in the class?
- Individualized work plans – does the system present pupils with work at the appropriate level automatically?
- Can the teacher select an appropriate sequence of units for individual pupils? Can specific sets of units be turned on or off within courses? Can individual pupils be given menu access to specific sets of units?
- Third party software – can the system launch third party software?
- Timed units – can the time on units be set for a system? Can the response time be adjusted for individual tasks? Can teachers ensure pupils complete tasks before moving on to the next unit?
- Assessment – does the system provide initial and summative assessment?
- Reporting – is a range of reports available: individual, class, group, to pupil, teacher, parents?
- Monitoring and tracking – does the system log pupil performance within a specified set of units? Can pupils check their performance at any stage? Are pupil responses to every task attempted recorded?
- Diagnostic feedback – does the system provide feedback on performance within a range of applications and skills?

The latter point is very important. We need measures of how valid the learning is. If 'success' is only defined in its own terms it may not be that reliable or useful. For example, one system moved a low-scoring learner on to the next stage automatically without remediation or repetition of the module.

Possible advantages:

(1)   Lewis (1998) suggested that children with special needs using the ILS system became more self-regulated in their learning. They were taking control of their learning.
(2)   ILS systems can increase the availability of IT within an institution.
(3)   They can increase the amount of time a learner has using a computer.
(4)   They can enable more flexible grouping. Whilst some children are engaged using ILS, the teacher can work with a smaller group who are not on the system.

Possible disadvantages:

(1)   Does the ILS follow guidelines for universal design so that the following learner characteristics are taken into account?
    (a)   The level of attention of the user.
    (b)   Their preferred input method.
    (c)   Language demand of the instructions.
    (d)   The modality of output – i.e. use of speech, visual clarity.
(2)   If the system does not incorporate third party software, it will not support some access software.

Points to consider:

(1)   Will the hardware run the software and be able to take upgrades to the system?
(2)   Do they disable the teacher from developing IT capability and therefore using the potential of IT within his or her teaching area? (The NCET evaluation reports teachers being more favourable towards IT usage but this may not have the depth of understanding specified in Peter Dorman's Chapter 2 in this book.)
(3)   Is what is learnt on the ILS generalizable, relevant or exploited in other areas of learning? (Do ILS systems provide scaffolding for worthwhile units of work that will help the child engage in the other learning activities of the school?)
(4)   What training will be undertaken for staff to help them do this?
(5)   Some suppliers have used the evidence about their rival as evidence for their system.
(6)   Are they being used as a managerial 'bolt on' to remedy the lack of technology within the school?
(7)   Is the ILS being used as a 'bolt on' to remedy the lack of curriculum differentiation or universal curriculum design?

> Much attention has been given to ILS. The mathematical elements of such software do not sit easily with the learning intentions of current National Curriculum orders . . . Their educational potential seems to be in the instrumental instruction in those routine skills which other aspects of IT make largely redundant.
> (Mathematics Group Report in NCET, 1997, p. 8)

> What was not useful were decontextualised exercises, not connected to the English curriculum whose outcomes were of uncertain value.
> (Harrison, 1995, p. 38)

See also Chapter 2.

Internet
It is becoming rare to find an educational computer that cannot be used to communicate with most other computers in the world. The Internet is the network that enables this.

Using the facilities of the Internet it is possible for teachers and pupils to:

- find information on almost anything
- access a range of multimedia learning resources
- send and receive email
- contribute to group discussions about most areas of learning
- order books and resources
- obtain news, weather and travel information
- communicate with others who have similar interests
- publish and view information for and from other people around the world

(after Poole, 1998).

See also **browsers**.

Intranet
An intranet is a local network of computers which may have connections to the global network known as the **Internet**. Information and resources stored on the intranet may only be available locally.

J

Joysticks
A joystick is an alternative method of controlling the computer, consisting of a stick with a handle or switch that can be moved in a number of directions. A number of heavy duty switched joysticks are available to produce single, double, three- or four-way switching using push and pull for people with strong gross movement. These may be used to directly control a pointer or may be used with an on-screen selection set. These tend to be digital joysticks which have a switching action according to the direction of push.

A wide range of commercial joysticks and games-pads are available which are intended for controlling computer games. Software utilities are available to make them control a mouse pointer.

K

Keyboards
The standard keyboard:

> Some individuals may have difficulty writing because of fatigue or minimally impaired motor control. A standard keyboard on a computer may be all that is needed to allow them to complete written tasks effectively.
>
> (Cook and Hussey, 1995, p. 25)

Cook and Hussey suggest that the following questions should help in evaluating whether the standard keyboard alone is sufficient for the user (but see the entry on **positioning** and **seating** first):

(1) Can the user reach all of the keys on the keyboard? If not, consider positioning and then alternative keyboards.
(2) Is the size, spacing and sensory feedback of the keys appropriate? If not, consider an alternative keyboard or alternative keyboard layout.

(3)   Is the user's speed of input adequate to the task or activity? If not, consider the use of word prediction.

(4)   Does the user target keys with approximately 75 per cent accuracy? Consider keyguard and/or alternative keyboard.

(5)   Is the user able simultaneously to hold down the modifier key and select another key? If not, consider using **sticky keys** or a hardware latch.

(6)   Is the user able to control the duration for which a key must be pressed before it repeats itself? If not, adjust **input filtering** for repeat delay, consider using a keyguard.

(7)   Does the user make efficient use of the standard keyboard layout? If not, consider an alternative keyboard layout rather than QWERTY; for example, using a Dvorak keyboard driver that reassigns the key layout so that commonly used keys are more accessible. This has versions for two hands, single left or right hands.

In addition, the motivation of the user to be seen as the user of a keyboard that is most widely used is an issue. This may mean that the user could overcome minor difficulties identified in the use of the keyboard especially if used in conjunction with modifications outlined below:

- Modifier keys: keys such as ALT, Control and Shift have to be used in conjunction with other keys in order to produce a command or character. If the user cannot do this with two hands then **sticky keys** should be considered.
- Layout and lettering: the QWERTY layout is standard **selection set** but alternative ones are available. Some commercial suppliers provide an alphabet-based keyboard but this may cause confusion if the user is going to use a standard keyboard later on.
- Protection from moisture: keyboards can be protected from moisture by the use of a see-through flexible plastic moisture guard.

See also **positioning and seating, input filters, keyguards, sticky keys** and **macros**.

Expanded keyboards:
There are currently two types of expanded keyboard.

(1)   For users who have large forceful sweeping movements or who need to use a head or mouth pointer. The keys on such a keyboard are larger and more widely spaced than standard keyboards and are recessed so that the user might be able to 'dip into' them. Because of the nature of their use they tend to be made of very robust materials.

(2)   Less expensive versions for learners or those who would benefit from a larger keyboard but who do not have large-scale forceful movements and so do not require such a robust design; for example, younger learners who need larger keys to target.

With the first type of expanded keyboard the feature of mouse control through mouse keys on the keyboard may be useful in most cases. Sometimes the overlay keyboard can be configured as an expanded keyboard.

Ergonomic keyboards:
The advent of repetitive strain injury (RSI) has focused the minds of hardware and software developers on the individual needs of users for appropriate input devices.

Principles of flexibility and customization which have been widespread in software design are now being applied to the input devices used to control the software. Ergonomic keyboards have been produced in response to this. They are reminiscent of the Maltron ergonomic keyboards which have been in production for more than ten years. Why has it taken so long to learn that standard keyboards may be a bad idea? This is the beginning of a promising trend. A recent yuppie computer magazine bemoaned the lack of configurability of the standard keyboard layout. This will probably be responded to by the computer industry but has already been met to some extent by the overlay keyboard.

Miniature keyboards:
These are keyboards which may be of use to someone with a very limited range of hand/finger movement and/or with little strength to press keys. The keys are arranged around a central space key according to frequency of use rather than the more usual 'QWERTY' format. Alternatively, a palmtop computer may be of use both as a computer in its own right and also to act as a keyboard for a desktop computer.

Keyguards
Keyguards are available for some computer keyboards including alternative and overlay keyboards. They are usually made of metal with a plastic covering and fit over the keyboard to provide a matrix of round holes each above a key. They help to prevent the wrong keys from being pressed accidentally by a head pointer, mouth pointer or typing aid, or when the user's hand travels across the keyboard. They can also provide a support for the hand when a finger is targeting a desired key. Keyguards can be used alongside **predicting** software, **macros** and **sticky key** software.

L

Laptops
Laptops are getting lighter and more powerful but currently have less functionality than contemporary desktop machines of a similar price. Their advantage is that they are portable and can be attached to a wheelchair. Less expensive laptops will have cut-down versions of the large applications found on desktops or may just have a built-in word processor. These will be useful if the learner needs basic word-processing without extensive support features.

Points to consider (after Stansfield, 1997 and Woolfe, 1996):

(1) Does the user want to use it? If not, why bother getting it? Introduce the idea at a later date?
(2) Do the peer group know what the laptop is for? Are there rules for if and when they can have access to it?
(3) Can the user open up the machine and start it? (If users are one-handed they may not be able to open a laptop with two side clips that have to be pushed simultaneously.)
(4) Is the software at the cognitive level of the user?
(5) How long does the battery last before it needs recharging? (It may mean that an extra battery has to be purchased and kept charged up for lessons where there is no convenient mains point.)

(6)   Who will teach the learner how to use it?
(7)   Who will brief teaching and support staff on how it can be best used to support learning objectives? (If teaching staff do not see the point of the laptop, its effective use may be hindered.)
(8)   Who will provide technical support for its use at school and/or at home?
(9)   How and when will printing out be achieved?
(10) Who will maintain or upgrade the equipment?
(11) Does the learner have the appropriate space at home to use it with good lighting and correct working position?
(12) Will the machine have to be insured if taken home? (If so, by whom?)
(13) Will work need to be transferred to another computer? (If so, what are the arrangements for this?)
(14) Is the machine used efficiently to support the learner?
(15) Is the learner isolated because of its use, i.e. is she or he expected to 'get on with it' on their computer rather than engaging in social learning activities?

The mobility and versatility of a laptop can help a learner to engage in many learning opportunities which she previously may not have had access to.

Logo
Originally the computer was considered a teaching machine whose function was to deliver a knowledge base using a limited range of preprogrammed heuristics. In other words, the programmes were heavily based upon drill and practice with a narrow and specific content. In the early 1980s Papert (1980) turned this on its head: instead of the child being programmed by the computer, why not help the child programme the computer? Logo was developed as computer language for children so they could encounter different knowledge bases or microworlds, the most popular being Turtle Graphics which dealt with geometry. Logo was also intended to encourage the development of different heuristics alongside an understanding of the knowledge base but this required quite a lot of teaching skill from the teacher. From DeCorte's model in Chapter 1, they would have to provide contexts and activities to facilitate this learning.

Williams and Williams (1986, p. 17) suggested that a benefit from Logo work with floor **robots** for their students with physical disabilities was that it 'enabled them to perform formal thinking in concrete ways'.

Buckland's (1986) work with children with learning difficulties suggested that the use of a sequence of **overlay keyboard selection sets** with a floor **robot** (Figure R.3) met her expectation that 'teaching experiences should be challenging and demanding, they should only aim to stretch a child to the limits where success is still possible' (ibid., p. 121).

Using Buckland's materials with older children with severe learning difficulties, Haigh (1990, p. 8) suggested that it was valuable in that, 'Its use allows the teacher to see the extent of the language and thinking skills. Some children have thinking skills well in advance of their language skills and adults often underestimate their capabilities.'

This is a view that Weir (1987) would support from her case studies of teaching using Logo with children having a variety of special educational needs. She suggested that Logo helped to represent thinking that was often inaccessible using the language ability of the child. It could overcome difficulties in 'introspective awareness' that is often implicit in learning.

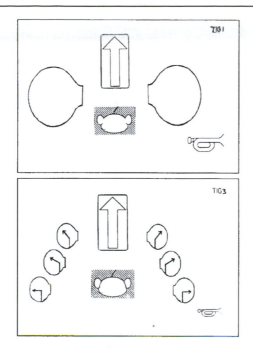

Figure R.3   Two of Buckland's selection sets for use with Logo and a floor robot

M

Macros
A macro is a sequence of actions that can be initiated by typing in a keyword or letter sequence or by clicking on a button. Most software that involves complex operations will allow you to create or use existing macros to complete long or involved tasks relatively simply. At its basic level, a word processor will have an abbreviation expansion facility which will replace 'Ikb' with 'Isambard Kingdom Brunel' when I am typing my essay about the English Victorian engineer.

At a more complex level the operating system can 'record' a sequence of actions such as opening a programme with a particular set of menu options, a specific input device and a particular file. This macro can be 'played back' later. Such a facility can aid the customization of software.

Magnification
This is discussed at length in Chapter 8.

Mathematics
The NCET consultation report on software in mathematics identified the following categories of activity that could be supported by the use of IT in the subject:

- Learning from feedback – the computer provides fast and reliable feedback which is non-judgemental and impartial. This can encourage students to make their own conjectures and to test out and modify their ideas. For example, **Logo** or **Macros** in generic software.

- Observing patterns – the speed of computers and calculators enables students to produce many examples when exploring mathematical problems. This supports their observations of patterns and the making and justifying of generalizations. For example, small software packages to explore number grids, or spreadsheets.
- Seeing connections – the computer enables formulae, tables of numbers and graphs to be linked readily. Changing one representation and seeing changes in others helps students to understand the connections between them. For example, spreadsheets and graphic calculators.
- Working with dynamic images – students can use computers to manipulate diagrams dynamically. This encourages them to visualize the geometry as they generate their own mental images. For example, Dynamic Geometry Software which allows the user to alter figures and perform animation.
- Exploring data – computers enable students to work with real data which can be represented in a variety of ways. This supports interpretation and analysis. For example, databases and spreadsheets can be used to display and analyse data which may be obtained from CD-ROM, the Internet or data logging equipment.
- 'Teaching' the computer – when students design an algorithm (a set of instructions) to make a computer achieve a particular result, they are compelled to express their command unambiguously and in the correct order; they make their thinking explicit as they refine their ideas. For example, Logo, Dynamic Geography Software and the macro facilities in spreadsheets.
- Practice, assessment and reinforcement – for example, ILS modules and drill and practice or precision teaching software and other small pieces of software that focus upon a particular area. For example, angles, place value, vectors.

(NCET, 1997, p. 4)

For a learner who has difficulty in using pencil and paper, software may be required that allows the user to carry out traditional mathematical exercises (see Figures R.4 and R.5).

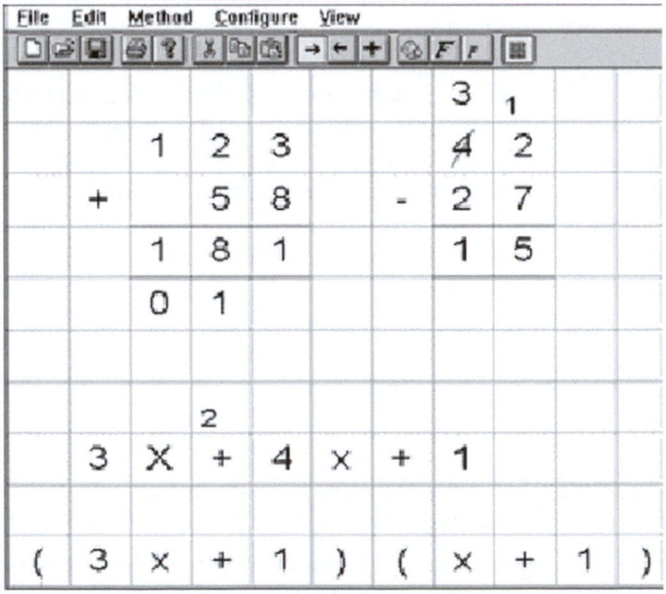

Figure R.4   A piece of software imitating squared paper (Courtesy of the ACE Centre)

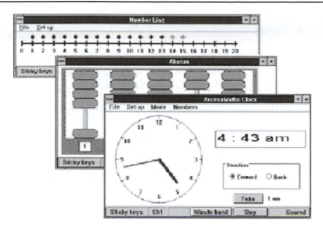

Figure R.5   Software tools providing functions of a number line, a clock and an abacus (Courtesy of the ACE centre)

Mice and mice alternatives

Using a mouse as an input to the computer is becoming increasingly common because many computers use graphical user interfaces for their operation. A graphical user interface displays pictures or icons on the screen and the user moves the mouse to move the onscreen pointer to the required icon and then presses a button on the mouse once or twice to make something happen.

All mice work on the same principle – a rolling ball makes a pointer move around the screen and selections are made by pressing the buttons on the mouse. The ball is usually underneath the mouse and is controlled by moving it across a surface.

The way the mouse moves is affected by the surface it rests on. Mouse mats can be made with a resistance to suit the user.

If a user finds using a mouse difficult, some programs and operating systems allow keyboard alternatives to be used. There are also **mouse key** access utilities available which transfer the vertical, horizontal and diagonal movements of the mouse to other keys such as the numeric keypad.

The relationship between the distance that the cursor moves on the screen and the distance that the mouse moves across the work surface is called the mouse speed, and can be altered in most computers through their configuration or control panels, or by additional access utilities.

As well as moving the cursor around the screen, the user needs to make selections by pressing a mouse button. This causes a problem for potential users who cannot reach the mouse buttons, or who cannot press them without moving the mouse. One way of overcoming this problem is to connect the buttons to a separate switch through a **mouse port switch adaptor**.

Some programs require the user to press a button twice in a given space of time in order to make a selection. This 'double-clicking' may cause difficulties if the user cannot make the second press in the time allowed. The maximum time allowed between clicks is called the double-click speed and most computers provide a way of adjusting this through their configuration or control panels. Some mice have extra buttons which can have functions such as 'Double Click' allocated to them.

Another mouse action that users may often need is 'click and drag' – holding the button down at the same time as moving the mouse. It is used to draw lines in painting programs or to move items from one place to another. If the click-and-drag action presents problems, a 'latching' mouse or **trackerball** can be used, which enables the user to lock the switch button on while moving the mouse, then release it again when the cursor has reached its destination.

Mouse mutations:
You can get a wide variety of alternatives to the mouse which just plug into the same place on your computer and will work straight away with your programs. A wide range of mice with different shapes and sizes of body and buttons are available.

Alternatives to the mouse:
These include:

- Stylus or mouse pen: this is a stylus with a ball in its tip or a graphics tablet so that the screen pointer will move in response to the pen's movement. It is useless for people with gross and fine motor difficulties in the arm or hand but is indicative of the fact that many other people would use anything other than a standard mouse. Therefore, alternative input devices are not only necessary but a matter of personal preference, self-image and style.
- Head operated mouse: this is a headset coupled with a suck and blow switch or other preferred switch so that the screen pointer can be controlled by moving the head. Typing is done in Windows using on-screen keyboard software. This requires a good deal of head control.

See also **trackballs**, **joysticks**, alternative **keyboards**, **overlay keyboards**, **switches** and **touch screens**

MicroMike
An obsolete analogue sound input device which responded just to the amplitude of noise monitored by a Citizen's Band-style microphone. See **voice activated software**.

Microworlds
These are a small coherent domain of objects and activities implemented in the form of a computer program which provides a representation or abstraction of the real world. 'They are places "to get to know one's way around" a set of concepts, problem situations, activities; places in which the student and teacher can test out ideas in a subject domain of interest' (Weir, 1987, p. 12).

One of the first examples of a microworld was Turtle Graphics (see **Logo**). More recently highly visual and interactive microworlds have been developed which respond to different learning styles and cognitive levels.

Simple pictorial microworlds may consist of a set of component images on a screen or series of linked screens which can be combined in a variety of ways to represent a scene (Figure R.6). They may include matching, labelling, sorting, grouping and odd-one-out activities as well as pictorial cloze procedure where the missing part of a diagram or picture has to be selected from alternatives and then moved into place.

They mirror many traditional off-computer based activities but take advantage of the technology in that they have a rich range of visual resources, a high degree of provisionality and the results can be saved or printed out as part of a developing portfolio of work.

Figure R.6 An example of a pictorial microworld from SEMERC

Scenario programs are a version of this approach which are controlled by written commands.

A wide range of these activities are available from commercial suppliers covering many curriculum areas but they can also be created using **multimedia authoring** software. **Virtual reality** could have a contribution to make in the development of this area.

More abstract microworlds are available which provide interactive and dynamic representations of systems and mathematical functions. See **modelling** and **mathematics**.

Miniature keyboards (see **keyboards**)

Modelling/models
Models are concerned with the investigation of real and imaginary situations and models, learning how to control them, how they work and their underlying rules. They include financial models, simulations and adventure games. Models can help people in all walks of life explore possibilities and reach decisions. For example:

- A spreadsheet for the accounts of a tuck shop or mini business (see **handling information**).
- An adventure game where the learners take the part of a character and make decisions which direct the course of events.
- A simulation of a geographical or historical event.

The power of these forms of software is in the way that they generate 'what if . . .?' and 'why did . . .?' questions in response to a developing understanding of the underlying variables and rules that control a model. See also **microworlds**.

Modern languages
ICT can support the development of skills in another language by providing access to authentic materials from the **Internet** and interaction with **multimedia** resources to

consolidate and refine skills. Study in this area has been found to increase social skills and understanding through the use of structured turn-taking activities with prompts.

Selection sets in the target language on **overlay keyboards** or **onscreen keyboards** can support writing activities. See also **English** and Chapter 3 on literacy.

Monitoring (see **sensing**)

Moon
Moon is made up of a small number of basic shapes that are related to the Roman alphabet. Until recently Moon has been used by the elderly blind population who previously read print. However, it is now beginning to be employed with blind learners who have learning disabilities (Knight, 1998). You can write Moon with a Moon writer or use a hand frame. Special plastic paper called braillon is used.

Mouse port switch adaptor
An invaluable little device. You can use it to turn off any mouse buttons you want to prevent the user activating, e.g. the right-hand mouse button. You can also plug switches into it so when a user presses a switch, a mouse click is produced.

Multimedia
This is combination of several elements in a presentation – text, sound, images. The idea is not new – multi-sensory approaches have long been used in education, e.g. visual aids, atmospheric sound. Early computers could support multi-media in the form of crude text, graphics and sound but they lacked quality.

Multimedia machines now include text (fonts, colours), sound (recorded and synthetic), and pictures (drawing, painting, still video, moving video). What do you need?

A multimedia-capable machine with the ability to store and manipulate different media as well as the ability to capture media is necessary if you want to use **multimedia authoring**. The better specification the machine the more it is able to use multimedia efficiently.

For learners with special educational needs it can enable the presentation of information in a wide range of modalities. Examples include multimedia encyclopaedias, reference works and **talking books**.

Multimedia authoring
Enables teachers and students to make relevant presentations based on their own experiences, knowledge and culture.

This software ranges from sophisticated applications that require a high level of technical competence, to simple applications that should not be beyond the ability of anyone who is a reasonably competent computer user. Planning is the key with multimedia authoring. Collect the necessary artwork, photographs, sound samples, etc. and save these together on your hard disc. Remember where you have saved them! Then you should be able to incorporate them in a presentation quite easily. Using multimedia authoring software does require time and careful planning.

Capturing media can be achieved by using a digital camera and possibly a video board to directly transfer video or still images, a scanner to process printed text, photographs, prints or drawings, a microphone and possibly a sound card. The last two can be used to sample sound, whilst music can be obtained from a midi interface.

A **serial port extension lead** may be useful.

Music

The teaching of music can be facilitated through the use of ICT, as musical synthesizers can be linked to sequencing software which is the musical equivalent of a word processor. For example, students can:

- develop critical listening skills
- try out and perform musical ideas using a sequencer
- use karaoke-type or multimedia authoring applications which can support the performance of songs or combine musical composition alongside video clips.
- use graphical tools to notate and display compositions (most sequencers will do this automatically)
- explore different styles of music from different times and cultures, e.g. using MIDI music files from collections on CD or the Internet; however, their accompanying descriptions may not be detailed enough or at the correct level
- compose and control a range of digital sounds, e.g. recording or processing a sound effect file.

Points to consider:

(1) Does the use of the technology have to preclude the development of skills in playing an instrument? (ICT may be the only way in which a learner can gain access to playing an instrument.)
(2) Is the notation system configurable to the level of the learner?

My world (see **microworlds**)

N

Networks

Networks mean that computers can be connected together to share access to resources and information. For example, computers in a room may be connected to share a printer but they may also be connected to the rest of the computers in the school to share access to the Internet, email or CD-ROMs. Networks can enable all students to have access to common facilities but the manager of the network has to acknowledge that the people who wish to use the network may have differing requirements. They may not be able to press the Control, Alt and Delete keys simultaneously which is the current requirement of many networks. A user should be able to use the computer in the way they want and not the way the network manager thinks is the most convenient. Having said this, most network managers want people to use the network and so will try their best to accommodate diversity.

Points for consideration:

(1) Can all users log on to the network when and where they need to use it?
(2) Can the network allow **customization** which is stored and used from session to session?

Note-taker

The note-taker has a Braille keyboard, speech output and, in some cases, Braille output also. Note-takers boast a range of software but most of them will contain at least a word processor, a calendar, a diary and a calculator. They connect to a printer and print out in the normal manner.

O

On-screen keyboards
Many programs provide toolbars or selection palates to help the user carry out tasks by clicking with the mouse or other pointing device. They can also provide a visual prompt as to the range of facilities available.

An on-screen keyboard displays a selection set within a window. The selection set may mimic a standard keyboard, provide a set of commands to control a specific program or provide any key words and phrases needed. The items in the selection set may be selected by a pointing device such as a mouse, trackball or touch screen or may be scanned for selection by switches. A learner with a visual impairment or who is blind may be able to use key presses to step through each option and hear each item spoken with speech synthesis.

The selection set within an on-screen keyboard can be linked to other selection sets. We are hesitant to use the term 'on-screen keyboard' as it is a little like the term 'horseless carriage' which states what it is not rather than what it is. Perhaps 'input window' or 'dynamic keyboard' may be more appropriate?

Overlay keyboards will have the facilities and features of onscreen keyboards.
Points to consider:

- Can the onscreen keyboard be used to control different applications?
- Can the window be resized to avoid clutter on the screen?
- Does the display dynamically resize text and graphics to fit its new area?
- Alternatively, does it allow the user to retain the text and graphic size, and allow scrolling instead?
- Can the window be positioned anywhere on the screen?

See also **selection sets**.

Organizers (see **planners**)

Outliners (see **planners**)

Overlay keyboard
This is a flat board or shallow box with a matrix of touch sensitive keys. This matrix may be made up of a grid of cells or keys ranging from ten to over 4,000 depending upon the type of overlay keyboard. Some come with ready-made overlays (**selection sets**) complete with barcodes that inform the board which overlay is being loaded. Selection sets can be created for the overlay keyboard using dedicated overlay editing software (Figure R.7). The user is shown the selection set layout on a paper or plastic overlay which is placed on top of the overlay keyboard. This indicates what happens when the user presses an area of the overlay.

Many programs now offer the overlay keyboard as an alternative means of access, and include ready-made paper overlays.

Another advantage is that overlay keyboards can often be used alongside standard keyboards. This is particularly useful for students who can use a standard keyboard but find it laborious – overlays can be prepared with whole words and phrases assigned to areas so that students can type text in the normal way on the standard keyboard but also insert whole words or chunks of pre-prepared text by pressing the overlay keyboard. This saves them the physical or intellectual effort of typing every word letter by letter.

Figure R.7 A selection set for use with an overlay keyboard with digitized speech and pictures to sequence a nursery rhyme (Courtesy of the Advisory Unit)

These keyboards have the advantage of being able to structure a task and offer a limited number of options within a complex program which are then added to as the learner becomes more familiar with the software.

Keyguards should be available for the overlay keyboard with differing sizes of matrix. **Input filtering** may also be needed.

Features to consider in the selection of overlay keyboards are:

- What is the size of matrix required and how is it arranged?
- What is the size of each individual cell and what is the spacing between cells?
- How is the overlay keyboard connected to the computer? Is it daisy chained from the keyboard socket or does it require another card slot in the computer?
- Is an infra-red option required so that the overlay can be used on a nearby wheel-chair and/or passed around a group of learners?
- Is the range of predesigned overlays flexible enough to be used with a number of different programs and learning activities?
- Are sequences of overlays available that offer progression through different levels of tasks?

Features to consider if overlay creation software is needed: can the overlay creation software make overlays that:

- insert text?
- use modifiers and cursor control?
- allow mouse pointer control and selection?
- insert graphics into programs that are able to handle them?
- provide auditory feedback for key presses?
- produce digital sound?
- use synthetic speech?
- allow designs to be produced using the board directly?
- print out an overlay so it can be used on the board?

The criteria for overlay design have much in common with any selection set design.

P

Painting and drawing
Graphics and drawing programs can help learners become more confident and adept in art and design activities. They can stimulate learning not only about art but through art as a medium which has so many spin-offs for children with special needs.

This can include the development of language through the discussion of colour, shape, size, texture and relative position but, most importantly, the learner can be engaged in learning about art by doing art.

Palmtops
These are pocket-sized computers which usually have cut-down versions of software for desktop computers. They have limited capabilities compared to bigger computers but are very portable. Files can usually be transferred between palmtops and other computers or printers using an infra-red link or cable.

Criteria for selection are:

- Is the palmtop robust in design?
- Does it have software that is compatible with other machines in use within the institution?
- Does it have a clear presentation on the screen?
- Is the keyboard layout similar to other keyboard layouts used by the intended students?
- Can the intended user manage the keyboard and is he or she able to understand how to operate the software?
- If it requires operation by means other than the keyboard, can the intended user carry these out?
- How long can it run on a set of batteries?

Physical education (PE)
The development of co-ordination can be facilitated through the use of digital video to record an activity which can then be used to provide high-quality frame-by-frame feedback on performance.

Traditional timers can be used to obtain personal performance scores which the learner can then use to chart their progress on a spreadsheet. As PE takes on the rigour of sports science, sensors and monitors are becoming more commonplace so training can be more individualized and realistic targets could be shared with physiotherapists or occupational therapists.

Planners
Word processors tend to be linear with a text organized in a sequential fashion. Some learners prefer to organize their thoughts in a spatial or visual manner using a flow diagram or mind map (Figure R.8). Relationships can be established between the elements on the screen, and the resulting diagram can be printed out, used as a graphic in another program or converted to a text outline.

Planners may be used alongside a speech synthesizer if the learner has difficulty decoding text. (The outline facility within some word processors is also a powerful planning resource that is under-used.)

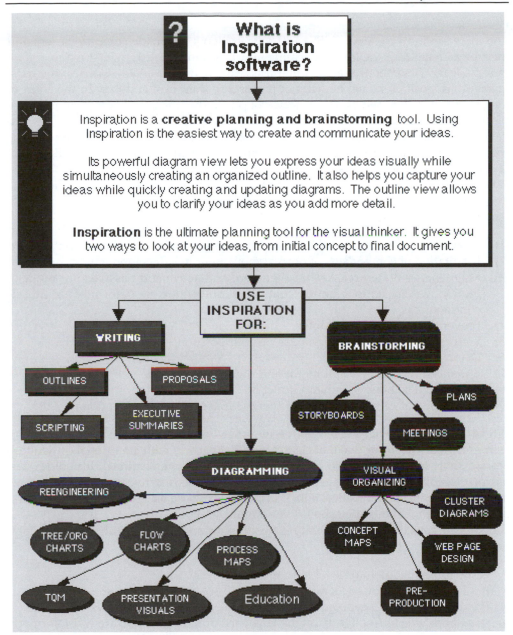

Figure R.8 An example of a mind map produced by the supplier of the visual display planner 'Inspiration'

Multimedia authoring can also be used for the production and publication of a non-linear presentation as a alternative to a text-based product.

Portables (see **laptops** or **palmtops**)

Positioning and seating

The increase in awareness of RSI and back problems has made computer users and their employers take the issue of seating and position seriously whilst using a computer. Clearly if someone engaged in a task on a computer is not seated in the most appropriate position he or she will not perform to their best and may in the short or long term injure themselves. The concerns of physiotherapists and occupational therapists have moved into the mainstream. Most computer systems and input devices have introductory software or documentation that outline ergonomic and seating considerations. Ensure that these are considered when a child has a difficulty in accessing a computer keyboard or device.

From their research on the positioning for function of wheelchairs and other assistive devices, Bergen *et al.* (1992) suggest the following advantages of appropriate seating and positioning:

(1)   Normalization or decreased influence of abnormal tone and reflexes on the body.
(2)   Facilitation of components of normal movement in a developmental sequence.
(3)   Maintenance of neutral skeletal alignment and active and passive joint range of motion within normal limits; control or prevention of deformity or muscle contractures.
(4)   Prevention of tissue breakdown.
(5)   Increased comfort and tolerance of desired position.
(6)   Decreased fatigue.
(7)   Enhanced respiratory, oral-motor and digestive function.
(8)   Maximized stability to enhance function.
(9)   Facilitation of care provision (e.g. therapeutic, medical or educational goals).

Whilst all the advantages listed above may not be relevant to the vast majority of learners, there are one or two that clearly would. Learners with attentional difficulties, limited short-term memory, co-ordination difficulties, organizational difficulties, visual processing difficulties, hypersensitivity or hypo-sensitivity, to name but a few, may benefit from such consideration. If difficulties persist, advice from a physiotherapist or occupational therapist should be sought.

Points to consider when evaluating positioning and seating with standard computer usage:

- Is the top of the monitor level with the user's eyes?
- If a laptop is being used, is the screen easy to see and at an angle?
- If using a standard keyboard, are hands at the same level as elbows?
- Are hands able to rest lightly on the keyboard or mouse? If not, are wrist supports for keyboard or mouse required?
- Are feet supported with feet resting on the floor or a footrest?
- Are arms and thighs parallel to the floor?
- Are arms supported by the table? If not, could a more appropriate table be obtained or do arm supports or grab bars need to be considered?
- Are the back and head upright or forced into a hunched position?

Considerations for the selection of tables and furniture (many trolleys and tables bought to support computer use in educational settings are unsuitable for their purpose) are:

- If the computer has to be used with a range of children, including children using wheelchairs, can the height be adjusted so that the child can reach the computer and use it in the way suggested above?
- If the height of the trolley has to be adjusted frequently, can this be carried out easily and safely with equipment loaded on the trolley?
- Does the working surface of the trolley have enough space to include the alternative keyboards that are needed?
- Does the trolley have enough room under the working surface to accommodate a wheelchair?

If the answer to the above three questions is 'no', then the options may be to:

- use infra-red connections or extension leads (beware of trailing leads) so that the keyboard, mouse switches or alternative keyboard can be located on a desk or wheelchair tray if available and big enough
- consider the use of monitor arms and keyboard shelves that can be added to trolleys and computer tables to swing out and adjust to the user's position and level, but if you are in any doubt as to the safety and stability of the resulting system . . .
- consider obtaining a more flexible trolley.

If a wheelchair or specialist seating is being used, Cook and Hussey (1995) suggest that the following questions may need to be addressed in consultation with seating specialists when considering how appropriate the seating system is in enabling computer use:

(1) Does the seating system meet the consumer's goals and needs, e.g. postural control, deformity management and pressure relief?
(2) Does it provide stability and allow for maximum performance in functional activities, e.g. transfers, weight shifts, wheelchair mobility, removal from wheelchair?
(3) Is the seating system comfortable for the user?
(4) Is the seating system durable enough to meet the user's needs for a reasonable period of time?
(5) Are the resources available to ensure appropriate maintenance of the seating system?

Precision teaching programs
These are pieces of software which teach a specific set of skills or knowledge in a structured way. They may be considered as components of an **integrated learning system**.

Predictors
A learner who is able to deal with a number of alternatives presented on screen while she is writing may benefit from the use of predictive typing in which the program uses its knowledge of what has been typed before in order to guess what the writer is trying to write after she has typed only the first letters of a word or phrase. Predictors appear alongside the text document (Figure R.9). When a letter is entered the box changes to show a list of words beginning with that letter. If the desired word is in the list it can be entered as a whole by selecting it from the list. If it is not on the list a second letter must be entered and the list changes to show words beginning with the first two letters, and so on.

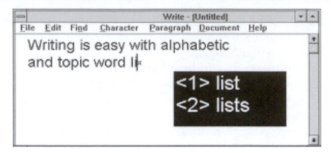

Figure R.9   A predictor working with a word processor (Courtesy of the ACE Centre)

In some cases the program may be set to remember new words so that the predictions gradually become more appropriate to the user's vocabulary.

Publishing
Desktop publishing is concerned with the production of publications such as newspapers, posters, keyboard overlays, worksheets and newsletters by combining pictures and words on the screen to create pages which are then printed out for possible further duplication. Most word processors worth their salt will allow text and images to be readily combined on the screen.

Most desktop publishing can now be carried out with integrated programs which incorporate many different facilities such as word-processing and drawing. Watch out for programs with the word 'works' in their title.

Desktop publishing can now encompass:

- the creation of interlinked web pages
- **multimedia authoring**
- musical composition
- a combination of all of the above.

R

Refreshable Braille display
A refreshable Braille display consists of a line of special cells. Each cell contains six or eight pins controlled electronically to move up and down to represent the characters which appear on the 'screen'. Many units also contain router buttons which show the position of the cursor on the line. Displays can be stand-alone units for use with a computer keyboard or can be integrated into another device, as in the note-taker described above.

Remote control (see **control technology** and **environmental control**)

Robots
The most widely used robots are 'floor robots' which can move over the floor in response to user commands (Figure R.10). They can be given personalities or functions and decorated as sailing ships, dogs or clowns. They can be given series of instructions via their keyboard symbols. These include the commands forward, back, left and right which need to be followed by a number to specify the degree of movement or turn. Most new robots have their own computer built in so that they do

not need to be used in conjunction with a desktop or laptop computer. In some cases sets of commands or programs can be transferred to and from a computer using an infra-red ink or an interface cable so that long sequences of instructions set up by a child or teacher do not have to be re-typed. Some children will learn a lot about orientation and spatial awareness from these activities by instructing an object moving in the real world. Some children with physical disabilities have benefited from the use of 'smart wheelchairs' which enable mobility by automatically slowing down or turning to navigate in collaboration with the wheelchair user (e.g. Kristofferson, Odor and Pinkerton, 1995). (See also **Logo, microworlds**.)

Figure R.10   An example of a floor robot

S

Scanners
These are devices which enable photographs or text within books or magazines to be transferred to a computer. Scanned text needs to be processed using OCR (Optical Character Recognition) software before it can be manipulated within a word processor or screen reader. This text can then be spoken using text-reading software with speech synthesis. There are a number of specialist suppliers of these systems. The process is rather like photocopying type directly into the computer. This means that worksheets can be read directly into a file which can be spoken by the speech synthesizer software or can be printed on a Braille embosser. (An alternative would be for a school or college to offer course notes on disc or as web pages.)

Scanning
This is a special term within assistive technology and should not be confused with the 'scanning' that goes on when someone is using a **scanner** to input an image or text document into a computer.

Within assistive technology scanning is 'a technique for the sequential display of a group of items to be selected from a selection set using a small number of switches' (after Nisbet and Poon, 1998, p. 127).

Scanning methods are ways through which a selection set is navigated. These include:

- Autoscan: each item in a selection set is highlighted in turn at a set rate. The user waits for the desired item to be highlighted and then activates a switch to select it. Other features include:
  - Toggle scan; waits for the user to press a switch before starting to scan when the program is first started or after a selection has been made (Colven and Detheridge, 1990). This gives the user more control so that the scanning does not go on all the time but it requires an extra switch activation by the user to restart the scanning again.
  - Scan delay is the time each item is highlighted.
  - Usually autoscan is used by a single switch user but when a second switch can be used it may have one of the following functions: start and/or stop the scan without selecting an item; delete the last entry; increase or decrease the scan speed; swap the direction of scanning.
  - Critical overscan is where the scan delay is shorter that can normally be coped with by the user so that when the user activates a switch, an item or group after the one desired will be highlighted but not selected. The direction of scanning reverses and slows down. The user then selects the desired item or group he or she has just passed.
- User scan: the scan begins and highlights each item or group in turn in response to a switch activation which continues while the switch activation is maintained (e.g. while the switch is held down). When the switch is released the scanning stops at the currently highlighted item or group. This can then be selected by activating a second switch if available, or by waiting for dwell selection if only a single switch is available.
- Step scan: this is when a switch activation and release moves the highlight on one item or group at a time. An item is selected by waiting for dwell selection if only one switch is available or by activating a second switch if two switches are able to be used.

Scanning movements dictate how items or a group of items within a selection set are highlighted during scanning. These include:

- Simple scan movement (Figure R.11). Each item with a selection set is highlighted in turn and can be selected by the user through a single switch action.
- Group scan movement. The selection set is divided into groups of items according to conceptual, functional or spatial criteria. These groups are highlighted in turn. Once a group is chosen an item from that group can be chosen using simple scan movement where each item of the group is highlighted in turn. Mistakes when choosing a group can be rectified by either having a cancel item within the group or setting the number of times the items in the group are scanned before returning to scanning the groups. Group scanning can take a variety of forms. For example:
  - Row-column scan (Figure R.12), where the row is scanned first. When a row is selected it is followed by a simple scan of items in the selected column (Figure R.13). Some users prefer this for letter grids.

Figure R.11 A simple scan (Courtesy of Widget)

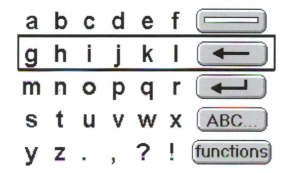

Figure R.12 An example of a row-column scan (Figures R.12–16c courtesy of Advisory Unit)

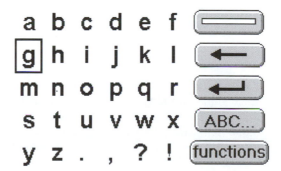

Figure R.13 An example of a scan of items in the selected row

- Column-row scan (Figure R.14), where the column is scanned first. This is followed by a simple scan of items within the selected row (Figure R.15). Some users prefer this for word lists.

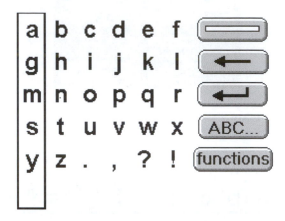

Figure R.14   An example of a column-row scan

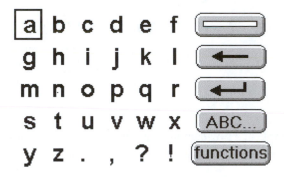

Figure R.15   An example of a scan of items in the selected column

- Nested scanning, where a selection set is divided up into a hierarchy of groups and subgroups. Each subgroup may in turn contain further subgroups (Figure R.16 a–c). This can be useful when a large number of items are in the selection set and can be faster than other scanning movements, but may require more switch presses as well as a clearly understood rationale and structure for subgrouping.

  The letter grouping in Figure R.16 is not very efficient as it is not based upon frequency of use.

  An alternative arrangement for frequency of use based upon selection by this scanning method could be that shown in Figure R.17.

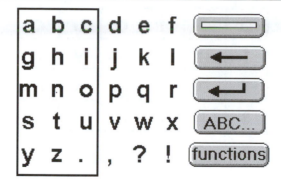

Figure R.16a An example of a nested scan starting with a group

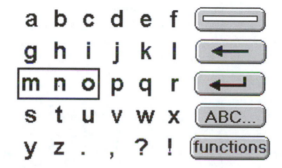

Figure R.16b Each row in the group is then scanned

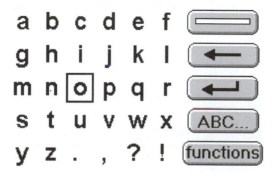

Figure R.16c Upon selecting a row, each item is scanned in turn

a	e	i	o	u	q
t	n	d	m	y	b
r	h	c	g	w	k
s	l	f	p	v	j
x	z	.	,	?	!

Figure R.17 An alternative arrangement for the frequency of use

- Directed scan movement. This is where the direction of scan through a selection set is controlled by the user usually with four or more switches or a switched joystick. The item can be selected either by one of the switches or by a dwell delay. This is similar to the use of the standard mouse controlled pointer system and requires the ability to view a selection set whilst simultaneously monitoring the position of the screen pointer. Figure R.18 is a selection set of letters that might improve the efficiency for such a system (especially with a joystick which centred itself after a selection) as the characters are grouped according to frequency from the centre.

Z	F	B	S	L	Y	V	1	2
X	P	O	T	H	C	K	3	4
J	U	A		E	D	↵	5	6
Q	W	R	I	N	G	M	7	8
'	;	,	←	.	-	=	9	0

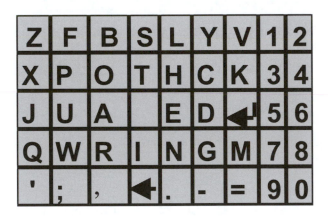

Figure R.18 An alternative arrangement with characters grouped according to frequency of use from centre

Points to consider in the selection and use of scanning systems include the following:

(1) Cognitive complexity

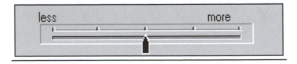

Figure R.19

(a)   Can the user understand the layout and functions of the selection sets?
(b)   Does the user understand how the selection method works?
(c)   Does the user know what switch action is required and when (i.e. does the user know what scanning movement is being used)?
(d)   Has the user received training in the use of the system?

(2)   Speed of operation

Figure R.20

(a)   Is the scanning too fast for the user, or too slow?
(b)   Could the arrangement of the selection sets be made more efficient?

(3)   Degree of accuracy required

Figure R.21

(a)   Are the input filters set appropriately so that errors and unintentional movements are masked out?
(b)   Have the switches been selected and appropriately positioned to ensure accurate use over time?

(4)   Amount of physical effort required

Figure R.22

(a)   Is the range and amount of movement needed to use the system achievable by the user over time?

(5)   Degree of concentration required (Figure R.23)

Figure R.23

(a)   Is the amount of time taken to achieve something longer than the attention span of the user? (If so, consider reducing the level of complexity and increasing the degree of clarity of the system.)

(6)   Clarity of display (Figure R.24)

Figure R.24

(a)   Can the user see the highlighted object?
(b)   Are the colour, size and style of the items appropriate?
(c)   Does the scanning need to be augmented with digital or synthetic speech?
(d)   Is the selection set organized logically, making best use of the available screen space?

(7)   Degree of user comfort (Figure R.25)

Figure R.25

(a)   Is the user positioned correctly in relation to the switches so that he or she does not undergo discomfort or pain through prolonged use?

(8)   Community commitment (Figure R.26)

Figure R.26

(a)   This is the commitment of the staff, parents and peers to the system's use. Have these people had opportunities to use the system so they empathize with the aims of its use, are confident that its use is a realistic goal for the learner, realize the difficulties in its use and are trained in how to support its inclusive use?

See also **switches**, **positioning and seating**, and **selection sets**.

Scenario programs

These were a suite of software, developed for the BBC computer, that enabled the user to build up a visual scene using 'written' commands. These commands could be typed into the computer using the standard QWERTY keyboard, an overlay keyboard or a mixture of both. An important aspect of the programs, for teachers, was that only grammatically correct sentences produced results. Pupils found them great fun and were able to explore language structures in an interesting, non-threatening way. Scenarios were available to suit various age groups and on a range of subjects that could be integrated into the curriculum. Additional overlays could be produced using standard software and used with the programs. Although one or two titles from the series were produced for the newer platforms, their use has declined over recent years.

Science

Word-processing can support the planning, data collection and writing up of experiments and projects.

Modelling software can immerse the learner in an area of scientific study, e.g. outer space, inside a body. **Virtual reality** may be able to take this further to facilitate investigating, classifying, pattern finding and data analysis. These models can become very compelling and generate 'What if?' type questions that are important to scientific enquiry.

Spreadsheets at an initial level can help in the production of tables of results which may be displayed graphically to highlight trends. Spreadsheets and charting software can also be used for the analysis obtained from data logging, the Internet or provided on CD-ROM.

Data logging allows data collected from sensors to be displayed graphically. The sensors may be monitoring an experiment live in the classroom or be located in a weather station on the roof of the building or attached to a scientific outpost in the Gobi Dessert or Polar station accessible via the Internet. This data can be replayed and analysed in a variety of visual ways to show the relationship between two or more variables. Such systems can increase the reliability of data gathering in experiments, and learners often display a keen sense of ownership of the data 'they have gathered'.

Branching Tree Databases can facilitate group work and collaboration by eliciting the learner's classification of a set of objects or concept through the generation of questions so that the computer is able to play a 'twenty questions' game to identify a particular object or concept.

Standard databases may also help in handling large sets of data which can be searched and sorted to find trends and exceptions. These data sets would not normally be available before CDs and the Internet.

Multimedia on CD can provide opportunities for re-enforcement and alternative presentation. A number of animation of scientific processes can be played, paused and rewound with a spoken commentary.

Screen readers

For a blind learner the central problem in using a computer is that of gaining access to information which is primarily visual. A screen reader uses digital or synthetic speech to convey information about the content of a screen. The advent of multimedia means that high-quality sound and speech are being employed more and more to channel information. However, visual aspects of a computer environment can be a barrier in that images and video may not have accompanying narrative or text that describes the content. Elements on the screen such as windows, buttons and menus may need to be spoken out.

Points to consider:

(1)   Can the text displayed be spoken out via speech synthesis?
(2)   Can this be spoken at the appropriate rate, e.g. letter by letter (using sound, name or the 'bravo' 'charlie' system), word, sentence and/or paragraph?
(3)   Can the user navigate through the text at the appropriate rate?
(4)   Can the style of voice used be customized (see speech synthesis in **speech output**)?
(5)   Can menus and buttons be spoken out?
(6)   Do the spoken button labels mean anything to the user? Do these need to be changed or taught? Can they be changed?
(7)   Does the user need feedback about the location of the cursor or mouse? If this is needed and provided, is it in a form useful to the user?

Such a system has options to read the current line, every letter pressed, each word in turn or the selected sentences. With a screen reader linked to a text-based web browser it can be possible, but not always easy, to access the vast wealth of information now available on the world wide web. See also Chapter 8.

Seating (see **positioning and seating**)

Selection sets
A selection set is an arrangement of items within a window, palette or toolbar and may contain links to other selection sets. An item may be a letter, word, phrase, picture or symbol which will do something when it is selected, e.g. put that word, phrase or image into a word processor, print out something on a printer or move to another selection set.

A standard keyboard is an example of a fixed selection set. A paper overlay on an overlay keyboard is another example of a selection set. An onscreen keyboard can contain a selection set which may include links to other selection sets, and is sometimes called a nested or dynamic keyboard.

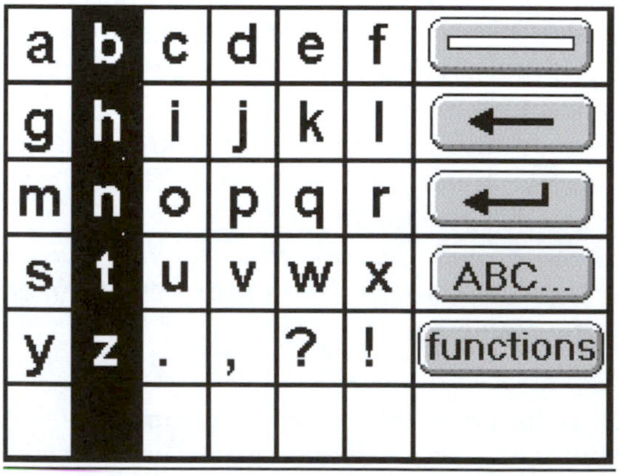

Figure R.27   A selection set used for scanning with one or more switches

It is sometimes said that 95 per cent of users of a complex application only use 5 per cent of its functionality. The task of the selection set maker is deceptively simple. Find which 5 per cent of functionality is needed by the user and arrange it sensibly within one or more selection sets. It is therefore most effectively a co-operative endeavour.

Examples of selection sets are provided in Figures R.27–R.33.

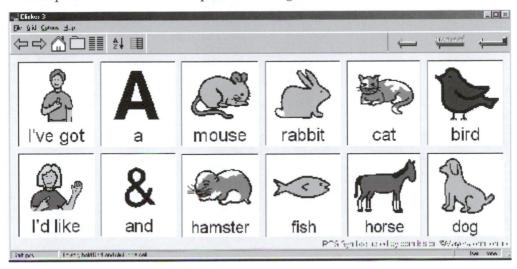

Figure R.28   Mayer Johnson symbols used within an onscreen keyboard (Courtesy of Crick Software)

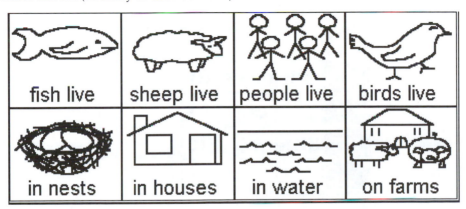

Figure R.29   A topic-based selection set that links to further selections sets with words about the beach and sea (Courtesy of Crick Software)

| fish live | sheep live | people live | birds live |
| in nests | in houses | in water | on farms |

Figure R.30   A selection set containing rebus symbols for use with a word processor (Courtesy of the Advisory Unit)

Figure R.31   A selection set for use with the basic commands in Logo. This would be used to drive a turtle around a screen or on the floor, but little else (Courtesy of the Advisory Unit)

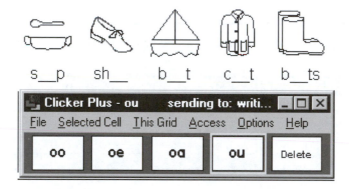

Figure R.32   A selection set used alongside symbol-supported reading software (Courtesy of Crick Software)

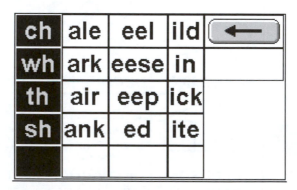

Figure R.33   A scanned selection set for use alongside a talking word processor in a phonic-matching activity (Courtesy of the Advisory Unit)

Seating (see **positioning and seating**)

Sensing (see **science**, data logging)

Serial port extension lead

If you have a digital camera, an overlay keyboard, switch interface boxes and lots of other things that need to be plugged into the back of your computer then a serial extension lead will be invaluable. You simply plug one end of the lead into the serial port at the back of your computer and put the other end somewhere you can reach easily. Then you can plug and unplug all your different devices quickly and easily.

Short cuts

These are keyboard alternatives to mouse operations. They were originally developed because laptop users did not have access to a pointing device. It was then found that keyboard alternatives could be a very useful access feature especially for some users with visual difficulties. They can be assigned to items within a selection set so that operations normally carried out using the mouse can be done using an alternative input device.

The following are keyboard equivalents for Windows 95. Unfortunately, some operating systems and software may not use keyboard equivalents:

Work in windows

To switch to the	*Press*
Next application	ALT + TAB
Previous application	ALT + SHIFT + TAB
Start menu	CTRL + ESC

Basic editing

To	*Press*
Cut a selection	CTRL + X
Copy a selection	CTRL + C
Paste a selection	CTRL + V
Undo an action	CTRL + Z
To select all	CTRL +A

Working with menus

To	*Press*
Display the shortcut menu	SHIFT + F10
Display the application Control menu	SPACEBAR (when the menu bar is active)
Select the next or previous command on the menu	DOWN ARROW or UP ARROW (with the menu displayed)
Select the menu to the left or right; or, with a submenu displayed, toggle the selection between the main menu and the submenu	LEFT ARROW or RIGHT ARROW

Filing

To	*Press*
Save the current document	CTRL + S

Print the current document   CTRL + P

Working within a window

To	Press
Close the window	CTRL + F4
Restore the window size	CTRL + F5
Switch to the next window	CTRL + F6
Switch to the previous window	CTRL + SHIFT + F6
Carry out the Move command (Control menu)	CTRL + F7
Carry out the Size command (Control menu)	CTRL + F8
Maximize the window	CTRL + F10
Select a folder in the Open or Save As dialogue box (File menu)	ALT + 0, and then use the arrow keys
Choose a toolbar button in the Open or Save As dialogue box (File menu)	ALT + number (1 is the leftmost button, 2 is the next, and so on)
Refresh the Open or Save As dialogue box (File menu)	F5

Work in dialogue boxes using shortcut keys

To	Press
Switch to the next tab in a tab dialogue box	CTRL + TAB or CTRL + PAGE DOWN
Switch to the previous tab in a tab dialogue box	CTRL + SHIFT + TAB or CTRL + PAGE UP
Move to the next option or group of option buttons	TAB
Move to the previous option or group of option buttons	SHIFT + TAB
Move within the active list box or group of option buttons	Arrow keys
Select the active command button or check box	SPACEBAR
Move to the next item beginning with that letter in an active list box	Letter key
Select the item with that underlined letter	ALT + letter key
Display a drop-down list box	ALT + DOWN ARROW
Close a drop-down list box	ESC
Choose the default command button	ENTER
Cancel the command and close the dialogue box	ESC

Within a text box

To	Press
Move to the beginning or end of the entry	HOME or END

Move one character to the left or right	LEFT ARROW or RIGHT ARROW
Select from the insertion point to the beginning of the entry	SHIFT + HOME
Select from the insertion point to the end of the entry	SHIFT + END
Select the character to the left	SHIFT + LEFT ARROW
Select the character to the right	SHIFT + RIGHT ARROW

Simulations (see **modelling**)

Speech input (see **voice activated software**)

Speech output
Synthetic speech is produced by translating written speech into phonemes using phonic rules. This electronic sound is being improved all the time through the use of higher-quality sampling of speech sounds plus the addition of stress and frequency change so that the voice is less monotone. The advantage of synthetic speech is that it does not take up much space in comparison to digitized speech which is a direct reproduction of a digitally recorded voice. Text on the screen can be spoken using the speech synthesis capabilities of the computer or by an external speech synthesizer. The fact that the latter is being used less and less is indicative of the way in which computers continue to increase their capabilities so that specialist facilities for a few are becoming standard features for the majority.

Synthetic speech is still being criticized for its American or 'Dalek' accents. This will become less of a problem as intonation, stress and the rhythm of speech (prosody) improve. People may have noticed how Steven Hawking's voice has continued to improve as his speech synthesis is upgraded. A number of different voices are being made available (e.g. English female, French male). Unfortunately, these are termed 'voice fonts' by the producers rather than simply 'voices'. Hopefully, whatever they end up being called, there should be a growing range of voices reflecting cultural diversity. There will be a market for a piece of software that lets you choose who you want to sing your emails and with the appropriate emotion according to content.

Digital speech is recorded speech and can comprise a range of qualities depending upon the sound capabilities of the computer and the quality of recording. Digital speech is usually used when a set number of phrases need to be produced with clear emphasis or a regional accent. It can be of high quality but takes up a lot of storage space. Communication aids can only store a few minutes of it using current technology and so they tend to use synthetic speech as well.

Educational issues:

(1)   More important than a technical consideration of synthetic speech technology is the fact that text produced by a speech synthesizer is not talk and should not be seen as a panacea for reading difficulties. Human speech takes into account the listener, sometimes. It alters its phrasing, stress and rate of production in response to cues from the listener. It makes guesses about common understanding to take short cuts. 'You get my drift?' It is dynamic and not a monologue. (This is a deliberate pun as one of the current speech utilities is called monologue.)

(2)   Speech and text processed by a speech synthesizer are ephemeral. Text has value because it is stable over time. It is not transitory like speech. However, you have to be able to decode it and some people have difficulties in doing this, so speech synthesis can help them. This is not a total solution because you do not understand everything you hear. There are a number of learners who can read beyond their own level of understanding. Speech synthesizers also do this but no one is fooled. Reading is more than decoding text to sounds. To derive meaning the reader has to actively engage with a text. If text is spoken then this task can become more difficult because it is there and gone. With small chunks of text this is not so much of a problem, depending upon the learner, but with larger chunks of text it is rather like listening to a story on the radio told by the most boring person in the world. It is difficult to concentrate on and understand.

Readability (Harrison, 1980) is a rough and ready measure of the difficulty of a text which takes into account the length of sentences, average number of syllables in each word, the number of unfamiliar words and the lengths of words. I repeat, just because a text is spoken out by a speech synthesizer does not mean it can be understood by the listener. He or she has to be able to engage with the text.

A vital part of study skills is the ability to skim and scan through a text. Skimming involves quickly reading the text to get a flavour of it, whilst scanning involves the search for key words or a phrase within the text. Using a speech synthesizer, skimming can be achieved by either speeding up the speech synthesizer or selecting key paragraphs to be spoken out. Scanning can be simply achieved by using the search facility with the word processor to find each occurrence of the words or phrase so that the surrounding text can be highlighted and then spoken out.

Spell checker
This is a facility within a program (usually a word processor) or device to check the spellings of words and then suggest alternative correct spellings if an error is found. Some word processors can inform the writer of a misspelling by underlining it in red as soon as it is typed. Most spell checkers look for typing errors rather than real spelling errors, so they may not always offer an appropriate set of alternatives. It is worth checking if the spell checker can be configured to be more responsive to poor spelling or be replaced by one which is.

Many spell checkers cannot spot homophones in the wrong sentence but some may alert the user to the fact that a homophone has been used and leave any amendment up to the user.

In some cases the number of alternative corrections on offer may be indistinguishable to the writer so that the facility to speak out each word using speech synthesis might be helpful. Alternatively, the option of using a spell check word list that is more suited to the written vocabulary of the writer could be explored with the software supplier.

A range of pocket-calculator sized spell checkers are available whose corrections are based upon spelling errors. Their advantage is that they are unobtrusive, 'look cool' and the simpler models are inexpensive. The more sophisticated ones may include spelling games, a dictionary and/or a thesaurus according to what the user can cope with and afford to pay. Some spell checkers are now supported by both speech and symbols.

Spreadsheets

A spreadsheet is a grid into which labels, values and calculations can be laid out in tabular form. They have advantages over calculators in that new values can be easily added and graphs can be produced. They can be used for simple and more complex financial modelling.

Sticky keys

'Sticky keys' is an option on most computers which allows the modifier key to remain activated after it is pressed until a further key is pressed so the user does not have to hold the modifier key down. This provides support for a one finger typist or someone who uses a head pointer.

A modifier key is a special key such as 'ALT', 'Control' or 'Shift'. In standard use, the user is required to hold down a modifier key at the same time as the desired key is pressed and released, e.g. 'Shift' and 'g' to obtain 'G' or 'Control' and 'C' to 'copy' text.

Subject teaching (see **curriculum, mathematics, English, science, history, music, modern languages, physical education** or **geography**)

Switches

'A switch is a device for making an electrical connection between two contacts (Nisbet and Poon, 1998, p. 152). Switches may have a momentary action where they are activated as long as they are held down or they may have a toggle action where the switch remains activated until it is pressed again. A radio button would be an example of the latter whilst a doorbell switch would be an example of the former. Such actions are often mimicked by buttons within a computer environment. See Figure R.34.

Figure R.34 An example of a simple block switch

There are many types of switch available which can be triggered by different parts of the body.

(1) Contact switches (alternatively known as passive switches) vary in size, pressure needed to activate the switch, travel (the amount of movement required before activation) and the extent and modality of feedback given on activation. Some switches will provide a click, resistance or movement to indicate that they are activated so that the user may not need to check if it has been successfully activated.

   (a) Paddle switches can be activated by most parts of the body. They have movement in one direction and their sensitivity may be adjustable.

   (b) Wobble and leaf switches are usually activated by hand, arm, knee or head, and consist of a 2–4 inch shaft that can be activated in two directions.

(c)   Levers are similar to wobble and leaf switches but they can only be activated in one direction.

(d)   Pillow or grasp switches respond to air pressure when they are squeezed or
pressure is applied to a bulb or cushion.

(e)   Puff and sip switches are activated by the individual blowing or sucking air
out of the switch.

A user might find it more comfortable and efficient to hold a switch down and
then release it to activate it. In such a case, options on the software should be
explored or the hardware option of a switch inverter could be used. A switch
inverter, as you might guess, reverses the standard operation of a switch when
it is connected between a switch and a computer. See also **joysticks**.

(2)   Non-contact switches (alternatively known as active switches) work by monitoring movements of body parts, e.g. eye blink, mercury tilt switches which can
detect if a body part is raised, sound operated switches, movement sensing by
breaking a light beam and proximity switches.

A single switch used to cause an effect is one of the first control experiences most
children meet – doorbells, light switches, television controls, for example. Switches
can also be one of the simplest or most complex ways of accessing software.

(1)   Direct entry: the triggering of a switch initiates a discrete action such as the
turning of a page on the screen or the display or building of an image or cartoons,
or the production of music or toy play. This may be used to teach cause and effect
or to train a user to use a switch.

> This is the ability of the individual to understand that he can control things in his
> environment and can make something happen. It encompasses the prerequisite
> skills of attention and object permanence. The individual must be able to attend to
> and be aware of his environment and the permanence of objects in that environ-
> ment. Information can be gathered on the individual's ability to understand cause
> and effect through the use of a single switch.
>
> (Cook and Hussey, 1995, p. 369)

(2)   Scanning (see **scanning** entry).

(3)   Encoded selection: this takes two forms.

(a)   Time encoded. This is a cognitive demanding form of switch input but some
have argued that it can be very efficient. It requires the user to memorize an
extended version of the Morse code which takes into account the special
keys on a keyboard such as 'return' and 'space' as well as mouse pointer
movement.

Nisbet and Poon (1998) pp. 131–132 state that a user of this system needs
to:

- be literate, as codes generate letters in the main
- have sufficient memory and sequencing skills to learn the codes
- have good switch control for either one or two switch use.

For a single switch user the switch is held down for a specified short duration to produce a 'dit', alternatively holding it down for a longer duration
will produce a 'dat'. With two switches one key is assigned to 'dat' and the
other to 'dit'. After waiting for a specified time the Morse code is then input
as text or a command by the computer.

(b) Multiple switch encoding (see **chording keyboards**).

See also **positioning and seating**.

Points to consider:

(1) Are switches positioned securely in such a way that the user can operate them reliably? (Use a flexible switch mounting system in collaboration with specialists.)
(2) Can the user wait for the appropriate highlighted option?
(3) Can the user activate the switch at the correct time?
(4) Can the user hold the switch (maintain activation)?
(5) Can the user release the switch?
(6) Is the user in a comfortable neutral position so that they can use the switches without pain or fatigue? Can the person reliably carry out the operations required?
(7) A person's ability to use a switch system might change during the day due to fatigue, ability to concentrate and change in their ability to control their own movements.

See also **mouse port switch adaptor**.

Symbol software
Symbol software that enables the user to create symbol enhanced text is a must for schools and colleges offering courses for students with severe learning difficulties. Teachers and supporters can use it to produce resources – worksheets, notices, record sheets, etc. Students can use it in conjunction with an overlay keyboard or on-screen word bank as a writing tool. Symbols will not be suitable for all students, but for those who are able to use them, symbols provide a powerful gateway to literacy. See Figure R.35.

Figure R.35 Rebus symbols produced with symbol-processing software

You should expect a symbol processor to provide most of the facilities that a word processor has, including the ability to use speech.

T

Talking books

A large range of talking books are available which combine text, pictures, animation and speech on the computer screen as an interactive page. The text can be read out using synthetic, but more usually digitized, speech. Words can usually be selected and read out in context.

Learners who have struggled to develop literacy skills may be encouraged to engage with text in meaningful and enjoyable ways (see Chapter 3 on developing literacy).

Talking books can be used in many ways. Sometimes you can get 'big book' versions of the stories as well so the talking book can be used to support work around a familiar story. Some talking books come with support materials for teachers; while these are usually designed for limited range mainstream students, the ideas can sometimes be adapted to suit the needs of students with learning difficulties. There is further need for talking books that are appropriate for older students. Talking books are easy for teachers and parents to install and use.

For learners with more cognitive difficulties who find it difficult to use a mouse, a **touch screen** will enable the learner to touch a word on screen and hear it.

Switch users can engage with these books through the use of selection sets that scan through **hotspots**. (See Richard Walter's Chapter Six)

Multimedia authoring and **talking word processors** mean that teachers and learners can create their own talking books and presentations relatively simply, including photographs or video.

Talking word processors

Many word processors have the facility to speak each letter, word or sentence as it is typed in. This can provide useful auditory feedback for the writer. A visually impaired learner or someone who is starting to write may want to have all these features switched on at the same time but other writers will usually prefer to have each word and sentence spoken. This will often alert the writer to syntax and spelling errors. Some writers will not have these automatic speech options switched on at all but will select text to be read back for review and checking after typing in a few sentences.

Text can be obtained from CD-ROMs, the Internet and from email. A talking word processor may be useful to speak out the text for someone who has difficulty in directly decoding print. (See speech output)

Text editors (see **word processors**)

Touch screens

Touch screens are devices which enable a user to control a computer by pointing or touching an area of the screen. Touch screens are a direct way of controlling software and may be suitable when the learner finds the use of the mouse too cognitively demanding.

Touch screens are very useful with early learning software dealing with comparisons, matching and odd-one-out activities. It must be remembered that mouse-driven programs are designed for small pointers rather than large fingers so, although it is a very direct method of access, some students may not be able to locate the precise, often small, areas required. The touch screen has advantages especially when used with multimedia such as talking books – learners can point at a word and then hear it spoken.

The earliest touch screens consisted of a frame around the monitor, reacting when an object such as a finger passed across the frame towards the screen. The frame contained a matrix of infra-red beams which were broken by a pointer or finger. Problems arose if the screen was not appropriately positioned so that the screen registered the wrist rather than the finger when pointing.

The best touch screens are those designed for industrial displays. These touch screens are built into the monitor and are far more robust that those that you have to attach separately. They are also more expensive.

Many laptops and palmtops will have an option for the use of a stylus with their small touch sensitive screens. It may be that such a system could be used with an **onscreen keyboard** in conjunction with a desktop computer instead of an **overlay keyboard**.

Points to consider:

(1) How is the touch screen to be positioned? If it is to be used in the usual oblique position, ensure that the user is slightly higher than the screen and directly in front so that the arm does not get exhausted and parallax effect errors are avoided.

(2) Will the user use their finger to point, or a pointing device? If a pointing device is used, check if the screen will withstand it.

(3) How will the user make a choice? Can the software be set to have **dwell selection**, does the user remove their pointer from the screen to select or does he or she tap the screen twice?

(4) Can this be configured for the user?

Trackballs or trackerballs

A trackerball looks like a large upside-down mouse but it remains stationary on the table. The pointer is controlled by moving the ball on its surface with a finger, thumb, foot or palm of hand and selections are made by pressing one of the buttons. The ball can be in a variety of sizes depending on the size of the trackerball.

Less gross hand and arm movement are required than a standard mouse. A large trackerball with a billiard-sized ball plus an extra middle button is available. Some trackerballs are available which have control over x and y mouse movement and can temporarily 'lock' into vertical or horizontal movement. Some also have extra toggle switches for holding the left and right buttons down. Trackballs are also available for foot operation. In some cases overlays are available so that the user's hand can be supported over the ball whilst a finger dips on to it.

Mini-trackerballs can be mounted on the edge of a notebook keyboard and controlled by the thumb and first finger or held in the palm of a hand. Although slightly strange to use at first it can become very intuitive. There are also left- and right-handed mice as well as thumb operated mini-trackballs that provide palm support.

See also **joysticks**, alternative **keyboards**, **overlay keyboard**, **switches** and **touch screens**.

Turtles (see **robots**)

Typing tutors

These can teach a learner to type with a QWERTY keyboard if they are able to cognitively or physically access the keyboard. For some learners it may help with keyboard familiarity and letter patterns if they are able to follow the teaching method employed by the software. An alternative viewpoint is that some schools use ICT so infrequently it is a waste of valuable time to teach typing skills. This in turn can be countered with the view that it is still a worthwhile investment.

Features of typing tutors and points to consider are listed below:

- Uncluttered screen presentation without horizontal text scroll.
- Does the program assess and store the level of the learner and allow the learner opportunities to repeat (overlearn) a previous lesson?
- Does the software provide feedback concerning progress made?
- If the training starts with letter sequences does it move quickly on to meaningful words which are of use to the learner?
- Does the instruction move on to include continuous text as soon as is possible?
- Does the program include speech feedback of target letters and words if required by the user?

See also Chapters 5 and 7.

U

Universal design

Universal design for the curriculum echoes many of the debates in the UK concerning curriculum differentiation. Whereas, the concept of differentiation grew to have a multiplicity of meanings for different interest groups, the principles of universal curriculum design have clearly stated principles and definitions that can be used to evaluate resources.

> Universal design is an approach to creating environments and products that recognises the diversity of users regardless of their ability or age. Universal design is a value not a set of dimensional requirements. It challenges designers to think beyond code compliance and special features for specific users towards more inclusive solutions that incorporate the needs of diverse users without segregation or separate accommodation. Designing special solutions for different segments of the population is a costly and cumbersome way to design places and products.
> . . .
> Universal design, however, is not a euphemism for accessibility. It is an idea that re-establishes a critical and fundamental goal of good design: meeting the needs of as many users as possible.
> (Universal Design Education Project, Http://darkwing.uoregon.edu/uplan/UDEPweb/MainUDEP.html)

Stating that universal design is efficient and cost-effective resonates with the Salamanca statement (1994) which states that inclusion can also be achieved in a cost-effective manner.

The Trace Research and Development Centre has outlined seven principles of universal design which are listed below to provide guidelines which may be usefully applied to evaluate educational practice and provision.

> Principles of Universal Design (Note not all guidelines may be relevant to all designs)
>
> Principle One: Equitable Use
> The design is useful and marketable to any group of users:
> Guidelines:
> 1a)   Provide the same means of use for all users: identical whenever possible; equivalent when not

1b)   Avoid segregating or stigmatising any users
1c)   Provisions for privacy, security, and safety should be equally available to all users

Principle Two: Flexibility of Use
The design accommodates a wide range of individual preferences and abilities
Guidelines:
2a)   Provide choice in methods of use
2b)   Accommodate right or left handed access and use
2c)   Facilitate the user's accuracy and precision
2d)   Provide adaptability to the user's pace

Principle Three: Simple and Intuitive Use
Use of the design is easy to understand regardless or the user's experience, knowledge, language skills, or current concentration level
Guidelines:
3a)   Eliminate unnecessary complexity
3b)   Be consistent with user expectations and intuition
3c)   Accommodate a wide range of literacy and language skills
3d)   Arrange information consistent with its importance
3e)   Provide effective prompting for sequential actions
3f)   Provide timely feedback during and after task completion

Principle Four: Perceptible Information
The design communicates necessary information effectively to the user, regardless of ambient conditions of the user's sensory abilities
Guidelines:
4a)   Use different modes (pictorial, verbal, tactile) for redundant presentation of essential information
4b)   Provide adequate contrast between essential information and its surroundings
4c)   Maximise 'legibility' of essential information in all sensory modalities
4d)   Differentiate elements in ways that can be described (i.e. make it easy to give instructions or directions)
4e)   Provide compatibility with a variety of techniques or devices used by people with sensory limitations

Principle Five: Tolerance for Error
The design minimises hazards and the adverse consequences of accidental or unintended actions
Guidelines:
5a)   Arrange elements to minimise hazards and errors: most used elements, most accessible; hazardous elements eliminated, isolated, or shielded
5b)   Provide warnings of hazards and errors
5c)   Provide fail safe features
5d)   Discourage unconscious action in tasks that require vigilance

Principle Six: Low Physical Effort
The design can be used efficiently and comfortably and with a minimum of fatigue
Guidelines
6a)   allow user to maintain a neutral body position
6b)   use reasonable operating forces
6c)   minimise sustained physical effort

Principle Seven: Size and Space for Approach and Use
Appropriate size and space is provided for approach, reach, manipulation, and use regardless of user's body size, posture or mobility
Guidelines:
7a)   Provide a clear line of sight to important elements for any seated or standing user
7b)   Make reach to all components for any seated or standing user
7c)   Accommodate variations in hand and grip size
7d)   Provide adequate space for the use of assistive devices or personal assistance

Trace also note: 'It must be acknowledged that the principles of universal design in no way comprise all criteria for good design, only universally usable design. Certainly, other factors are important, such as aesthetics, cost, safety, gender and cultural appropriateness, and these aspects should be taken into consideration as well.' (Trace.wisc.edu/world/gerund.html). Many pieces of legislation use cost or the 'efficient use of resources' as the limiting factor for funding of inclusion.

CAST have proposed three principles for universal design which are considered in the introductory chapter.

V

Video (see **digital video**)

Virtual reality
Like speech recognition, virtual reality until recently had seemed to be within the realms of science fiction. However, this nascent technology is currently being researched within the entertainment industry, the military, aviation, oil and nuclear industries.

Virtual reality (VR) involves the representation of salient three-dimensional environments which a user can interact with using alternative control devices based upon standard ways of interacting with the environment. For example, an input glove can be used to point to a virtual destination and manipulate virtual objects. Feedback can be supplied on a screen or from a VR helmet or goggle which provides stereo visual feedback. This could also be combined with being tilted and moved on a chair or platform.

Like all technology, virtual reality is not neutral. It could be used in disturbing ways with vulnerable learners. However, the virtual swords and laser guns can become virtual plough shares if they exploit the field of enabling technology to enable alternative forms of representation, control and engagement which underpin **universal design** for learning. For example, papers presented at the 2nd European Conference on Disability, Virtual Reality and Associated Technologies included:

- the use of videoed panorama of pictures linked to speech to support communication for a person with aphasia
- the design of a virtual city with and for people with learning difficulties to teach and rehearse life and mobility skills
- the creation of a virtual worlds using haptic (textural) feedback with three-dimensional sound for visually impaired or blind users to play video games
- the creation of a virtual keyboard to control other applications for a switch user
- a virtual invisible keyboard which can be 'played' via movement.

This technology could give a physically disabled user the freedom and mobility to work without the use of cumbersome tools like mice, keyboards or switches. Actually surfing the Internet might become a virtual reality.

There are, as usual, ethical considerations:

- Do some learners have only a right to access virtual experiences rather than reality?

- Should some children have access to 'real' reality first?
- How 'real' is reality for some learners anyway?

See also **microworlds**.

Visual feedback
This is an accessibility feature that can augment or replace some of the auditory prompts from a computer. The 'sound-sentry' accessibility feature instructs the computer to flash part of the display (usually the caption bar or border) every time the system's built-in speaker plays a sound. The 'show-sounds' feature instructs programs that usually convey information only by sound to also provide all information visually, for example, displaying text captions or informative icons. To what extent this is actually implemented in programs making extensive use of sound has yet to be seen.

Voice activated software (VAS)
There are different types of voice recognition systems.

- Simple voice activated software: at the simplest level a voice can be used to activate a switch to cause some action to be performed (the micromike on the Acorn BBC computers). At a slightly more sophisticated level the computer can react to the user's control of the characteristics of his or her voice by producing displays and animation in response to amplitude, frequency or degree of airflow. An example of this would be the voice print produced in the use of a sound recording software or the IBM speech viewer software utilized by a few speech therapists teaching deaf and partially hearing children in the late 1980s and still available.

  Points to consider:

  (1) How useful was/is this software for learners with severe/profound learning difficulty, children with elective mutism or those with speech articulation difficulties?
  (2) Are upgraded or alternative software available now? How are they used?

- Speech recognition allows people to control computers using their voice.
- Speaker independent systems are intended to work with any voice without training. As a consequence they have a limited vocabulary. These are used for environmental home appliance control. Do these systems have potential for included learners in control activities or are they inappropriate in education?

  Voice navigation on some systems is intended to be speaker independent and built but, unless it is localized for regional accents, age and gender for our potential users, it has to be trained.

- Speaker dependent systems adapt to the characteristics of the user's voice. They require an enrolment where the computer learns the basic characteristics of the user's voice by soliciting a range of sentences to be spoken. This can be followed by a further period of training in which the voice recognition accuracy is significantly increased. An accuracy of over 90 per cent is claimed by manufacturers which means one word in ten is guessed wrongly and must be corrected.

  If this is a fault, is this any more accurate than word-processing systems? (The software also uses 'predictive' processes and contextual clues – it will also continue to learn and get better at recognition as it goes on.)

Speaker Dependent Systems divide into Voice Navigation Systems which can be used to mirror the usual tasks of operating a computer, e.g. selecting from menus to open a document and in some cases control of the mouse pointer, and Speech Dictation Software which in turn consists of two broad types: discrete and continuous.

– Discrete software works through classic dictation with pauses between words and consistent intonation. Elliot (1998) suggests that these systems may be most suitable for users who have difficulty retaining and expressing thoughts clearly, race ahead or have an erratic speech pattern or a tendency to language blocks, need direct contact with the written word so that they can bridge the gap between speech and writing, or want to improve and develop spelling, reading and writing.
– Continuous software works with speech at the speed of normal conversation. There is a slight lag between speech and the words appearing on the screen so there is no immediate link between the words spoken and the words displayed. Elliot (1998) suggests that continuous speech systems may be most suitable for users who have clear controlled thoughts, no difficulties finding words to express themselves, poor spelling and just want to get down thoughts quickly, strong reading skills.

Point to consider:

(1)   Is this the case? (Thorough evaluations have not yet been completed)

Features to consider in selecting a speech recognition system:

- What is the minimum specification machine required (because you really must exceed the minimum in terms of memory, disc space and processor power)?
- How many words are active compared to the word archive on disc?
- Does it allow correction by voice? (or does it involve using the keyboard?)
- Does it allow more than one user?
- Can it have different topic sets (e.g. for different subject areas or styles of writing)?
- Can the text that has been guessed be played back using speech synthesis?
- Can the recorded speech be played back? (As a prompt for correction)
- Can the mouse and operating system be controlled directly by speech? (Is this needed?)
- Can it use macros (so that the user can say 'Take a letter Mr Jones' and a new page is opened with the address and current date in place)?

Factors perceived to influence successful use:

- The quality of the microphone is very important. Get a very good microphone and follow the instructions so that it is positioned correctly. There are two kinds of microphone that can be used: either a close-talk or headset microphone that is held close to the mouth, or a medium-distance microphone that rests on the computer 30 to 60 centimetres away from the speaker. A headset microphone is needed for noisy environments. It has been suggested that dictation works best with close-talk microphones.
- The type of sound card used needs to be good at sound input and compatible with the software.

- Some laptops cause noise and interference with sound input. Check to see if this is the case.
- Motivation to undertake the training and support for its use. The more a user trains the system to their voice, the more accurate will be the recognition.
- The enrolment and training may require the user to follow complex multi-syllabic sentences and also to speak them. This requires a high level of cognitive skills. (It can be anticipated that computer-based games will be used for enrolling children in the near future.)
- The complexity of screen layout and error correction. Some also make use of the aviator's alphabet. Can the user deal with these successfully?

User considerations (after Cook and Hussey, 1995; Litterick, 1998; and Nisbet and Poon, 1998):

- Can the user consistently utter the range of sounds that are required to use the system?
- If discrete recognition is to be used, can the user dictate with pauses between words using a consistent monotone?
- Often users are learning to dictate at the same time as learning to use voice recognition.
- Conversely, is the recognition vocabulary adequate for the user?
- Are templates available that are representative of the user's age and dialect?
- Can the user articulate the words in a consistent manner over time?

Implementation issues:

- Is there likely to be background noise in the user's setting?
- Can the user make some use of the keyboard and screen for simple editing of mistakes and basic rewriting?
- Where will it be used? If it is to be used in a noisy setting, then that is where the training needs to take place.
- How many users will there be? Can each user have their own recognition profile so it is maximally configured for their voice? Each profile will take up significant disc space in the near future.
- Laine and Breen (1996) suggest that the user should not spend more than 30–40 minutes at a time using discrete speech recognition as it is exhausting on the voice and eyes. Nisbett and Poon (1998) advise the drinking of plenty of water.

Setting targets, monitoring and evaluation:

- Why is the system being used? Is it to increase work rate, writing quality and/or writing quantity?
- What does the learner think the system can offer?
- What do the parents think the system can offer?
- What does the teacher and LSA think the system can offer?
- From this establish a baseline and set realistic targets which are monitored by those involved.
- Can the use of VAS link with concerns expressed within any IEP for the learner?
- Monitor the amount of writing, is it enough? The style of writing, is it appropriate? The content, does the resultant text meet the requirements of the curriculum? Is the learner excluded or included academically and socially as a result of its use?

- Does the monitoring link into existing systems?
- Does the monitoring result in action?
- Is the monitoring manageable?
  (After Tod, Castle and Blamires, 1998.)

Educational and ethical issues:

- Writing is not always speech written down. Laine and Breen (1998) note that the style of writing with a dictation system changed to a more oral style.
- It may be that the text composers (can we call them writers?) have to think more than users of other input devices. They may also have less cognitive processing demands made of them if they do not have to worry about finding keys and generating letter sequences, so they consider composition. Smith (1982) distinguishes between 'composition' and 'transcription' elements of the writing task stating that concentration on one of these elements will be to the detriment of the other. It may be that voice recognition offers support in transcription so that the speaker can devote more cognitive resources to composition.
- Provisionality, the ability to write and change what you have written, has been a vital factor in the success of word-processing. Refining and rephrasing a text for an audience is a central part of the writing process. Does voice recognition facilitate or inhibit this?
- Could a discrete system be more effective for some learners than continuous speech?
- Pilling (1998) and Laine and Breen (1998) both report that VAS was effective with learners whose voice was not easily understood by peers. The software appeared to be more skilled than peers in interpreting the users' speech.
- Are there times when a scribe would be a better solution?
- Some users of word prediction programs find that the words offered may limit the development of a wide vocabulary as the suggestions are based upon words they have used before. Does voice recognition have the same effect especially when the user is motivated to get the software to be accurate?
- Is the use of voice activated software being limited to one area of need – that of specific learning difficulty? Is this because learners with these difficulties are more tolerant of the technology than others?
- Could the use of simple voice activated software be fostered for learners with more complex needs?
- The use of simple voice control with floor robots has not been consolidated in the new technology.

W

Word banks (see **selection sets**)

Word processors/word-processing
Word-processing is powerful mechanism for many learners as it enables them to draft and edit their ideas without the finality of pen on paper. Mistakes can easily be rectified and risks can be taken because text can be removed and inserted. **Selection sets** can be used in conjunction with word-processors to provide an appropriate level of support.

A variety of typefaces (fonts) are available which may be suited to different writing and reading needs. Some are freely copiable from shareware or can be purchased from commercial suppliers. Different learners have preferences for particular fonts.

Word-processors can be used to create stories and articles containing recorded sounds attached to words, pictures or on-screen buttons. **Multimedia** support can thus be provided alongside the text.

Many educational word processors will include a speech facility. See **talking word processors** and **symbol software, selection sets, planners, predictors, multimedia**.

World wide web

The world wide web is that part of the Internet which is available to be viewed using web **browsers** in the form of pages containing text, possibly multimedia and links to other pages. There is pressure from some proprietary vendors to make users use resources within their web pages which are not part of the open agreed standards that form the web. This may be convenient in the short term but could exclude many people from using that web page.

Web pages can be made more accessible to different users by ensuring that the page is still usable when all the images are turned off in the browser.

- Ensure that all images have an ALT property set which contains a text description of the image as far as it is possible.
- Avoid using frames or provide an alternative without frames.
- Ensure that the text of a link conveys what it is a link to.
- Avoid using columns and tables or provide an alternative.
- Avoid using none standard features. You can check if your pages confirm to the current standard by having it checked at CAST's web site.

CAST have a utility which can asses the usability of a web page:

Http://darkwing.uoregon.edu/uplan/UDEPweb/MainUDEP.html

Web pages can be made more usable by following the principles of **universal design** for learning.

Wrist rests

These are widely available for keyboards and mice and may provide support for the wrists and arm but also for those who do not need full arm support. See **arm supports, positioning and seating**.

Bibliography

Abbott, C. (ed.) (1995) *IT Helps, Using it to Support Basic Literacy and Numeracy Skills*, Coventry NCET.

Ackerman, D. (1991) *Literacy for All*, London: David Fulton.

Ainscow, M. (1991) *Effective Schools for All*, London: David Fulton.

Arditi, A. (1998) *Print Legibility and Partial Sight*, available at URL: http://www.lighthouse.org/print-leg.htm.

Armstrong, D. (1998) Changing faces, changing places: policy routes to inclusion, in P. Clough (ed.) *Managing Inclusive Education: From Policy to Experience*, London: Paul Chapman Publishing.

Arnold, M. (1995) The semiotics of Logo, *Journal of Educational Computing Research*, Volume 12, No. 3.

Astington, J.W. (1993) *The Child's Discovery of Mind*, Cambridge, MA: Harvard University Press.

Barker, K. (1998) Using ICT in the literacy hour, in R. Dick (ed.) *MAPE Focus on Literacy*, Birmingham: MAPE.

Baron Cohen, S. (1996) *Mindblindness, An Essay on Autism and Theory of Mind*, Cambridge, Mass: MIT Press.

Barton, L. (1998) Markets, managerialism and inclusive education, in P. Clough (ed.) *Managing Inclusive Education: From Policy to Experience*, London: Paul Chapman Publishing.

Bearne, E. (ed.) (1996) *Differentiation and Diversity in the Primary School*, London: Routledge.

Bednar, A. K., Cunningham, D., Duffy, T. M. and Perry, J. D. (1991) Theory into practice: how do we link? in G. J. Anglin (ed.) *Instructional Technology: Past, Present and Future*, Colorado: Libraries Unlimited.

Best, A. (1992) *Teaching Children with Visual Impairments*, Milton Keynes: Open University Press.

Bonk, C. J. (1995) Searching for social constructivism in learning environment surveys and social interaction coding schemes. Paper presented at the 6th European Conference for Research on Learning and Instruction (EARLI), University of Nijmegen, The Netherlands.

Breuker, J. A., Winkels, R. G. F. and Sandberg, J. A. C. (1987) A shell for intelligent help systems, *Proceedings of the 10th International Joint Conference on Artificial Intelligence*, Vol. 1, pp. 167–73. USA Massacheusetts: MIT Press.

Brooks, J. G. (1990) Teachers and students: forging new connections, *Journal of Educational Leadership*, Vol. 5, pp. 68–71.

Bruce, I., McKennell, A. and Walker, E. (1991) *Blind and Partially Sighted Adults in Britain: The RNIB Survey*, London: HMSO.

Bruner, J. S. (1986) *Actual Minds, Possible Worlds*, London: Harvard University Press.

Buckland (1986) Danny: using Logo, in M. Hope (ed.) *The Magic of the Micro: A Resource for Children with Learning Difficulties*, London: CET.

Clough, P. (ed.) (1998) *Managing Inclusive Education: From Policy to Experience*, London: Paul Chapman Publishing.

Collins, J., Longman, J., Littleton, K., Mercer, N., Scrimshaw, P. and Wegerif, R. (1995) *CD-ROMs in Primary Schools; An Independent Evaluation*, Coventry: NCET.

Colven, D. and Detheridge, T. (1990) *A Common Terminology for Switch Controller Software*, Oxford: ACE Centre.

Cook, A. M. and Hussey, S. M. (1995) *Assistive Technologies: Principles and Practice*, St Louis: Mosby.

Cooper, P. (1998) (ed.) *Understanding and Supporting Children with Emotional and Behavioural Difficulties*, London: Jessica Kingsley.

Crystal, D. (1995) *The Cambridge Encyclopedia of the English Language*, Cambridge: Cambridge University Press.

Curry, N. E. and Johnson, C. N. (1989–90) Beyond self esteem: developing a genuine sense of human value. Research monograph of the National Association for the Education of Young Children, Vol. 4.

Day, J. (1995) *Access Technology: Making the Right Choice* (2nd edition), Coventry: NCET.

DeCorte, E. (1990) Learning with new information technologies in schools: perspectives from the psychology of learning and instruction, *Journal of Computer Assisted Learning*, Vol. 6, pp. 69–87.

Dennet, D. (1996), *Kinds of Minds*, London: Phoenix.

DES (1978) *Special Educational Needs* (The Warnock Report), London: HMSO.

DES (1988) Education Reform Act, London: HMSO.

Department for Education and Employment (1988) *The National Curriculum*, London: HMSO.

Department for Education and Employment (1994) *Special Educational Needs – Code of Practice*, London: HMSO.

Department for Education and Employment (1997) Green paper, *Excellence for All Children: Meeting Special Educational Needs*, London: HMSO.

Department for Education and Employment (1998) *The National Literacy Hour*, London: HMSO.

Dijkstra, S. (1995) The integration of instructional systems design models and constructivist design principles. Unpublished paper presented to the European Association for Research and Instruction, Nijmegen, The Netherlands, August.

Duffy, T. M. and Jonassen, D. H. (1996) *Constructivism: New Implication for Instructional Technology*, Dallas: Lawrence Erlbaum.

Eklund, J. (1997) *Adaptive Learning Environments: The Future of Tutorial Software?*, Faculty of Education, University of Sydney, eklundj@edfac.usyd.edau.

Elliot, E. (1998) Breaking down barriers, *Ability*, Vol. 26, Autumn.

Engel, G. L. (1977) The need for a new medical model: a challenge for biomedicine, *Science* Vol. 196 (4286), pp. 129–36.

Feuerstien, R. (1976) Mediated learning experience: a theoretical basis for human modifiability during adolescence, in P. Mittler (ed.) *Research and Practice in Mental Retardation*, Vol. 2, Baltimore: University Park Press.

Foster, R. S. (1996) Telecommunications and the written language development of deaf students, in Sitko, C. M. and Sitko, C. J. (eds) (1996) *op. cit.*

Foucault, M. (1967) *Madness and Civilisation*, London: Tavistock.

Gagné, R. M. and Briggs, L. J. (1979) *Principles of Instructional Design*, New York: Holt, Reinhart and Winston.

Gardner, H. (1985) *The Mind's New Science. A History of the Cognitive Revolution*, New York: Basic Books.

Gardner, J. (1996) *Tactile Graphics: An Overview and Resource Guide*, available at URL: http://dots.physics.orst.edu/tactile/tactile.html.

Gill, J. M. (1997) *Equipment for Blind and Partially Sighted Persons: An International Guide*, London: RNIB.

von Glaserfeld, E. (1995) *Radical Constructivism: A Way of Knowing and Learning*, London: Falmer Press.

Goleman, D. (1995) *Emotional Intelligence*, London: Bloomsbury.

Gray, C. (1994a) *The New Social Story Book*, Arlington: Future Horizons.

Gray, C. (1994b) *Comic Strip Conversations*, Arlington: Future Horizons.

Green, F., Hart, R., Robson, C. and Staples, I. (1982) *Microcomputers and Special Education*, London: Longman for Schools Council.

Haigh, D. (1990) Developing thinking skills, in T. Detheridge (ed.) *Technology in Support of the National Curriculum*, Coventry: NCET.

Hall, N. (1987) *The Linguistic and Social Background of Emergent Literacy*, London: Hodder and Stoughton.

Harrison, C. (1980) *Readability in the Classroom*, Cambridge: Cambridge University Press.

Harrison, C. (1995) *Evaluation of ILS among Students for Whom English is a Second Language*, Nottingham: University of Nottingham School of Education and NCET.

Hart, S. (1996) *Beyond Special Needs: Enhancing Children's Learning through Innovative Thinking*, London: Paul Chapman Publishing.

Heppell, S. (1994) Multimedia and Learning: Normal Children, normal lives and real change in J. Underwood (ed.), *Computer Based Learning: Potential into Practice*, London: David Fulton.

Hodgon, L. (1995) *Visual Strategies for Improving Communication: Volume 1*, Michigan: Quirk Roberts.

Holdsworth, J. (1991) Unpublished draft of Hearing IT, Coventry: NCET.

Hope, M. (1986) *The Magic of the Micro: A Resource for Children with Learning Difficulties*, London: CET.

Hope, M. (1987) *Micros for Children with Special Needs*, London: Souvenir Press.

Horton, W. (1991) *Illustrating Computer Documentation. The Art of Presenting Information Graphically on Paper and Online*, Chichester: John Wiley.

Hutchins, J. (1998) *Literacy Software*, Reading: British Dyslexia Association.

IDEA (1990) Individuals with Disabilities Act, Public Law, pp. 101–476.

Jeffrey, J. (1996) ICT multimedia and specific learning difficulties. Unpublished dissertation, Canterbury: Christ Church University College.

Jonassen, D. H. (1994) Thinking technology: toward a constructivist design model, *Journal of Educational Technology*, April, pp. 34–63.

Jonassen, D. H. (1995) Supporting communities of learners with technology: a vision for integrating technology with learning in schools, *Journal of Educational Technology*, August, pp. 60–3.

Jones, C. (1986–87), The Listening Eye, *Learning to Cope: Computers in Special Education Year Book 1986/7*, London: EMAP, pp. 46 and 47.

Jordan, R. and Powell, S. (1995) *Understanding and Teaching Learners with Autism*, London: John Wiley.

Kelly, G. (1955) *A Theory of Personality: the Psychology of Personal Constructs*, New York: Norton.

Knight, C. (1998) Moon – a route to communication and literacy, *Focus*, July, www.rnib.org.uk/multdis/Focus/jul88.htm.

Knox-Quinn, C. (1995) Student construction of expert systems in the classroom, *Journal of Educational Computing Research*, Vol. 12, pp. 243–62.

Kristofferson, K., Odor, P. and Pinkerton, S. (1995) *Moving Smartly Through 5–14: Smart Powered Wheelchairs and Special Educational Needs*, Edinburgh: CALL Centre.

Laine, C. J. and Breen, M. (1996) Writing by talking to the computer: experience with speech recognition systems, in M.C. Sitko and C.J. Sitko (eds.) *op. cit.*

Latham, C. and Miles, A. (1997) *Assessing Communication*, London: David Fulton.

Lawler, R. (1985) *Computer Experience and Cognitive Development*, Chichester: Wiley and Sons.

Lawrence, D. (1996) *Enhancing Self-esteem in the Classroom*, 2nd edition, London: Paul Chapman Publishing.

Lemke, J.L. (1988) Towards a social semiotics of the material. *Subject*, Vol 2, no. 1, pp. 1–17.

Lewis, A. (1998) In the appendices of NCET, *Integrated Learning Systems: A Report of Phase Two of the Pilot Evaluation of ILS in the UK*, p. xiii.

Litterick, I. (1998) *A Comparison of Features of Speech Recognition Systems*, Cambridge: Iansyst.

Lodge, J. (1998a) Preparing a laptop for a visually impaired computer novice, *New Beacon*, issue 82: pp. 4–9, July/August.

Lodge, J. (1998b) Improving access to Windows 95, *Visability*, Vol. 22, pp. 12–15, Spring.

Lodge, J. (1998c) The Mouse Pointer Page, available at URL: http://www.jlodge.demon.co.uk/web/pointer.htm.

Lunzer, E. and Gardner, K. (1979) *The Effective Use of Reading*, London: Heineman Educational Books for Schools with the Schools Council.

Maddison, A. (1982) *Microcomputers in the Classroom*, London: Hodder and Stoughton.

Mandl, H. and Reinmann-Rothmeier, G. (1995) From system-mediated vs. situated learning environments to flexible learning environments. Paper presented in the Symposium on the Integration of Instructional System Design Models and Constructivist Design Principles at the European Association for Research on Learning and Instruction, Nijmegen, The Netherlands, August.

Mandl, H., Gruber, H. and Renkl, A. (1995) *Situeiertes Lernen in Multimedialen Lernumgebungen (Forschungsbericht Nr. 50)*. Munchen:lugwig-Maximilians-Universttat, Lehretuhl fur Empirische Padagogiische Psychologie.

Mano, A. and Horn, P. (1998) Children and computers: prerequisite skills and basic concepts, in M. N. Henderson, *Closing The Gap*, June/July. www.closingthegap.com/library/June-July/mano-horn.html.

Margerison, A. (1996) Self-esteem: its effect on the development and learning of children with EBD, *Support for Learning*, Vol. 11, no. 4, November, pp. 176–180.

McDevitt, A. (1998) An investigation into the use of CD-ROM technology by students in mainstream primary schools. Unpublished M.Phil. thesis, Middlesex University.

Miles, M. (1998) Voice activated software for dyslexic students. Paper presented at the NASEN Special Needs Exhibition Seminars, London.

Mittler, P. (1991), *Literacy for All*, London: David Fulton.

Moore, J. (1992) Good planning is the key, *British Journal of Special Education*, Vol. 19, no. 1, pp. 16–19.

Moy, B. (1984) Personal communication.

Murray, D. K. C. (1997) Autism and information technology: therapy with computers, in S. Powell and R. Jordan (eds.) *Autism and Learning*, London: David Fulton.

Musselwhite, C. and King-DeBaun, P. (1997) *Emergent Literacy Success: Merging Technology and Whole Language*, Park City, UT: Creative Communicating.

Myles, B. S. and Sampson, R. (1998) *Asperger Syndrome: A Guide for Educators and Parents*, Austin: ProEd.

Nash, C., Steadman, S. and Eraut, M. (1992) *CD-ROM in Schools. Evaluation Report*, Coventry: NCET.

National Council for Educational Technology (1995) *Extending Horizons, Imagination Technology*, Coventry: NCET.

National Council for Educational Technology (1997) *Review of Software for Curriculum Use*, Coventry: NCET.

National Council for Educational Technology (1998) *Integrated Learning Systems: A Report of Phase Two of the Pilot Evaluation of ILS in the UK*, p. xiii, Coventry: NCET.

NCET (1997) Review of Software for Curriculum Use, svently: NCET.

Nisbet, P. and Poon, P. (1998) *Special Access Technology*, Edinburgh: CALL Centre.

Norwich, B. (1990) *Reappraising Special Needs Education*, London: Cassell.

Norwich, B. (1996) Special needs education or education for all: connective specialisation and ideological impurity, *British Journal of Special Education*, Vol. 23, no. 3, pp. 100–3.

Olson, J. (1988) *Schoolworlds/Microworlds: Computers and the Culture of the Classroom*, Oxford: Pergamon Press.

Orford, P. (1995) Multimedia on CD-ROM: what is it and can hearing impaired children use it? *Focus on Deaf People Conference*, May, Coventry: NCET.

Papert, S. (1980) *Mindstorms: Children, Computers and Powerful Ideas*, Hemel Hempstead: Harvester Press.

Papert, S. (1991) Situating Constructionism, in I. Hare and S. Papert (eds.) *Constructionism*, New Jersey: Ablex.

Papert, S. (1992) *The Children's Machine: Rethinking School in the Age of the Computer*, New York: Basic Books.

Papert, S. (1997) *Computers, Constructionism, Constructivism*, available at http://metric.ma.ic.ac.uk/~pkent/construction/construction.html.

Papert, S. (1998) Obsolete skill set: The Three Rs, Literacy and Leteracy in the Media Age, WIRED ONLINE: Wired Ventures USA Ltd.

Paveley, S. (1997) *Getting Started with Symbols*, Hatfield: The Advisory Unit: Computers in Education.

Pester, K. (1990) *Hearing I.T.* Coventry: NCET.

Pilling, M. (1998) Personal communication to the editor.

Poole, P. (1998) *Talking about Information and Communication Technology in Subject Teaching: A Guide for Student Teachers, Mentors and Tutors*, Canterbury: Canterbury Christ Church University College.

Rahamim, L. (1993) *Access to Words and Images*, Coventry: NCET.

Reigluth, C. M. (ed.) (1983) *Instructional Design Theories and Models*, Hillsdale: Lawrence Erlbaum.

Resnick, L. B. (1987) Learning in school and out, *Educational Researcher*, Vol. 16, No. 19, pp. 13–20.

Reynell, S. (1977) *Reynell Developmental Language Scales (Revised)*, Windsor: NFER.

Ridgeway, L. and McKears, S. (1985) *Computer Help for Disabled People*, London: Souvenir Press.

Schön, D. (1987) *Educating the Reflective Practitioner: Toward a New Design for Teaching and Learning in the Professions*, San Francisco: Jossey Bass.

Schopler, E. and Mesibov, G. (eds.) (1985) *Communication Problems in Autism*, New York: Plenun Press.

Scrimshaw, P. (ed.) (1995) *Language, Classrooms and Computers*, London: Routledge.

Seagrave, J. (1983) The use of micros by clients – communication, control and creativity. Transcription of a speech for The Group for Technology and Disability.

Self, J. (1985) *Microcomputers in Education: A Critical Appraisal of Educational Software*, Brighton: Harvester Press.

Sharkey, P., Rose, D. and Linström, J. (eds.) (1998) *Proceedings of the 2nd European Conference on Disability, Virtual Reality and Associated Technologies*, Skövde, Sweden.

Sheingold, K., Kane, J. H. and Endreweit, M. E. (1983), Microcomputer use in schools: developing a research agenda, *Harvard Educational Review*, Vol. 53, no. 4, November, pp. 412–32.

Silver, J., Gill, J., Labes, S., Martin, M., Sharville, C. (1998) A new font for digital television subtitles, available at URL: http://www.eyecue.co.uk/tiresias/design.html.

Sitko, M. C. and Sitko, C. J. (eds.) (1996) *Exceptional Solutions: Computers and Students with Special Needs*, Ontario: The Althouse Press.

Skinner, B. F. (1938) *The Behaviour of Organisms*, New York: Appleton Century Crofts.

Smith, F. (1982) *Writing and the Writer*, New York: Holt, Rhinehart and Winston.

Sparrowhawk, A. (1995) 'Report from a Field Officer', *CD-ROM TItles Review 1995*; 6–10, Coventry: NCET.

Stansfield, J. (ed.) (1997) *A First Handbook of IT and Special Educational Needs*, Tamworth: NASEN.

Strack, G. (1995) Curriculum constraints and opportunities, in B. Tagg (ed.) *Developing a whole school IT Policy*, London: Pitman.

Straker, A. (1986) *Time to Reflect*, London: CET .

Taylor, J. (1992) *Technology in Support of the National Curriculum for Students with Severe Learning Difficulties*, Coventry: NCET.

Teacher Training Agency (1998). Draft of the initial teacher training national curriculum for the use of information and communications technology for subject teaching, http://www.teach-tta.gov.uk/ictst.htm, accessed 4 October 1998.

Thomas, G., Walker, D. and Webb, J. (1997) *The Making of the Inclusive School*, London: Routledge.

Thoms, J. (1998) Starting up with the Braille Lite 40, available at URL: http://www.dorton.demon.co.uk/ATS/br140.htm.

Tingle, M. (1990) *The Motor Impaired Child*, Windsor: NFER Nelson.

Tod, J., Castle, F. and Blamires, M. (1998) *Individual Education Plans: Implementing Effective Practice*, London: David Fulton.

Twachtman-Cullen, D. (1997) A Passion to Believe: Autism and the Facilitated Communication Phenomenon, Oxford: Westview Press.

Underwood, J.D.M. and Underwood, G. (1990) *Computers and Learning: Helping Children Acquire Thinking Skills*, Oxford: Blackwell.

United Nations (1989) Convention on the rights of the child, United Nations.

UNESCO (1994) The Salamenca Statement and Framework for Action on Special Needs Education, Paris: UNESCO.

Vygotsky, L. S. (1978) *Mind in Society; the Development of Higher Psychological Processes*, Cambridge, MA: Harvard University Press. (Original material published in 1930, 1933 and 1935.)

Ward, D. B. and Ward, T. (1993) The assessment of self esteem, in G. McEachron-Hirst (ed.) *Student Self Esteem*, Lancaster: Basel Technomic Publication.

Ware, J. (1994) *Educating Children with Profound and Multiple Learning Difficulties*, London: David Fulton.

Webster, A. (1988) Deafness and learning to read 1: theoretical and research issues, *Journal of the British Association of Teachers of the Deaf*, Vol. 12, no. 4, pp. 77–83.

Webster, A. (1989) Deafness and learning to read 1: literacy across the curriculum, *Journal of the British Association of Teachers of the Deaf*, Vol. 13, no. 3, pp. 82–92.

Weir, S. (1987) *Cultivating Minds: A Logo Case Book*, New York: Harper Row.

Wells, G. (1987) *The Meaning Makers; Children Learning Language and Using Language to Learn*, London: Hodder and Stoughton.

Wells, G. and Chang-Wells, G. L. (1992) *Constructing Knowledge Together: Classrooms as Centres of Inquiry and Literacy*, Portsmouth, NH: Heinemann.

Wertsch, J. V. (1991) *Voices of the Mind: A Sociocultural Approach to Mediated Action*, Cambridge, MA: Harvard University Press.

Williams, A. and Williams, R. (1986) Using microcomputer technology to develop reasoning abilities in special education students, *Australian Journal of Special Education*, Vol. 18, no. 4, pp. 17–20.

Woolfe, A. L. (1996) Laptop support for learning disabled student in a mainstreamed classroom, in M. C. Sitko and C. J. Sitko (eds.) *op. cit.*

Xiaodong, L., Bransford, J. D., Hickey, D. T. and Kantor, J. (1995) Instructional design and development of learning communities: an invitation to a dialogue, *Educational Technology*, September, pp. 53–61.

Name Index

Abbott, C. 104, 186
Ackerman, D. 41, 186
Ainscow, M. 7, 186
Arditi, A. 85, 186
Armstrong, D. 8, 41, 186
Arnold, M. 25, 186
Astington, J.W., 35, 186

Barker, K. 30, 186
Baron-Cohen, S. 35, 186
Barton, L. x, 7, 41, 186
Bearne, E. 28, 186
Bergen, 154, 186
Best, A. 83, 186
Blamires, M. 1, 27, 37, 54, 114, 133, 184, 191
Bonk, C.J. 22, 186
Breen, M. 183, 184, 188
Breuker, J.A. 23, 186
Briggs, L.J. 21, 187
Brooks, J.G. 22, 186
Bruce, I. 83, 186
Bruner, J. 14, 22, 186
Buckland, M. 142, 143, 186

Castle, F. 114, 184, 191
Collins, J. 104, 186
Colven, D. 132, 158, 187
Cook, A.M. 139, 155, 174, 183, 187
Crystal, D. 26, 187
Curry, M. 53, 187

Day, J. 4, 5, 41, 187
Decorte, E. 1, 2, 187
Dennet, D. 35, 187
Dickinson, D. 57
Dijkstra, S. 23, 24, 187
Dorman, P. 19, 113, 138
Duffy, T.M. 22, 187

Endreweit, M.E. 43, 190
Eklund, J. 23, 24, 187
Elliot, E. 182, 187

Feuerstein, R. 32, 35, 187
Foster, R.S. 109, 187
Foucault, M. 41, 187

Gagné, R.M. 21, 187
Gardner, H. 19, 187
Gardner, J. 187
Gardner, K. 23, 189
Goleman, D. 35, 188
Gray, C. 35, 188
Green, F. 37, 188

Haigh, D. 41, 143, 194
Hall, 96, 188
Hardy, C. 35, 52, 105
Harrison, C. 138, 172, 188
Hart, S. 8, 9, 113, 188
Heppell, S. 105, 188

Hodgon, L. 36, 188
Holdsworth, J. 98, 99, 188
Hope, M. xiii, 11, 19, 44, 188
Horn, P. 132, 189
Hussey, S.M. 139, 155, 174, 183, 187
Hutchins, J. 28, 188

Jacobs, J. 38
Jeffrey, J. 31, 188
Johnson, C.N. 53, 187
Jonassen, D. 19, 21, 22, 187
Jones, C. 19, 103, 188
Jordan, R. 62, 188

Kane, J.H. 43, 190
Keane, P. 11
Kelly, G. 38, 188
King-DeBaun 28, 189
Knox-Quinn, C. 23, 188
Kristofferson, K. 157, 188

Laine, C.J. 183, 184, 188
Latham, C. 125, 188
Lawrence, D. 53, 188
Leedale, R. 99
Lemke, J.L. 25, 188
Lewis, A. 138, 189
Lodge, J. 83, 85, 88, 93, 118, 189
Lunzer, E. 29, 189

Maddison, A. 43, 189
Mandl, H. 19, 21, 23, 189
Mano, A. 132, 189
Margerison, A. 52, 189
McDevitt, A. 96, 104, 129, 189
McKears, S. 77, 140
Mercer, B. 38
Mercer, N. 19, 186
Mesibov, G. 133, 190
Miles, A. 125, 188
Miles, M. 16, 189
Mittler, P. 40, 187, 189
Moore, J. 7, 113, 189
Moy, R. 29, 189
Murray, D. 57, 189
Musselwhite, C. 28, 189
Myles, B.S. 35, 189

Nash, C. 104, 189
Nisbet, P. 158, 173, 174, 183, 189
Norwich, B. 3, 13, 39, 189, 190

O'Callaghan, D. 49
Odor, P. 157, 188
Olson, J. 56, 190
Orford, P. 104, 190

Papert, S. 23, 24, 25, 26, 142, 190
Paveley, S. 35, 37, 190
Pellegrino, N. 38
Perry, J.D. 19 190
Pester, K. 19, 190

Pierce, C. 25
Pilling, M. 184, 190
Pinkerton, 157, 188
Poole, J.P. xiii, 139, 190
Poon, P. 158, 173, 174, 183, 189
Powell, S. 62, 188

Quist, J. 38

Rahamim, L. 73, 75, 190
Reigluth, C.M. 21, 190
Reinmann-Rothmeier, G. 19, 21, 23, 189
Resnick, L.B. 8, 21, 24, 35, 26, 190
Reynell, S. 35, 190
Ridgeway, L. 77, 140
Ryan, K. 49

Sampson, R. 36, 189
Schon, D. x, 9, 190
Schopler, E. 133, 190
Sheingold, K. 43, 190
Scrimshaw, P. 19, 190
Seagrave, J. 43, 190
Sitko, C.J. xi, 10, 14, 39, 190
Sitko, M.C. xi, 10, 14, 39, 190
Skinner, B.F. 20, 190
Smith, F. 15, 184, 190
Sparrowhawk, A. 104, 190
Stansfield, J. 141, 190
Strack, G. 52, 191
Straker, A. 117, 191

Taylor, J. 127, 191
Thomas, G. 7, 191
Tingle, M. 5, 77, 132, 191
Tod, J. 114, 184, 191
Twachtman-Cullen, D. 36, 191

Underwood, G. 15, 57, 58, 60, 191
Underwood, J.D.M. 15, 57, 58, 60, 191

von Glaserfeld, E. 22, 191
Vygotsky, L. S. 13, 22, 96, 191

Walker, D. 7, 191
Walter, R. 10, 35, 40, 61
Ward, D.B. 53, 191
Ward, T. 53, 191
Ware, J. 77, 191
Warnock, M. 3, 5, 191
Webb, J. 7, 191
Webster, A. 96, 97, 99, 103, 191
Weir, S. 10, 142, 146, 191
Wells, G. 22, 96, 191
Wertsch, J.V. 22, 191
Williams, A. 142, 191
Williams, R. 142, 191
Woolfe, A.L. 141, 191

Xiaodong, L. 20, 22, 191

Subject Index

AAC 61
Access Technology 4, 13, 124, 187
Accessibility Options 79, 131
acuity 83
Adulthood 41
advocacy 37, 38, 44, 49
Affirmation/Criticism 115
Alternative keyboards 139
American Sign Language 102
analogic phonics 32
Arm Supports 123
Armrests 66, 119
Art 16, 44, 47, 114, 152
Asperger Syndrome 35, 189
Assistive Technology 5, 124, 132, 157
attention (Given or Expected) 116
audiograms 103
Auditory Feedback 124, 131
Augmentative communication 29, 83, 124, 128
authentic Learning 15
Autism ix, 35, 57, 133, 189, 190
Autocorrect 59, 125
Available time for tasks (work load) 115

basics 3, 29
behaviourist 19, 21, 22, 30
biological/psychological/social model 4
braille 84, 89, 90, 91, 93, 94, 102, 157, 191
Branching Tree Databases 126, 165
bricolage 24
British Sign Language 102
Browsers 126, 185
BT Fax Buddy Scheme 109

CAST 10, 11, 118, 180, 185
CCTV 85, 87, 89
Chording Keyboards 126
Circular 4/98 15
Clarity 86, 87, 109, 114, 133, 138, 164
Cloze Procedure 13, 29, 30, 32, 126, 133, 147
Code of Practice 5, 6, 39, 75, 113, 187
Coded Communication 127, 128
Cognitive Access 5
Cognitive Flexibility Theory 22
Colour 88
Communicating Ideas 127
communication aid 4, 22, 61, 71, 72, 80, 83, 84, 117, 121, 122, 124
communication skills 46, 51, 58, 61, 75, 101, 117
CD-ROM 51, 91, 95, 103, 104, 105, 106, 129, 176, 186, 189
constructionist 22
constructivist 21, 22, 23, 187, 188
Content Specific 44
Continuity 117
Contrast 85
control hypothesis 59
Control Panel 79, 131
Control Technology 124, 129
Curriculum xi, 3, 5, 8, 10, 11, 17, 25, 27, 28, 29, 38, 40 43, 45, 52, 53, 54, 56, 57, 58, 75, 77, 82, 83, 84, 89, 92, 95, 99, 100, 103, 104, 110, 113, 114, 117, 129, 130, 136, 138, 146, 165, 178
Customization 131

DARTS 30
Data bases 131

Data logging 144, 165
de-professionalisation 7
Design Stance 35
Desk Top Computers 131, 152
Developing Literacy 176
Developing Tray 126
DFEE 6, 27, 28, 52, 104
dictaphone 89
differentiation 113, 127, 130, 138, 178, 186
Digital camera 37, 46, 48, 71, 72, 123, 148, 169
Digital Storage 131
Digital Video 35, 132, 152
Direct entry 174
direct switch access 66
drill and practise 44
DVD 95
Dvorak 140
Dwell Selection 132
dyslexia 28, 33, 89, 188
dyspraxia 75, 82

Early Intervention 77
early learning 12, 35, 40, 55, 62, 98, 101, 127, 132, 176
Electronic Mail 28, 31, 37, 38, 49, 50, 64, 65, 109, 133, 139, 149, 171, 176
Enabling Learning 17
Enabling Physical Engagement 73
Enabling Socialization 35
Enabling Software and Devices 13
Enabling Technology 16
Encoded Selection 174
engagement 1, 5, 6, 7, 8, 11, 13, 16, 28, 29, 30, 33, 52, 58, 66, 73, 96, 123, 130, 135, 180, 113,
English 133
Environmental Control 134
Ergonomic keyboards 55, 119, 139
Expanded keyboard 54, 55, 78, 119, 139
Expert systems 2, 3, 188
Extending horizons 5

Facilitated Communication 35
facilitator 5, 64, 76
field 83
floor robot 5, 35, 41, 45, 130, 134, 142, 156, 184
Font style 87
Four Block Model 29
frames 185
Framework Software 44

Geekdom 113
Generalisation and 'Transfer' 11
Geography 32, 134, 144
Grab Bars 134
Grammar Checkers 135
Grammatical Knowledge 27
Graphic Knowledge 27
GUI 84, 85, 88, 95, 135

Handling Information 135
headphones 33, 88, 103, 105
hearing impairment 73, 96, 101
Henry VIII 103
History 64, 103, 105, 135
hotspots 66, 69, 72, 80, 119, 136, 176
Hypertext 30, 99

ID 20
IDEA 6, 8, 78, 84, 188
Inauthentic labour 15, 16, 28, 60

Inclusion x, 6, 7, 40, 77, 117, 130
independence 52, 93, 97, 117
Individual Education Plan 55, 191
Information Communication Technology (ICT) 8, 15, 19, 25, 29, 31, 32, 35, 36, 38, 39, 40, 41, 42, 43, 44, 45, 47, 48, 49, 50, 52, 54, 55, 58, 60, 61, 62, 63, 64, 65, 72, 73, 75, 76, 77, 78, 82, 84, 85, 92, 109, 114, 123, 124, 134, **136**
Information Handling 13, **135**
Information Technology (IT) 4, 5, 24, 41, 42, 45, 52, 54, 81, 97, 98, 100, 101, 107, 138,
Innovative Thinking 8
Input Filter 78, **136**
Integrated Learning Systems 3, 119, **136**, 144, 189
Intelligent Courseware 23
Intelligent software 2
Intentional Stance 35
Interaction/group work 115
internet x, 1, 10, 29, 31, 33, 66, 71, 95, 110, 126, 133, 134, **138**, 144, 147, 149, 165, 176, 180
'Isambard Kingdom Brunel' 143

joysticks 66, 72, 127, **139**, 162

keyboard alternatives/equivalents 78, 84, 145, **169**
Keyboards 31, 78, **139**, 141, 180, 185
keyguard 55, 78, 79, 119, 140, **141** 151

language demand 116
laptop **141**
LCD 85, 91
learning characteristic 39
learning difficulties 57, 59, 66, 69, 75, 76, **142**, 175, 176, 180, 184
Letter spacing 91, 88
level of work/complexity 116
lip-reading 102, 110
Literacy 27–30, 34, 39, 40, 41, 44, 47, 50, 75, 77, 81, 99, 103, 109, 126, 134, 175, 176, 179, 113, 186, 187, 188, 189, 191
Literacy for All 40, 189
Literacy Hour 28
Logo 10, 24, 25, 97, 98, 129, **142**, 144, 146, 157, 168, 186, 191
low technology 1, 65, 128

Macros 108, 131, 140, 141, **143**, 182
Magnification 86, 87, 123,
Makaton 102
Margins 88
Mathematics 2, 94, 138, **143**, 147
Mediation 28, 42, 46, 68, 126, 131
Meta-Cognition 2, 3, 5, 10, 19, 24, 37
Mice and Mice Alternatives 47, 51, 66, 79, 101, **145**, 150, 154, 177, 180, 185, 189
Micromike 97, **146**, 181
microphone 46, 48, 71, 77, 100, 103, 146, 182
microworld 10, 13, 24, 61, 66, 97, 98, 133, **146**, 147, 157, 180
Miniature keyboards 119, 141
Minicom 109
modality 116
Modelling **147**, 165, 173
models 2, 4, 6, 7, 9, 10, 19, 20, 22, 23, 29, 31, 32, 39, 54, 57, 76, 77, 97, 130, 134, 136, 142, 187, 190

Models of learning 1
Modern Languages **147**
Modifier keys 140, 173
Moon 93, 94, 188, 190
Motoric Level 133
Mouse (See Mice etc)
Mouse Port Adaptor 51, **148**
Mousekeys 67, 79, 131, 145
Multi-Media 10, 41, 42, 55, 66, 103, 123, 127, 132, 133, 135, 138, 148, 156, 165, 176, 184
multi-media authoring **148**
Music 4, 10, 39, 53, 62, 76, 94, 104, 148, **149**

N.C.E.T 34, 45, 137, 138, 143, 144, 186, 187, 188, 189, 190, 192, 194, 195, 197, 198, 199
National Curriculum 8, 27, 40, 41, 43, 92, 100, 104, 129, 138, 187, 188, 191
National Grids 116
negotiation/conflict (choice) 115
Networks **149**
note-taker **149**
nystagmus 83

Object Level 133
on-screen keyboard 30, 44, 78, 102, 136, **150**
overlay keyboard vii, 30, 31, 37, 41, 43, 44, 49, 51, 54, 56, 66, 68, 69, 77, 78, 79, 82, 97, 98, 99, 102, 128, 136, 141, 142, 165, 166, 169, 175, 177, 119
overlearning 97

painting and drawing 12, 51, 123, **152**
Palm Tops 31, **152**, 177
paper and pencil 8, 55, 59, 144
Pen Portraits
    Adele 61
    Amira 80
    Amy 99
    Anne 80
    Ben 101
    Claire 54
    Eve 32
    Fazila 59
    Greg and Lee 105
    George 94
    Jacob 64
    Jean Paul 33
    John 46
    Julie 103
    Kirsty 106
    Kulvinder 62
    Mathew 76
    Maurice 64
    Moira 75
    Neil 98
    Phillip 56
    Rajik 81
    Reg 48
    Tony and Sarah 63
    An After School Keyboard Club 57
    An online community 49
    A Timetable for John 46
    Group Communication 63
    Making Books with a Reception Class 46
    School Web Site 65
    She used to tear up her work 54
    Talking books 47
    The Student Helper/Expert 56

    Using a braille note-taker in lessons 94
    What colour shoes do you wear? 59
    Writing and Telling a story 69
    Writing with symbols 48
    Zebra Crossing 47
People First 37, 38, 42, 49
Perkins Brailler 89, 90,
Phonic Knowledge 27
Physical Access 5, 75, 77
Physical disability 39, 75, 82
Physical Education **152**
Physical Stance 35
Picture Level 133
planner 31, 33, 36, 96, 109, 133, 134, 184, **152**
Point size 86
portable computer 77, 78, 90, 91, 107
Positional mouse clicks 66, 67, 136,
Positioning and Seating **154**
Pre School (See also Early Years) 39
Precision Teaching Programs 144, **155**
Predictability/Novelty 114
Prediction 30, 67, 76, 140, **155**, 184
provisionality 4, 39, 55, 57, 102, 133, 146, 184
proximal zone 13, 100, 102,
Publishing 45, 71, 85, 86, 123, 126, 133, **156**

QWERTY 78, 91, 140, 141, 165, 177

Readability 44, 88, 172, 188
Rebus 64, 67, 97, 102, 167, 175
Record of Achievements 64
Reflective Practitioner 9
retinitis pigmentosa 83
Robots 130, 120, 134, 142, **156**, 184

Salamenca Statement 8
scaffolding 5, 13, 14, 15, 22, 32, 39, 138
Scanners 157
Scanning 30, 67, 80, 86, 136, **157**, 172, 174
scenario programs 97, 147, **165**
Science 2, **165**
Screen Readers 84, 88, 157, **165**
selection set 32, 41, 49, 51, 61, 64, 66, 67, 68, 79, 82, 97, 98, 99, 101, 102, 120, 126, 127, 134, 136, 139, 142, 143, 148, 150, 151, 158–163 **166**, 169, 176, 184
self-esteem 52, 53, 55, 101, 188, 189
semiotics 25, 186
Serial port extension lead 51, 148, **169**
Shakespeare 66
shared attention 40, 61, 67 75
Short Cuts 153
Show-sounds 105, 131, 181
signs, signing 96, 99, 101, 102, 104, 124
single switch 1, 61, 62, 71, 72, 80, 158
Skimming & Scanning 30, 71
sliced bread xiii
social awareness 61
Social understanding 61
Socialisation 35, 125
Sound-sentry 181
Speech Output 89, 90, 94, **171**
Speech Recognition (see Voice Activated Software)
speech synthesis 28, 32, 88–89, 126, 150, 152, 157, 166, 171–172, 182

Spell Checkers 126, 152, **172**
spelling 15, 25, 28, 32, 33, 56, 57, 81, 98, 106, 172, 176, 182
spina bifida 75
Spreadsheets 4, 13, 32, 51, 60, 134, 144, 165, **173**
SQ3r 30
Sticky Keys 78, 131, 140, **173**
Supportive Access 5
switch 1, 5, 6, 40, 44, 51, 55, 61, 62, 63, 64, 66, 67, 71, 72, 76, 77, 79, 80, 82, 100, 120, 136, 145, 148, 150, 154, 158, 163, 164, 166, 169, **173**-175, 176, 177, 180, 181, 187
symbol 1, 20, 25, 27, 31, 37, 41, 44, 46, 48–49, 50–51, 61, 64, 72, 82, 93, 97, 102, 116, 124, 125, 127, 128, 133, 157, 166, 167, 175, 190
symbol software 44, 82, **175**
synthetic speech (see speech synthesis)
system font 86

Talking books 12, 29, 31, 40, 41, 47, 51, 65, 66, 67, 100, 136, 148, **176**
Talking Word-Processors 32, 33, 54, 116, 120, 134, 168, **176**
tape recorder 72, 76
Target Drift 15
Teacher Training Agency (TTA) 4, 7, 39, 58, 191
Teaching Machine 44, 142
teletext 89
The fish who could wish 69
Toggle keys 124, 131
Touch Screens 46, 48, 51, 99, 101, 120, 150, **176**
Trace Centre 118, 163, 180
Trackballs or Trackerballs 66, 72, 150, **177**
Turtle Graphics 142, 146
Turtles 98, 142, 168, 177
typing tutors 12, 59, 82, **177**

Universal Design 5, 9, 10, 11, 29, 30, 44, 66, 84, 104, 113, 114, 117, 118, 126, 127, 130, **178**, 180, 185,
'Usupport' mailing list 38

verbal communication 64, 77
video conferencing 49, 109
Virtual Reality 61, 122, 165, **180**, 190
Visual impairment 83
Visual Feedback 105, 131, 180, **181**
visual perceptual difficulty 45
vocalise 100
Voice Activated Software 33, 81, 95, **181**, 189

Web 33, 37, 39, 42, 44, 49, 51, 55, 65, 71, 85, 106, 109, 123, 126, 133, 157, 166, 185
Word Processors/Word-processing 5, 11, 12, 15, 25, 28, 30, 31, 32, 33, 44, 48, 54, 55, 56, 57, 59, 75, 77, 78, 82, 87, 88, 90, 91, 94, 96, 98, 101, 102, 107, 108, 114, 125, 126, 127, 129, 132, 133, 135, 141, 149, 152, 156, 157, 166, 167, 172, 175, 176, 181, **184**
Word Recognition 27
World Wide Web **185**
Wrist rests **185**
Written Level 133